D1562629

Erratum

PARALLEL SYSTEMS
Redundancy in Government
By Jonathan Bendor

P. 286, para. 2, should read:

There is a second reason governmental ineffectiveness may not induce decision-makers to think of using redundancy: money. This period of fiscal retrenchment is an inhospitable budgetary climate for bureaucratic duplication. As noted in Chapter One, economizers have oft decried redundancy (read "waste") in government, and the 1980s is no exception. It is not that there are solid data showing that redundancy is cost-ineffective; rather, the conventional wisdom, enduring in an evidential vacuum, is bolstered by short-sighted efforts to economize.

Parallel Systems

Parallel Systems

Redundancy in Government

Jonathan B. Bendor

UNIVERSITY OF CALIFORNIA PRESS

Berkeley • *Los Angeles* • *London*

JF
1411
.B36
1985

University of California Press
Berkeley and Los Angeles, California

University of California Press, Ltd.
London, England

Printed in the United States of America

1 2 3 4 5 6 7 8 9

Library of Congress Cataloging in Publication Data
Bendor, Jonathan B.
Parallel Systems
  Bibliography: p.
  Includes index.

  1. Public administration.   2. Organizational
effectiveness.   3. Performance.   4. Reliability.
I. Title.
JF1411.B36   1984   353.0087'84   84-2594
ISBN 0-520-05149-1

For my parents

Benami Bendor   Ruth Brodie Bendor
        Learning was joyful in their home

Contents

Tables, Figures, and Maps

Acknowledgments

One of the most pleasant aspects of completing this study is that I can finally thank in print the people and organizations who helped me in so many ways. First thanks go to Martin Landau, my dissertation chairman, for providing theoretical inspiration. His brilliant essay on redundancy seized my imagination early in graduate school and never relinquished it. I also benefited by receiving many pointed comments from Melvin Webber and Aaron Wildavsky. I am especially indebted to all three for having urged me to resist the temptation to write a scholarly tome. They wanted ideas, not bulk. If I have failed in this, the fault is mine.

A most important acknowledgment goes to the scores of transit officials and observers who talked, often with great frankness, about problems of organization and decision-making in urban transit. I am especially indebted to the interviewees from Minneapolis-St. Paul for their candor and their generosity in talking at such length with a stranger.

Many friends and colleagues at Berkeley and Stanford helped me enormously by criticizing earlier drafts of this work. I am particularly grateful to Thomas Hammond and Serge Taylor for their insightful comments on several drafts. Their patience was exceeded only by their acuity. I would also like to thank Suchitra Bhakdi, Mark Brucker, Michael Cohen, Alan Egan, John Ferejohn, David Jones, Alexander George, Jack Knott, Norton Long, Mark Mandeles, James March, Terry Moe, William Niskanen, Samuel Popkin, Steve Rosenstone, Stuart Ross, Arthur Stinchcombe, Russ Stout, and Dwight Waldo for their comments and critiques. Several decision-makers were kind enough to review the relevant case study chapters: David Graven, Douglas Kelm, Ted Kolderie, and three officials of the Washington Metropolitan Area Transit Authority. I also benefited from stimulating conversations with Sey Adler, Don Chisholm, Carol Heimer, Jane Fraser, Don Palmer, and Phil Viton. Robin Gaster, Paul Pfleiderer, and Roland Van Gaalen provided timely pieces of advice.

The librarians of the Institute of Transportation Studies, at the University of California, Berkeley, know how to retrieve arcane pieces of information with extraordinary dispatch. Their expert and energetic assistance saved me a great deal of time.

For financial support I thank the Urban Mass Transit Administration, U.S. Department of Transportation, for giving a grant to the Institute of Urban and Regional Development, University of California, Berkeley. The grant funded a larger study, which included an earlier version of this book. I would also like to thank the Graduate School of Business, Stanford University, for providing the summer research support that enabled me to undertake significant revisions.

The manuscript was typed first by Cynthia Lehner and Candy Wynne of the Institute of Urban and Regional Development and later by Mollie Porter, Jane Castruccio, and Betty MacNeur of the Graduate School of Business. I thank them all for a meticulous job. I am particularly indebted to Mollie Porter for her boundless patience: she typed seemingly endless revisions with great cheerfulness. Grace Katagiri, Estelle Jelinek, and Joan Johnstone provided valuable editorial assistance.

Linda Rothenberg Bendor gave advice on the manuscript from beginning to end. Despite her own demanding work schedule, she was amazingly willing to talk about redundancy theory at midnight. I am a lucky man.

The rest of my family had the sensitivity to forego asking how the study was progressing, yet listened intelligently when I wanted to talk about it. For this and much more, my heartfelt thanks.

Despite the diligent efforts of this redundant set of error-detecting friends, mistakes undoubtedly still lurk in this work. Because the theory of redundancy is a technical theory of reliability rather than a moral theory of culpability, I alone am responsible for all errors of theory and fact.

Abbreviations

AB&W	Alexandria, Barcroft, and Washington
AC	Alameda-Contra Costa Transit District
BART	Bay Area Rapid Transit District
MTC	Metropolitan Transit Commission (Minneapolis-St. Paul)
NCTA	National Capital Transportation Agency
NRPB	National Resources Planning Board
NVTC	Northern Virginia Transit Commission
PRT	Personal Rapid Transit
PUC	Public Utilities Commission (California)
UMTA	Urban Mass Transit Administration
WMATA	Washington Metropolitan Area Transit Authority
WMATC	Washington Metropolitan Area Transit Commission

Introduction

"Failure of the military rescue mission in Iran resulted from an almost unbelievable chain of bad luck," House Democratic leader James Wright said Friday after a White House briefing. Americans are seldom happy with such explanations. Valiant failures are not admired. Why did three out of eight helicopters malfunction?

Wall Street Journal, April 28, 1980

It is only out of redundancy that one can buy security.

Warren McCulloch, 1960

To have just enough to do a job, and no more, is an oft-proclaimed virtue in American public life. Government agencies should be streamlined and lean, without extra men or equipment. To have more than enough constitutes redundancy, and redundancy, we all know, is wasteful.

Yet certain events alert us to the possibility that not all duplication is excess. When the American rescue expedition to Iran departed with eight helicopters, military planners expected that six would suffice. The planners prepared for the intrusion of Murphy's Law by including more helicopters than they deemed necessary. The two extra were sent as a reserve, in case a machine malfunctioned. Even this cautious plan proved optimistic: three machines malfunctioned, terminating the expedition. What seemed before the fact to be more than enough proved after the fact to be inadequate.

Such events remain isolated incidents. They do not disturb the conventional wisdom of American public administration that the bare minimum is the ideal. And as for hardware, so for bureaucracies. One agency must not intrude into another's domain, nor duplicate another's work. To do so is even more wasteful than to supply redundant equipment. It is too costly.

Yet Americans do not only want government to be inexpensive. They demand effectiveness as well. Effectiveness implies reliability; it means dependable performance in the face of the inevitable blunders that attend all complex ventures. And, as the Iranian expedition clearly reveals, reliability may entail having more than one thinks necessary. More than eight helicopters. More than one computer in a command-and-control system. More, perhaps, than one public agency in a given policy area.

This last possibility, of organizational redundancy, runs directly counter to accepted principles of public administration. Since the days of scientific management, scholars have advised decision-makers to reduce duplication and overlap in the public bureaucracy. Politicians have taken this advice to heart. In Congress and in many state legislatures, committees are charged with increasing efficiency by eliminating redundancy in the executive branch. In this search, to find an agency duplicating another's function is tantamount to uncovering waste.

The conventional wisdom has stood for decades without scrutiny. Recently, however, Martin Landau, a political scientist, and William Niskanen, an economist, have challenged the orthodox position from two theoretical vantage points. Landau (1969) has hypothesized that duplication—of effort, of organization, of authority—can provide a measure of reliability in the face of uncertainty. Where one agency fails, a second may succeed. Thus, he extends the principle of backup design, well known in reliability engineering, to organization theory. Niskanen (1971) conjectures that when public organizations compete for jurisdiction over programs, rivalry will stimulate them to greater efficiency than a monopolistic agency would attain. The monopolist, whether public or private, ever seeks "the quiet life."

These theoretical formulations do not, however, establish that the distinction between monopoly and competition have any empirical relevance in the study of American bureaucracy. Redundancy may be an interesting idea, but is it the organization theoretic equivalent of the unicorn: a concept without a referent? To ease the reader's mind on this score, we provide a quick tour on the natural occurrence of duplication in three program areas: weapons, water, and welfare.[1] In addition to their alliterative appeal, these three cases advance the argument by showing that redundancy, far from being an exotic structure unknown in American bureaucracy, appears in a wide variety of policy sectors.[2] After the tour, Chapter One will provide a closer look at the theoretical underpinnings of the idea.

Weapons, Water, Welfare

Case 1: The Armed Services Fight over Missiles

A former Secretary of Defense, observing the intense rivalry among the armed services, ruefully remarked: "They could at least treat each other as allies!" In fact, however, the services have not always been locked in competition or even in conflict. Before World War II, the War Department

1. I would like to thank Norton Long for suggesting a section on the natural occurrence of redundancy in American bureaucracy. Professor Long also suggested several examples not mentioned in the text: overlapping among federal law enforcement agencies and among intelligence agencies, competition between the Bureau of Labor Statistics and the Census Bureau for business, and competition among the departments of Housing and Urban Development, Commerce, and the Treasury to run an Urban Bank for ex-President Jimmy Carter. To these we must add the fascinating and important example of redundant economic forecasting by the Congressional Budget Office and the troika of the Office of Management and Budget, the Council of Economic Advisers, and the Treasury. These cases invite further study.

2. The dimension underlying this diversity (roughly, the degree of conflict in each policy sector) will be discussed in the final chapter.

and the Department of the Navy tended to go their own ways (Huntington, 1961, p. 370). Competition over weapon systems did not begin in earnest until after the war.

That interservice rivalry became such a prominent feature of postwar defense politics was of course unintended. Indeed, the combination of unifying the service into a single Department of Defense and the services' jurisdictional "treaty" of Key West in 1947 (which, roughly speaking, assigned land weapons to the Army, air weapons to the Air Force, and weapons moving on or under water to the Navy) was expected to prevent unseemly bickering over mission and hardware. But harmony did not prevail; the services, only a few years after the Key West agreement, were shortly to embark on the most intensely competitive era in American military history—the 1950s conflicts over Intermediate-Range Ballistic Missiles (IRBMs).

What brought this about? Close observers have isolated three conditions.[3] First, the "New Look" strategy of the Eisenhower administration, stressing massive nuclear retaliation and deemphasizing conventional warfare, shifted the budgetary allocations of the three major services: the Army's share fell; the Air Force's rose. As an Army general warned his colleagues: "You're fighting a losing game. If you put all your energy and effort into justifying these conventional weapons . . . even though I know we need them, I think you are going to get very little money. . . . It is far easier to justify a budget with the modern items that are popular . . ." (Armacost, 1969, p. 44). The implication was clear: if the Army wanted to prevent its budgetary share from declining further, it had to move from machine guns to missiles.

So much for motive. What about opportunity? The Key West agreement had presumably established nonoverlapping jurisdictions. Surely the Army could not brazenly enter the Air Force's domain of air weaponry. But the treaty had a serious flaw: it did not address every technological contingency. In 1947, the treaty's terms were clear enough: the division of labor meant that the Air Force controlled manned

3. I am relying heavily here, and throughout this case, on Armacost (1969) and Huntington (1961).

aircraft.[4] And in the beginning of the nuclear age, nuclear deterrent meant one weapon system, the bombers of the Air Force's Strategic Air Command.

Technology, however, is mischievous, creating organizational problems even as it solves technical ones. The idea of using guided missiles to carry nuclear warheads had been entertained as early as 1946; the Army was particularly well acquainted with the notion since it had several of the German V–2 missile scientists, including Werner von Braun, working at its Huntsville, Alabama, base. And missiles posed a problem for the Key West accords. Naturally, Air Force leaders claimed missiles were their province. But the Air Force's special competence was *flying*, and guided missiles were *launched* from the ground—as was artillery. The parallel between artillery and guided missiles was not lost on Army leaders: "Why should we throw away a hundred and fifty years of artillery experience merely to keep the Air Force fat and happy by handing them a weapon they are not suited either by training or temperament to use?" (ibid., p. 46). And it could be argued that the dividing line between long-range artillery and missiles was arbitrary, that the Army needed the depth of attack provided by the new technology. Hence the Army was given the right to develop and employ its own missile in 1954, subject to the constraint that the missile have only tactical range.

With its tactical missile, the Redstone, the Army edged sideways into the new technology. It thereby set a precedent: the Air Force did not have exclusive jurisdiction over missiles. True, the Army was hemmed in by a range limitation, but such constraints, being continuous, can always be eased gradually, thus making the service less vulnerable to accusations of blatant poaching. Indeed, this incremental expansion was discussed by Generals James Gavin and Matthew Ridgeway. Gavin recommended a range expansion large enough to make the modified weapon an IRBM; the more cautious Ridgeway suggested extending the Redstone's range from 200 to 500 miles. "Further extensions in range might, of course, be contemplated in the future" (ibid., p. 45).

---

4. The Navy, however, retained jurisdiction over carrier-based planes.

Ridgeway's strategy of gradual encroachment might have been the sensible one to pursue in normal times, but the 1950s were not normal. The third element of the story, the strategic context, permitted a bolder move. The arms race was heating up: the Soviet Union exploded an atomic bomb in 1949, earlier than U.S. officials had expected, and five years later the United States tested the first hydrogen bomb. The second event was particularly significant, for the hideously destructive potential of hydrogen bombs rendered the precise accuracy of the missiles less important. The question in 1954 was, how close were the Soviets to developing long-range missiles carrying hydrogen warheads? The answer of the prestigious Killian report in the following year was, "too close." The report deemed it crucial that the United States not wait until Intercontinental Ballistic Missiles (ICBMs) could be deployed, but it should develop IRBMs as rapidly as possible.

The stage was now set for full-blown competition between the Air Force and the Army. Present were three crucial elements for such rivalry: the budgetary incentive for the Army, the jurisdictional ambiguity created by the new technology, and the strategic context of haste, thus making the Secretary of Defense tolerant of duplication if it shortened lead time. Secretary of Defense Charles Wilson was so inclined (ibid., p. 75). Despite howls of protest from the Air Force, the Army began Research and Development (R&D) on a strategic IRBM, the Jupiter.

Although the Air Force was incensed that the Army would try to move into strategic weaponry, it had not previously been enthusiastic about missiles. As one Air Force general admitted: "I would say if anything helped the Air Force work like hell on that, it is the fact that we know the Army was clawing at our backs" (ibid., p. 56). So just as the Jupiter project got underway, the Air Force began work on the Thor. The race was on.

And a race it was thought to be because all parties expected that only one missile would go into production. The reasoning of the Office of the Secretary of Defense was straightforward. The two missiles' technical performance would be compared during the test phase of R&D, and the superior one chosen for full-scale production. Duplication during R&D

would stimulate the services to do their best; duplication in production would be too costly (ibid., p. 130).

If this strategy sounds a bit too neat, it is. Secretary Wilson proved unable to manage the competition in the above manner, of which more shortly. But part of the process played out as planned. In particular, the parallelism produced a valuable divergence on the solution to the critical problem of the missiles' reentry. At the beginning of the competition, no one knew how to build a missile's nose cone to withstand the tremendous heat of reentry into the earth's atmosphere. The Air Force's scientists bet on a heat-sink method; the Army chose an oblation solution. In Armacost's judgment: "The Army program may have paid for itself simply by ensuring against the possible neglect of the oblation . . . solution of the reentry problem" (ibid., p. 165), for not only was the Army's solution usable for the IRBMs, but ultimately for the ICBMs as well (ibid., p. 145). Without the duplication of the Jupiter project, this

> important technological opportunity may have been unrecognized or unexploited for an indefinite period . . . [for] the Air Force may have overlooked the potential of the oblation method and did not specifically encourage their contractors to study it. (ibid.)

The second major technical uncertainty addressed in divergent ways was that of launching. The Air Force thought in terms of fixed bases; the Army, perhaps because of the artillery analogy, perhaps because of the implications for organizational control of operations, wanted a mobile missile. Armacost notes that the different approaches to this subproblem generated an exploration of alternative ground tactics that would otherwise have been overlooked (ibid., pp. 146–148).

The third benefit of the rivalry pertained to the speed of development. Time was of the essence in this project, and both services were spurred on by the knowledge that delays could ruin their chances.

Therefore, in Armacost's judgment, the redundancy during R&D was well worth the reasonable financial costs. However, Secretary Wilson did not eliminate one of the contestants before production started; duplication continued on into the maufacturing stage. The secretary's indecisiveness was due to three reinforcing factors. First, the R&D phase ended without a clear-cut winner. Second, in those pre-McNamara days, the secretary was not backed up by a technically proficient staff. Had one of the missiles exhibited clear superiority in testing, the absence of staff would not have mattered, but since the race was close, the secretary needed help in assessing small technical differences. He lacked that help. Third, by the time production was close at hand, both services had mobilized their natural constituencies, the producer interests, and their congressional allies. The office of the secretary was not politically obtuse:

> If the Defense Department suggested canceling the Air Force's Thor program, a congressional delegation from California would be down our necks. And elimination of the Army Jupiter program would have half the Alabama delegation plus a couple of representatives from the Detroit area fighting us.
> (ibid., p. 177)

The major cost of the race was financial. By letting both missiles go into production, the Defense Department paid an estimated $100 million more than it would have paid for seven squadrons of the same kind of missile (ibid., p. 218). Wilson's successor considered that "the price paid for the compression of time," but as Armacost notes, it was also the price of a measure of interservice harmony.

The Thor-Jupiter controversy, though the most prominent instance of military competition in the fifties, did not exhaust the Defense Department's capacity to create redundant IRBMs. Entrepreneurial admirals with an eye for technological progress foresaw the possibility of launching missiles armed with nuclear warheads from submarines. Submarines, they claimed, were the perfect second-strike weapon: virtually undetectable, submarines guaranteed second-strike capacity even in the face of a completely surprising first strike by the USSR. Again the Air Force resisted this incursion into what it deemed its jurisdiction, but the admirals were not to be denied, and the Polaris project (a brilliant technological success) began in 1957.

Thus was the strategic triad of bombers, land missiles, and submarine missiles developed largely by organizations in competition with one another for budgets and status. Defense strategists came to regard the triad as a redundant system in the positive sense—in the sense of a reliable deterrent. If one is destroyed, two are left. And they are not all vulnerable to the same kind of first-strike attack, that is, they do not suffer from what reliability engineers call common failure mode. It is therefore worth remembering that "the value of multiple methods of delivering warheads . . . was not explicitly recognized in the late 1950s" (Sapolsky, 1972, p. 38).

Beyond the reliability of diversified strategic force, the interservice competition yielded process benefits: the rivalry opened up what might have been an arcane issue, accessible only to a few decision-makers in the Pentagon, to a wider array of officials. C. P. Snow warned democracies about the "closed politics" that he thought would characterize such arenas. But the interservice rivalry made closed politics impossible. The services, unable to negotiate stable divisions of labor among themselves, turned outside the Pentagon for support, thereby enhancing civilian control over the "experts of violence" (Huntington, 1961, pp. 378–380).

Case 2: The Bureau, the Corps, and the Kings River Project

The organization of federal water policy has elicited criticism for better than half a century.

> In 1959, when the Senate Select Committee on National Water Resources looked back upon this history, it found that in the fifty years preceding its own efforts no less than twenty different national commissions or committees had been charged with examining these problems and seeking solutions. . . . Despite many differences, most of those studies emphasized with remarkable consistency the need for coordination among the agencies dealing with water.
> (McConnell, 1966, p. 213)

One of the most famous cases of water agency conflict—indeed, one investigated by the Hoover Commission in 1949—was the Kings River Project in California. Both the Bureau of Reclamation of the Department of Interior and the Army Corps of Engineers sought jurisdiction over the project. Their vigorous rivalry between 1937 and 1947 provided the source material for one of the earliest studies of bureaucratic competition (Maass, 1951).

The setting for the conflict involved three elements. First, despite some functional specialization, the agencies' jurisdictions overlapped. Though the corps was oriented toward flood control and the bureau toward irrigation, both of those functions involved a common technology—dam construction. One could easily build dams that fulfilled both functions, and doing so produced more attractive benefit-cost ratios.[5] Hence, the incentives of the benefit-cost game combined with the agencies' similar expertises to create a functional overlap. Second, both agencies were at this time actively searching for new projects, thereby increasing the chance of a run-in. Third, the bureau and the corps were hierarchically equal: neither could simply order the other to abandon the project. Thus, there was ample room for the play of organizational interests.

Not only were the agencies independent, they operated under different laws, were staffed by a different mix of professions, and had somewhat different conceptions of their central missions. Hence it was predictable that they would produce plans that, though envisaging multipurpose reservoirs on the Kings River, differed in several important respects. The corps was heavily predisposed toward flood control. Its enabling legislation referred primarily to that objective; its legislative bills were handled by Congress's public works committees, themselves oriented to flood control; its hierarchy was dominated by civil engineers who thought in those terms. The Bureau of Reclamation, on the other hand, had been created to develop the arid West by alleviating the *scarcity* of water (Hart, 1957, p. 109). Irrigation reflected that charge. Hence the bureau and the corps regarded the Kings River Project from different perspectives. Of course these perspectives did overlap because flood control and irrigation are

5. I thank Serge Taylor for suggesting this point.

joint products of the same project. As the bureau saw matters, storing water for irrigation also serves the purposes of flood control; for the corps, once one built a dam to protect against floods, one might as well use the stored water for irrigation. But clearly the order of priorities differed.

This difference was probably known to water users in California's Central Valley. Contrary to the conventional wisdom that citizens are always confused by redundancy, neither the overlapping jurisdiction of the two agencies nor their different missions baffled the water users' association. Indeed, the association *instigated* this competition in 1937 by asking both bureaus to begin investigations of the project. The association members were sufficiently politically sophisticated to perceive that they might benefit from two agencies competing for their support (Maass, 1951, pp. 210–211). Stimulated by local interests, the regional offices of the corps and the bureau completed preliminary plans and forwarded them to Washington in 1939.

No one in Washington viewed the rivalry with the pleasure of the water users, and there were several attempts in the executive branch to resolve the conflict before the reports reached Congress. The Water Committee of the National Resources Planning Board (NRPB) strongly opposed the competitive planning, urging that the bureaus reconcile their differences by issuing a single report "reflecting their combined judgment." But the ill-fated NRPB, soon to be abolished, was incapable of enforcing its desire. Then a far more formidable decision-maker expressed opposition to the duplication. Franklin Delano Roosevelt himself initiated considerable redundancy in government,[6] but it was a different matter when instigated by someone else. Accordingly, Roosevelt moved to restore order. To prevent such incidents from recurring, he instructed the relevant departments to write, with the aid of the NRPB, a memorandum of agreement that would secure interagency cooperation in the early stages of project planning. And to settle this dispute, he requested the rivals to submit their reports to him *via* the NRPB.

6. As Schlesinger has described (1958), Roosevelt made a practice of using competing sources of information and often created agencies that overlapped older bureaus' jurisdictions.

Neither the short-run nor the long-run measure proved successful. The memorandum, the Tripartite Agreement, lacked an enforcement mechanism and did not eliminate future conflicts (ibid., p. 212). Even the matter at hand evaded White House control. The corps, by-passing the NRPB, sent its report directly to the White House, where, possibly by clerical error, it was approved for transmission to Congress. The dam was out of the executive bag and into the congressional bog.

For a bog it was. The committees of Congress were ill-organized to manage the conflict: in each chamber different committees had jurisdiction over the corps and the bureau. There was no natural arena (short of the floor of either chamber) where the plans could fight it out. Thus began several years of conflict, with the public works committees backing the corps and Roosevelt backing the bureau.

The plans were worth fighting about. Though the engineering designs were similar, the visions of the uses of the water differed. The corps saw the project in terms of flood control, the bureau in terms of irrigation. This basic difference in water use philosophy led to disagreements over all major legal, operational, and financial dimensions of the project. Legally, the corps wanted it built under the Flood Control law; the bureau, under the Reclamation Act. The Reclamation Act imposed acreage limitations on water recipients[7] and retained water ("over schedule" water in excess of contractural obligations) in the hands of the federal government whereas the Flood Control law restricted neither the acreage a user could own nor the amount of water he could receive. This difference in property rights and water rights would probably have sufficed to excite local passions, but the agencies also differed in their allocation of project costs among the uses of flood control, irrigation, and power. This could have become an enormous divergence since the amount local interest would have to pay for the project was linked to how the water was used. Whereas the proportion of a project's cost allocated to flood control was paid for largely by the federal government, the proportion going for irrigation was paid for by the

7. The 160-acre limit was a legacy of the egalitarian populist movement of the late 1800s. The populists were an important part of the coalition that produced the Reclamation Act.

users.[8] Naturally, the corps allocated a larger proportion of costs to flood control.

The third major difference concerned power—not political but electrical. The Bureau of Reclamation wanted to build a power plant immediately; the Army Corps of Engineers, disinterested in power, was content to let the Federal Power Commission license private development sometime in the future. This too had financial significance. As Maass commented: "The largest water users' association in the area preferred the Army scheme because it planned to file with the FPC for the license to develop the power and then to set power rates which would yield sufficient revenues to help retire the local contribution for irrigation benefits" (ibid., p. 219).

In summary, then, the two plans had pronounced distributional effects. Large water users would strongly favor the corps's alternative: they would be eligible to receive water, and their costs would be reduced by the double gambit of high-cost allocations to flood control and power revenues. Small water users, such as those composing the Grange, would be hurt by the loss of cheap power that the bureau would have provided and would not be helped by the corps's indifference to acreage limits (DeRoos, 1948, p.65).

Given the historic political strength of large water users in California's Central Valley, it is not surprising that the public works committees and appropriation subcommittees of Congress were able to resist, first, Roosevelt's strong preference of the Bureau of Reclamation and, subsequently, Truman's weaker opposition to the corps. Eventually a compromise was struck. The corps, getting the better of the deal, won the primary fight: it would build and operate the dam. Concerning finances, the corps made a concession and accepted the bureau's higher-cost allocation to irrigation.[9] Concerning power, it was a draw: no power plant was ever built on the project site.

The controversy over the law governing water rights

8. No interest was charged, however.
9. According to Maass (1951), the corps's cost allocation for irrigation had been $13,230,000, the bureau's $14,250,000. This difference, though not huge, was not insignificant in those preinflationary days. Unfortunately, Maass did not indicate whether the agencies' allocations had converged during negotiations.

proved most difficult to settle. The compromise had provided that the Reclamation Act would govern the operation of the dam (Maass, 1951, p. 235). The chief consequence of the act would have been that farmers could not receive water for more than 160 acres.[10] This restriction was unacceptable to the Kings River Water Users Association. It now appears that the large landowners, having taken the case to the courts and urging Congress to change the law, have avoided the restriction.

Proceeding now to the evaluation of bureaucratic competition, we can use, on the debit side, Maass's impressive list (see Table 1). Unfortunately, his eight points obscure the difference between the negative effects of competition per se and the effects of the corps's winning this particular race. Evaluations of the general features of the competitive process must be disentangled from more specific assessments of a winner's vices and virtues. To see this more concretely, try this thought experiment: how many of the negative effects listed in Table 1 would vanish if the winner of the competition had been selected by a coin toss in 1937, and if the corps had won the toss? This procedure, by driving the process costs of competition down to zero while retaining the same outcome, enables us to distinguish the (possibly general) costs of the process from the particular costs of the outcome.

I submit that though this mechanism would eliminate points 2a and 5–8 in Table 1, problems 1, 2b, and 3 would remain, for they reflect properties of the winner rather than of the rivalry per se. Further, points 1, 2b, and 3 are by far the most serious issues on the list. Though delay, the diversion of managerial attention, and the loss of face of the federal government are not trifles, they are outweighed by the policy questions of point 3 alone, which would *not* have been removed by eliminating the process of interagency competition. It appears, therefore, that Maass's evaluation rests chiefly on his dislike of the winner; had the bureau come out on top, his evaluation would read quite differently.

10. The restriction was actually more complicated. If a farm was jointly owned by a husband and wife, they could receive water for 320 acres. If water for excess land was received, that land would have to be sold within ten years.

TABLE 1 *Costs of the Bureau-Corps Competition*

1. It is uncertain whether the Kings River water is being used in the most cost-effective manner.
2a. Duplicate planning costs money.
2b. A significant portion of irrigation costs will never be repaid to the federal government.
3. Some beneficiaries of the project may avoid acreage restrictions; thus the outcome favors large landowners and water users.
4. The easing of acreage and repayment restrictions in this project sets a bad precedent for similar concessions in other water projects.
5. The conflict hardened the agencies' positions, making further policy development more difficult.
6. The project has been delayed.
7. The conflict absorbed executives' time and attention.
8. The "unbecoming conduct" of the agencies made the federal government lose face in the eyes of the public.

SOURCE: Maass, 1951, pp. 252–254.

Nevertheless, a sanguine assessment of this case is impossible. Unlike the Thor-Jupiter fight, this rivalry did not reduce technical uncertainty and though it presented decision-makers with the *opportunity* to think about several fundamental issues of water policy, the opportunity was apparently not seized. The committee structure of Congress was not suited to adjudicate this issue in a manner that would shed light on basic policy choices. Hence the competitive process did not generate benefits that would offset those costs of Table 1 that can properly be charged to the process. A coin toss in 1937 would have been better.

Case 3: Redundancy in Welfare Policy

Antipoverty programs provide a difficult testing ground for the concept of redundancy. Weapon systems clearly involve unproven technologies; hence recognizing the potential of redundancy is easy. But antipoverty programs do not produce tangible objects with specified performance criteria. Instead, they entail transfers of wealth from one part of the population to another. Does redundancy have any relevance in this kind of policy sector?

Descriptively, it surely does. Numerous studies of welfare policy have noted the multiplicity of programs that collectively constitute our welfare system and the multiplicity of departments that run these programs. One estimate is that "no fewer than 62 separate federal programs were providing social insurance and aid to the needy" (Salamon, 1978, p. 4), operated by nine different agencies or departments. From the beneficiaries' perspective, there is overlapping as well: over 40 percent of those receiving aid were assisted by at least three programs, nearly 20 percent by at least five programs.

The growth of this complicated system is a fascinating story in its own right. But for the purpose of illustrating the functioning of redundancy in different policy sectors, we need focus only on part of that story. From 1962 to 1965, this sector bubbled with an impressive variety of proposals, reaching a peak in the War on Poverty.

Of course, the proliferation of most of the proposals was not a deliberate plan to let alternative theories compete against each other, to "let one hundred flowers bloom." Rather, the causal factors of organizational, interest, and professional predispositions, the vagaries of presidential attention, and financial and political constraints combined to produce an unusually large and diverse number of rival solutions. Let us consider four of the most prominent antipoverty theories and their associated strategies (Aaron, 1978).

Theory 1: Poverty is caused, or at least maintained, by a culture of poverty, by the poor's ways of coping (or failing to cope) with their social environment. These behaviors are passed down from generation to generation. The solution is a program of intense casework, of social workers providing a battery of services designed to interrupt the intergenerational pattern. The natural organizational location for such a program was the Department of Health, Education, and Welfare (HEW).

Theory 2: Poverty is caused primarily by structural unemployment, by a mismatching between the skill requirements of available jobs and the skills of job seekers. The solution implied by this theory is a manpower program. Its obvious organizational home was the Department of Labor.

Theory 3: Though the proximate cause of poverty is unemployment, as theory two claims, the basic flaw is in our educational system. Children in poor school districts start falling behind in grammar school; once they reach high school, they are severely handicapped in the subsequent competition for jobs. This theory suggests that compensatory education is the prescription of choice. The obvious home of such a program, after a brief period of bureaucratic independence, was the Office of Education in HEW.

Theory 4: The poor are poor because they are powerless. Political systems, like markets, respond only to effective demand; unarticulated preferences do not count. The solution is to organize the poor against local power structures. The organizational home of such an effort clearly had to be outside a line department, for by hypothesis the old line agencies were part of the problem. Thus, a new entity, the Office of Economic Opportunity (OEO), was required.

Of these four strategies, the first, the social services approach, emerged as the leading solution of the administration of John F. Kennedy; the next three received more attention under Lyndon Johnson. The Kennedy years witnessed less competition in policy planning, for at that time social workers, led by HEW Secretary Abraham Ribicoff, enjoyed a virtual monopoly of advice. This monopoly was broken simultaneously by three new or quasi-new approaches following Kennedy's assassination. For Johnson's War on Poverty was not of one piece. There were serious disagreements among antipoverty scholars—and among departments whose chances of receiving new programs and expanding their jurisdictions depended upon which solutions were chosen.

These disagreements surfaced in interdepartmental meetings in 1964, the first year of the War on Poverty, but they were not resolved then or later. With hindsight we can argue that it was well that agreement was beyond reach. For though consensus could have been obtained by fiat, or based on faith, it could not have been founded on knowledge, for that was lacking. No one in 1964 knew which course to pursue. There were guesses, of course, variably informed by theories, but no one knew.[11]

And there were some surprises in store for the administration, surprises that showed how hard it was for officials to predict which programs would work. Several of the programs attracting the most attention, from politicians, the media, and scholars, turned out to have minimal impact on the problem. The social services approach, the Community Action Program, and several of the manpower programs fell well below their adherents' expectations. What kept poor people afloat or moved them across the poverty line was a combination of macroeconomic policy and welfare programs that no one had ushered onto the public policy stage with great fanfare—in particular, Aid to Families with Dependent Children (AFDC) and Food Stamps. By 1975 these two programs had become the mainstays of our welfare system, a result that few experts would have predicted in 1964 (Haveman, 1977). Under uncertainty some of the "one hundred flowers" became weeds; some of the weeds, flowers.[12]

11. Indeed, even well-accepted descriptions of the poor were mistaken. It was then assumed that almost all poor people stayed poor for long periods. Subsequent work by labor economists showed that though the total number of the poor is relatively stable, individuals shift in and out of poverty much more often than once thought. This descriptive inaccuracy indicates how much we had to learn about poverty in the mid-sixties.

12. Robert Haveman, in his overview chapter in *A Decade of Federal Anti-poverty Programs* (1977), summed up the findings of the massive University of Wisconsin study:

> While several of the measures explicitly designed to reduce income poverty proved to be rather ineffective, some of the unanticipated and unplanned changes were potent in increasing the economic welfare of those at the bottom of the income distribution. Hence, while the net result was a substantial reduction in poverty over the decade, many of the policy changes contributing to this were not anticipated in 1965, nor were they a central part of OEO's plans for poverty reduction. (pp. 1–2)

Not only were many of the individual programs surprising, so was their collective effect. It has become a ritual in American politics to declare that our welfare system is a mess, a patchwork quilt of poorly designed and poorly coordinated programs. And indeed many of the parts would not elicit the admiration of a dean of a public policy school. Yet the collective impact of this ungainly system was surprisingly strong. In 1965, 33 percent of the pretransfer poor were moved across the poverty line by cash transfers; by 1972, that figure rose to 44 percent, even though the absolute number of pretransfer poor had increased (Lynn, 1977, p. 91). Moreover, if we include in-kind assistance, the percentage lifted out of poverty is substantially increased (ibid., p. 94). Thus the welfare system is stronger, *in toto,* than its despised constituent programs.

Nevertheless, one could not pick a more unlikely policy sector to praise for its redundant robustness. Everybody despises our welfare system,[13] and I do not intend to praise it as the epitome of efficiency or compassion. Rather, it is to point out that given that it must function under extraordinary political constraints, its organizational properties of fragmentation and duplication are more a source of strength than customarily believed. But because this conclusion rests, as must all policy assessments, on valuational as well as factual premises, it is tendentious. The problem of evaluating alternative organizational designs in the face of sharp conflict over values will be taken up in the last chapter. For now it suffices to note two quandaries of redundancy in this sector. The first is clearly a disadvantage; the second poses thornier and more fundamental issues of evaluation.

First, the organizational fragmentation of our antipoverty ensemble hid a vexing problem of unintended interaction among programs. Most welfare programs have an implicit tax

13. Joseph Califano, recalling Jimmy Carter's 1976 campaign pledge to institute welfare reform, observed that this promise "always drew satisfying applause, whoever his audience: chic Manhattan liberals, street blacks in Detroit, Southern Baptist churchgoers, white hardhats on construction sites, conservative Midwest farmers, or the nation's governors in conference" (1981, p. 320).

rate: benefits decline, or are "taxed," as earnings increase. This raises the problem of work disincentives. Even within a single program, the matter is complicated by the trade-off between work disincentives and program cost.[14] But multiple programs aggravated the dilemma by boosting each other's implicit tax rates. For example, "since eligibility for Medicaid is based largely on eligibility for AFDC or SSI benefits, the point at which families or individuals earn the dollar that renders them ineligible for AFDC or SSI cash assistance is also the point at which they lose Medicaid benefits, worth hundreds, often thousands of dollars each year" (Califano, 1981, p. 333). This phenomenon was clearly a side effect of organizationally independent programs affecting the same people in a surprising way. The defect probably would have been discovered sooner had all the programs been operated by one department.

There is a second, exquisitely difficult problem of evaluation. Americans disagree over, first, who are the "truly needy" who deserve help and, second, how much should we assist each deserving person? In this type of political context, what is the *meaning* of programmatic reliability? A liberal rejoices that overlapping decreases the chance that some poor soul will fall through cracks in the welfare system; a conservative worries that overlapping increases the chance that the undeserving poor (pace Albert Doolittle) receive aid, or that the truly needy receive more than they should, or both. At the level of aggregate spending, the argument is whether the redundant structure affects the total welfare budget and, if so, in what direction, how much, and is it a "Good Thing"?

In this policy sector, one man's reliability is another's waste; hence evaluating redundancy is a delicate affair. In the last chapter we shall propose that a device invented by political philosophers, the "veil of ignorance," can help us assess organizational designs under these conditions of intense conflict of interest. But the dispute also involves matters of fact: does the organizational structure of welfare affect the

14. One diminishes the disincentive by lowering the implicit tax rate, thereby increasing the program's scope, per capita cost, and total cost. See Califano (1981, p. 333) for a vivid description of the pain this trade-off imposes upon would-be reformers.

flow of dollars? Though a definitive answer is unavailable, many who have considered the issue believe that the multiplicity of programs increases the total aid given. A former assistant secretary of HEW saw two reasons why this might be so: "The multiplicity of programs increases the total transfer to the poor because it brings some political allies on board who would not otherwise be there . . . and because it hides from the average congressman the true magnitude of the transfer" (Steiner, 1971, pp. 13–14).

If this claim is correct, then disagreements over the bureaucratic structure of welfare are not merely technical arguments about the reliability of alternative organizational forms; they are surrogates for fights over the redistribution of wealth, a most sensitive political issue. In such domains, organizational designers must move carefully.

These examples of bureaucratic competition do not, of course, prove that Landau's and Niskanen's criticisms of conventional wisdom are correct; they simply demonstrate that the structural alternative they are proposing is empirically relevant because it is a naturally occurring phenomenon in American bureaucracy. But one must establish much more than empirical relevance before Landau's and Niskanen's theories should be accepted. Thus, this work seeks to integrate their analyses, to modify them where necessary, and to probe them empirically. At this juncture, empirical work is essential, for evidence has not yet been brought to bear upon the matter. Numerous questions remain problematic, though in principle answerable, if only we address them to data. How, for example, do monopolistic and competitive bureaus behave? Are agencies that monopolize their jurisdiction efficient, as the traditional view suggests, or are they unreliable and sluggish, as Landau and Niskanen imply?

To remedy this empirical deficiency, I have undertaken a comparative study of competitive and monopolistic public organizations in the field of urban transit. To provide the needed structural variety, I have selected three cases. In the San Francisco Bay Area, two redundant transit agencies, Bay Area Rapid Transit (BART) and Alameda-Contra Costa Transit District (AC), supply parallel commuter services. In Washington, D.C., in contrast, the Washington Metropolitan Area

Transit Authority is a classically nonredundant, monopolistic agency. Metro, as it is called, runs nonoverlapping bus and rail service from a single, integrated headquarters.

For the third case, I have chosen to study the planning of a transit system rather than its operation. Redundancy is most palpable when it occurs in the operation of a system or the delivery of a service, such as parallel transit lines, redundant missile systems, and the like. But, plausibly, if bureaucratic monopoly risks unreliable performance during operations, then monopolistic planning risks the unreliable *design* of operations. Monopoly during planning may be no more benign than monopoly during operations. Indeed, to permit a single agency to monopolize the planning of a program may promote "groupthink" (Janis, 1972) whereas if competing agencies advocate alternative plans, the rivalry may generate a healthy diversity. Accordingly, for the third study I have investigated a case of competitive planning in Minneapolis-St. Paul, where, in the seventies, two regional agencies argued over their rival plans for the future of transit in the Twin Cities.

The three cases thus cover the requisite four organizational situations. Redundant operations are exemplified by the AC-BART relationship and nonredundant operations by the Washington Metro. Competitive planning is found in Minneapolis-St. Paul. In the case of monopolistic planning the Bay Area study did double duty, for the planning of BART was essentially monopolistic. Hence the Bay Area systems illustrate both redundant operations and nonredundant planning.

Plan of the Book

The basic theory of bureaucratic redundancy is presented in Chapter One. There the theoretical arguments for monopoly in the public sector are contrasted with those for redundancy. Chapter Two then places the general arguments in the policy context of urban transit. The differences between redundant transit planning and operation, on the one hand,

and monopolistic transit planning and operation, on the other, are specified.

Armed with the theoretical propositions developed in Chapters One and Two, we move into the empirical core of the book in Chapters Three, Four, and Five. These contain the comparative case studies. Chapter Three recounts the curious story of the parallel transit lines created in the Bay Area by a bus agency's stubborn refusal to yield to the space age wonders of BART. Chapter Four examines the competitive planning in the transit politics of Minneapolis-St. Paul. Chapter Five presents the orthodox monopolistic organization of the Washington Metro.

Chapter Six assesses the lessons of these case studies, the sometimes surprising virtues and defects of redundant and monopolistic structures. The feasibility and desirability of redundancy in government are scrutinized in the seventh and concluding chapter.

One should resist the natural temptation to write the conclusions of a study in the introduction. Let it suffice to say that the evidence gives reason to believe that the virtues of streamlined, monopolistic public bureaucracy have been exaggerated, the defects underestimated. Conversely, these studies reveal several highly practical benefits of redundancy. And, of course, field research brings its inevitable surprises, findings anticipated by neither theory. Thus, all in all, the studies yield a pleasing mixture of the expected and the unexpected.

1

The Theory of Bureaucratic Competition and Redundancy

The Argument for Redundancy: Man's Frailties

Max Weber believed that bureaucracy, despite its risks, embodied rational choice. More recently, social scientists have regarded bureaucracy with a more jaundiced eye. Indeed, some of the most interesting work in organization theory in the last thirty years has explored the *limitations* on rational choice (Merton, 1940; Simon, 1947; Cyert and March, 1963). Simon's theory of bounded rationality, focusing upon individual decision-makers, addressed the problem of how an organization, composed of rational but fallible persons, could function. His early work explicitly juxtaposed organizational and individual levels of analysis. This contrast caught the attention of the political philosopher Sheldon Wolin, who feared that Simon's focus on "irrational man[1] and rational organization" (Wolin, 1960, p. 380) would eventually repre-

---

1. There was a misunderstanding here: Simon postulated that decision-makers have *limited* rationality; he did not posit irrationality.

sent "the organization as the epitome of rationality, as being that which man is not." By so doing, "organization theory has succeeded in creating a standard of nonhuman excellence" (ibid., p. 381).

But Wolin failed to observe that, in fact, the Carnegie School had *not* pursued the intriguing question of whether organizations can offset (in Simon's words) the "limits of humans as mechanisms for computation and choice."[2] Aside from Simon's early work in the late forties and early fifties, the influential Carnegie tradition has focused more on how individual limits translate into organizational limits than on how the latter could compensate for the former.[3] Starting with articles in the late fifties and culminating in *A Behavioral Theory of the Firm* (1963), Cyert and March developed a theory explaining why *organizations* could not be as comprehensively rational as classical economic theories implied. And their theory of limited organizational rationality was based largely upon a theory of limited individual rationality.

When we reach second-generation interpretations, such as Graham Allison's Organizational Process model in his *Essence of Decision*, we see that Wolin has no need for concern. The question posed by Simon nearly thirty years before—how do organizations function if administrative man is more fallible than economic man?—is lost to view. The organization is as

2. March and Shapira contend that this pattern is typical of organization theory generally: "Students of organizations have a long tradition of moving rather cavalierly from theories of individual cognition and choice to theories of organizational cognition and choice" (1982, p. 11). Of those working in the Carnegie tradition, the major exception to this tendency of dubious analogizing is the significant work of Michael Cohen (1981; 1984).

3. Simon does show an awareness of the constraints operating at different levels:

> Individual human beings are constructed basically as serial information-processing machines. They can attend to only one or to a few things at a time. This fundamental fact has wide-ranging consequences for behavior.
>
> The body politic is composed of a very large number of human beings. Hence it is perfectly capable of operating as a parallel system, carrying on many activities simultaneously. (1966, p. 20)

Substituting "organization" for "body politic" leaves the sense of the quotation intact.

limited as the individual; there are no compensating features.[4] What began as an interesting tension ended as a commonplace observation: systems composed of imperfect parts are equally imperfect.[5]

This focus on the organizational difficulties that merely reflect individual constraints is less inaccurate than it is incomplete. Concerning organizational design and structural possibility, is it necessarily true that organizations must be as unreliable as their parts? Martin Landau, in an essay, "Redundancy, Rationality, and the Problem of Duplication and Overlap" (1969), gave a surprising answer—no. Following John von Neumann's pioneering work in reliability theory, Landau extended the idea of deploying redundant, functionally equivalent components into the design of organizations *more* reliable than their parts. Landau proposed that, contrary to historical strictures in public administration against duplication and overlap, a correct arrangement of independent and functionally equivalent channels of communication, decision, and action can provide a degree of reliability that a single channel could rarely attain. Consider the following analogy. Suppose an automobile had dual breaking circuits: each circuit can stop the car, *and* the circuits operate independently so that if one malfunctions it does not impair the other. If the probability of either one failing is 1/10, the probability of both failing simultaneously is $(1/10)^2$, or 1/100. Add a third independent circuit and the probability of the catastrophic failure of no brakes at all drops to $(1/10)^3$, or 1/1000.

The example could be extended, but the point should be clear: a system's reliability is *not* necessarily limited by its

4. See particularly Allison's Model Two (1971, pp. 68–96), and consider the following juxtaposition of levels of analysis: "Simon and the Carnegie School focus on the *bounded character of human capabilities.* Firms are physically unable to possess full information, generate all alternatives . . ." (ibid., p. 74; emphasis added). And: "The physical and psychological limits of man's capacity as alternative generator, information processor, and problem solver constrain the decision-making processes of individuals and organizations" (ibid., p. 71).

5. I am indebted to Thomas Hammond for discussing this problem with me.

components' fallibility.[6] Hence, though the strategy of redundancy is fully consistent with organization theory's emphasis on the proposition that "every actor is a risky agent" (ibid.), it goes beyond that idea by abandoning any easy equivalence between individual and organizational effectiveness. By doing so, the strategy takes us full circle, back to Simon's early, unexplored tension between the rationalities of the two levels, individual and organizational.[7]

A student of weapons development, Burton Klein (1962), has argued that successful projects exhibit precisely this disparity between unreliable organizational *units* and a reliable *organization*. Klein, finding that the design choices made in the early stages of a weapons project often fail to meet performance specifications, recommended that the development of crucial components should be assigned to competing teams. These redundant problem-solving units would work on different solutions to the same problem, increasing the probability of discovering a satisfactory design. The point of the strategy is to prevent premature programming, that is, to avoid committing the entire project organization to the flawed design of one of its subunits.

Some project managers have intuitively recognized the value of this strategy. In the Manhattan Project, several parallel teams worked on key components. Likewise, in the development of the Polaris missile, the Navy's Special Projects Office ensured that redundant teams worked on crucial parts (Sapolsky, 1972). In these successful ventures, officials understood that the success of any one team could not be taken for granted. Indeed, failure was an ever-present danger. Devel-

6. Lest one think this point obvious, consider that the well-known proverb, a chain is only as strong as its weakest link, is *false* when applied to redundant systems, for duplication generally makes systems more reliable than their *strongest* parts. In contrast, nonredundant series systems are virtually always weaker than their *weakest* link. For an analysis of how believing in the proverb leads to systematic errors in planning, see Chapter Seven.

7. There is a difference. Simon framed his problem as a query: how could a human of bounded rationality make decisions in an unbounded environment? His answer: organizations provide contexts for choice by supplying decision premises. Simon did not, however, directly address the issue of unreliability.

opment managers also intuitively recognized that the success of the entire project could not rest on the learning capacity of any single team, that is, on the ability of a subunit to find its mistakes and correct them. To rely on such error correction is risky, for one easily becomes committed to one's own choices, flawed though they may be (Janis and Mann, 1977). In short, far from the equivalence of individual and organizational limitations implied by Allison, the project organization had to have a higher probability of success than did its subunits. Hence, redundancy, by making the project organization less vulnerable to failures of its teams, created (paraphrasing von Neumann) a reliable organization from unreliable parts.

Klein's work compared the effectiveness of a single organization with that of its units, but one could easily extend the idea of redundancy to multiorganizational systems. Much empirical work indicates that public agencies are themselves risky actors, prone to develop rigid perceptions and programs maladapted to changing task environments. Redundancy theory therefore implies that encouraging bureaus to duplicate each other's functions will enhance overall reliability. This principle of interorganizational design conflicts, however, with a venerable argument against redundancy.

The Argument for Nonredundant Organizational Structures

Robert Merton (1973) has compressed a common reaction to new ideas into a pithy saying:

> If it's new,
> it's not true.
> If it's true,
> it's not new.

On which horn shall we impale the idea of redundancy? We shall demonstrate shortly that the idea is indeed novel to organization theory and public administration. The second horn is thereby blunted. What about the first?

Three major arguments have been presented in the case against redundancy:

1. *Efficiency.* Of these, the argument from efficiency is best known. The basic reasoning is simple: maintaining several agencies to do a job that one can do is wasteful.[8] If performance is assumed to be nonproblematic, it is hard to take exception to that point. Yet we must, of course, ask two questions here: what is the probability that a given task will in fact be performed, and what are the consequences if it is not?

A more subtle version of the economy-efficiency position appears in the suggestion that merging duplicate activities inside one organization produces economies of scale. This argument is particularly persuasive when economies of scale pertain to physical facilities, as these are more easily measured than *administrative*-scale economies.[9] Yet economists have warned that overlooking this difference confuses the optimal size of an industrial *plant* with the optimal size of a *firm*. Political scientists should avoid analogous confusions in the public sector. Blurring the distinction could result in recommending mergers at the wrong organizational level. Obvious physical scale economies result from merger at fairly low levels, but mergers are often aimed at higher levels, where the argument must rest on less easily measured administrative economies.[10] In the latter case, the political symbolism of reorganization is probably more important than substantive considerations.

2. *Gaps and overlaps.* The efficiency perspective is held more often by organizational outsiders than insiders. It is a budget-cutting move. Insiders are unlikely to wish to cut the budget, but they may be attuned to another difficulty that redundancy

8. Different types of redundancy are differentially vulnerable to the redundancy-is-waste criticism. Stand-by redundancy, where one agency takes over a function only if another one fails, is less vulnerable than active redundancy. For this reason stand-by redundancies are probably more legitimate in the public sector than are active ones. The federal system of independent state and national governments exhibits many cases of stand-by duplication (Landau, 1973a).

9. Curiously, the one scale economy of larger organizations is a more economical use of physical redundancies: "The big firm needs less proportionate reserve of machinery or of stocks to meet possible emergencies than does the small firm" (Robinson, 1958, p. 26).

10. In addition to these caveats, Niskanen warns that a monopoly might not pass the benefits of economies of scale on to taxpayers (1971, p.196).

can create, programmatic gaps. Given a fixed budget, more resources allocated to one problem mean less for another. Problem-solving overlaps, therefore, automatically imply problem-solving gaps elsewhere. One can call this the "internal opportunity cost" of redundancy.

An excellent example of the opportunity cost of duplication occurred in a dispute between engineers and scientists on a recent space project. Given a constraint on the weight of a probe, the design engineers and the scientists could not agree on how much redundancy to build into the probe. For the scientists, adding a backup system meant sacrificing scientific experiments. From their point of view, the redundancy was not ineffective; rather, it cost too much in terms of experimentation foregone.

3. *Pinpointing responsibility.* Organizations allocate blame as well as solve problems, and overlapping jurisdictions may make it more difficult to assign blame (Wallace, 1941). A nonredundant structure reduces this uncertainty.[11] A corollary holds that clear lines of responsibility, from elected officials down through bureaucrats, stimulate performance because they make it easy to detect who was at fault for failure.

Evaluating the Case Against Redundancy

To argue *against* bureaucratic duplication is, of course, to argue *for* organizational monopoly: for every program there should be one and only one agency. Anything more runs afoul of the three preceding arguments. But how well do these arguments stand up empirically?

Unfortunately, advocates of organizational monopoly have not deemed it necessary to substantiate their claim with evidence. The unmitigated wastefulness of bureaucratic redun-

---

11. But Gilbert Steiner, arguing against this concentration of responsibility in the antipoverty field, rejoins that "while there may be a focusing of responsibility, there is also an exclusive dependence. If the job does not get done, it is easier to decide who should be fired, but this does not much help the potential beneficiary of the nonperformed task" (1971, p. 16).

dancy is an untested axiom, sometimes explicitly stated (Coker, 1922), sometimes implied, but in neither case doubted or tested. Thus, there is *no evidence* that bureaucratic competition has the drawbacks attributed to it. On the contrary, a recent empirical study casts doubt "on the conventional wisdom that executive reorganization along the principles of classical organization theory introduced economies into bureaucracy" (Meier, 1980, p. 410). Specifically included in the set of classical organization theory principles was "reducing duplication and overlap." We can therefore infer that the reorganizations Meier studied included such "reforms" and that his data indicate that they did not save money.

Herbert Kaufman's overview of administrative reorganization reaches much the same conclusion: "The profound, determinable consequences (of reorganization) do not lie in the engineering realm of efficiency, simplicity, size, and cost of government" (1977, p. 403). Indeed, Kaufman proceeds to note that even "reorganizers have also grown wary of claiming massive savings in operations for their reforms" (ibid., p. 417). Of course, advocates of monopoly can claim, in Edward Tufte's felicitous phrase, that the absence of evidence is not the evidence of absence. In other words, if we were only to look harder, we would find the savings produced by eliminating duplication. Yet it is odd that the economies have not turned up yet.

A study by the Joint Economic Committee suggests that we will not find savings even if we do look harder. The committee's examination of federal output increases from 1967 to 1971 in different kinds of activities yielded the data in Table 2. As Niskanen commented:

> These estimates of the rate of increase of output per federal employee are almost perfectly correlated with the extent of existing competition with private firms and among bureaus. The federal government does not contract for any final services, and their output is difficult to compare across bureaus. The government contracts for some support services and most industrial services.
>
> (1975, p. 637)

At the level of local government, a review of ten empirical studies reports a similar finding: "Under conditions not un-

TABLE 2   *Increase in Federal Output per Man-Year*

SERVICE ACTIVITY	ANNUAL % INCREASE	
Final services	1.25	
Operating		0.84
Processing		3.62
Support services	3.24	
Management		1.32
Procurement		1.11
Maintenance		6.32
Industrial services	5.38	
Overhead and repair		5.05
Manufacturing		6.53

SOURCE: Niskanen, 1975, p. 637.

common among local governments, the average quasi-long-run cost function of horizontally integrated services tends to be reasonably horizontal over a wide range of operations" (Hirsch, 1970, pp. 183–184). If cost functions are horizontal, there are no economies of scale, and consolidating agencies does not save money.

The evidence reported by Meier, Kaufman, Niskanen, and Hirsch does not support the proposition that eliminating redundancy saves money. This is a serious blow to the monopoly theory because the argument from economy is easily its major pillar.

Theories, of course, do not need confirmation in order to survive, and thus far the stricture against bureaucratic competition has lasted very nicely in an evidential vacuum. But the persistence of this belief *is* puzzling when evaluated in the light of the generally positive attitude toward competition in American political history. We tend to favor competitive markets and competitive political parties. An adversary process is an integral part of our legal institutions. Our civil service is nominally competitive in terms of hiring and promotion. Our constitutional arrangement of checks and balances operates on a competitive principle.[12] Yet we condemn competition in

12. The constitutional design embraced competition in the sense of pitting competing ambitions, and institutions, against one another. The kind of

our public bureaucracies in a one-sided fashion.[13]

How can we explain this crazy quilt pattern of norms? The pattern is clearly not a product of data showing that redundancy has different effects in different settings, for, surprisingly, if undeniably, the requisite evidence concerning bureaucratic competition does not exist.

I propose that to put together the puzzle, we should investigate the history of public administration doctrine.[14] Our preference for competitive interorganizational arrangements in both public and private spheres dates back to the political economists of the 1700s whereas public administration strictures against redundancy represent an entirely different intellectual tradition, one originating with Woodrow Wilson (1887) and continuing through W. F. Willoughby (1927) and Leonard White (1939). These two groups were independent intellectual cohorts, and they bequeathed to us two inconsistent approaches to organizational design. The political economists focused upon competing independent firms or quasi-independent political institutions. Indeed, our concepts of a competitive market and of a competitive separation of powers have a common historical origin. Both date from eighteenth-century Enlightenment thought. Both received metaphorical inspiration from Newtonian mechanics and the principle of action and reaction, interpreted as countervailing self-interest (Laundau, 1972).

But the concept of interorganizational regulation via checks and balances was not extended to cover the *internal* structure of governmental departments. The question of how to manage the internal affairs of large-scale organizations did not arise then for a good and sufficient reason—such or-

---

reliability sought in this system differs from that of the others (see the discussion of type one versus type two errors below).

13. For a list of recent adherents to the conventional doctrines of public administration, see Meier (1980, p. 398). The list includes a 1972 Council of State Governments publication and a 1967 National Governors' Conference report.

14. Robert Kagan suggested that a legal doctrine is at work here as well. Norms of fairness mandate that agencies should treat citizens equally, and equal treatment implies a single set of uniformly applied rules and non-overlapping jurisdictions to clarify which agency makes and enforces the rules (personal communication).

ganizations did not exist in the 1700s. Early public administration, on the other hand, was contemporaneous with the emergence of a powerful organizational form, the corporate hierarchy.[15] The corporations' thrust then was consolidation, horizontally to reduce competition and vertically to coordinate specialized and interdependent processes. Early scholars of public administration, fascinated by the power of the new corporate form, were not influenced by the political economists' ideas on interorganizational competition.[16]

Admiration for the corporate structure was not confined to academics. The historian Louis Galambos has suggested it was a pervasive view in middle-class America at the turn of the century:

> As bureaucracy spread, more and more people became enamored of rationalization, system, and control; the traditional emphasis on individualism and competition began to wane. Frequently, the new values were reflected in a desire to emulate the large business corporation.
>
> (1975, p. 153)

And just as the "visible hand" of corporations would supersede the vagaries of markets, so would government based on a corporate model overcome the defects of chaotic organization.[17]

The corporate analogy became more explicit as public administration evolved. As far back as Woodrow Wilson, administration was considered a species of business. But Wilson, writing in 1887 before the properties of the great corporate hierarchies had become well known, could only sketch the desired administrative structure. By Willoughby's

15. Chandler states that the basic form of the centralized, single-product corporation was in place by the start of World War I. Hence it was available as an organizational model for our public administration forefathers (1977, p. 455).

16. The intellectual gulf between these two cohorts was not closed until the descendants of the classical political economists, the public choice theorists, turned their attention to bureaucracies. Public choice theorists such as Niskanen investigate the same phenomena studied by conventional public administrationists but use the framework of Adam Smith rather than W. F. Willoughby. See Ostrom (1973) for an analysis of this intellectual history.

17. The prestige of the corporation in the first third of this century was such that it was an organizational model even to some who criticized it. Even a (nominal) trustbuster like Theodore Roosevelt saw it as a vision of power:

time, the corporate form had been extensively described. His analogies between government and business were accordingly more detailed. He deliberately set up correspondences between existing corporate and prescribed government structures. Legislatures were equated with boards of directors, chief executives with general managers, and government departments with unifunctional divisions (1927, Chs. 2, 3, 5).[18] The correspondence was so clear to Willoughby that he *measured* governments by their approximation to the corporate ideal.[19]

> The government offering the closest approximation to the board of directors–general manager system of private corporations is probably that of Switzerland. . . . The actual working relations between the legislature and its administrative agents are almost identical with those obtaining in a private corporation. . . . It represents a system of administration toward which American practice is tending, notwithstanding the obstacles that stand in the way in the form of our doctrine of separation of powers.
>
> (ibid., pp. 50–51)

Once the comparison was made to corporations, the internal structure of government fell quickly into place: "there is no question" that an integrated structure with unifunctional departments has superior merit. Eliminating internal competition was an easy corollary to draw from the corporate model. Corporations had expanded partly to reduce competition, and Willoughby wrote long before the time when corporations used competing divisions internally. Not only did the one-to-one matching of functions to departments au-

---

"There is every reason why our executive governmental machinery should be at least as well planned, economical, and efficient as the best machinery of the great business organizations" (quoted in Hays, 1959, p. 125).

18. Prior to this, the corporate model had influenced municipal reform. While examining these, Leonard White noted that businessmen provided much of the opposition to "bad government" and that "looking about for a remedy, they were captivated by the resemblance of the city manager plan to their corporate form of business organization" (quoted in Hays, 1959, p. 159).

19. Ironically, only five years later Adolph Berle and Gardiner Means proclaimed the growing separation of managerial control and corporate ownership. Had Willoughby read their work, perhaps he would have been less sanguine about the "corporate ideal."

tomatically entail internal monopolies, Willoughby sought this outcome intentionally:

> A proper grouping of operating services departmentally furnishes the only means by which conflicts of jurisdiction, overlapping of functions, and duplications of organization, plant, and activities may be avoided.
>
> (ibid., p. 84)

The corporate model's implications were reinforced by the then popular machine metaphor.[20] Willoughby conceived administration as "a single integrated mechanism" (ibid., p. 81). Consider the following syllogism. The measure of a machine's performance is efficiency; friction constitutes inefficiency. Organizational conflict equals friction in the "machinery" of government; therefore, conflict is inefficient, and decreasing conflict by diminishing its causes such as overlapping jurisdictions will increase efficiency. Q.E.D.

Willoughby's explicitness in advocating the elimination of redundancy should not lead us to infer that he was the first to raise the issue. Congressional economy and efficiency committees preceded academic public administration theorists by thirty years, advocating cutting waste and shrinking government (Arnold, 1976). Although the committees' goals were to reduce government's size and expenses, the academics' goals were to strengthen the executive branch: "The root purpose of executive reorganization has remained the increase of presidential power over administration" (ibid., p. 26).

The difference in approach was signaled by a growing split between the concepts of economy and efficiency. Originally they were synonyms, referring to streamlined, simplified government. By the time of Taft's Commission on Economy and Efficiency in 1911, however, scholars such as Frederick Cleveland distinguished economy from efficiency. The latter

20. We should note that the *machine* metaphor of the early administrative theorists implied quite a different structure from the *mechanics* metaphor of the old political economists. The latter, relying on Newton's third law (for every action there is an equal and opposite reaction), sought designs that would minimize the effects, but not the existence, of self-interest (Landau, 1972). The former saw in the machine the model of perfectly coordinated parts: specialized, interdependent, and fundamentally harmonious.

connoted performance, not merely saving money. Adequate performance was in turn related to a strong chief executive, the president. Willoughby, who served with Cleveland on the Taft commission, testified that "the goal of economy was minor compared to the necessity for government to be able to plan its future expenditures and competently recommend policy to Congress" (ibid., p. 15). Thus, while congressional economizers wanted to *eliminate* wasteful programs, executive-oriented advocates urged *consolidating*[21] similar programs into single departments to augment managerial efficacy.[22] Both perspectives, however, pointed to the same outcome: increased departmental monopoly.[23] It is curious that in sixty years of reorganizations, reducing bureaucratic redundancy remained a constant tendency despite changing justifications.

In the decades after Willoughby, both machine and corporate metaphors ebbed in use. Even then political scientists began to criticize glib uses of the slogan of efficiency; the concept was altogether too ambiguous (Dimock, 1936, p. 120). But though the basic metaphors were receding, they left their imprint on the structural discussions of the thirties and forties. The dominant criterion remained organizing by major purpose, and except for Wallace (1941) and a few others, scholars of that period did not challenge the wisdom of establishing departmental monopolies via unifunctional organization.[24]

It was not until 1954 that the Willoughby tradition of basing structural reform on a corporate metaphor was broken. Norton Long, using a political party metaphor, suggested that the

21. For other examples of prominent public administration scholars advocating organizing by purpose, see White (1939, p. 106) and Macmahon (1937, p. 261).

22. Precisely why organizing by purpose would make bureaucracy more manageable was not spelled out in much detail. Reducing a chief executive's span of control was the reason cited most.

23. Theoretically, a department that monopolized a policy sector could be internally competitive, but this possibility was never considered.

24. The principle of unifunctional departments does not by itself eliminate redundancy since specialized departments could duplicate each other. But the unifunctionalists clearly implied the converse—only one department per function—as well.

conventional, monopolistic bureaucratic structure contained hidden dangers:

> We would all recognize the deficiency of a one-party legislature, yet many of us would applaud, and are applauding, a one-party top level bureaucracy. It may seem a forcing of the analogy to suggest that a loyal opposition in the upper levels of the bureaucracy could serve a function well nigh as socially useful as that performed by the loyal opposition in Parliament. We have only begun to think of how best to staff and organize administration if a major part of its job is to propose policy alternatives—alternatives that have run the gauntlet of facts, analysis, and competing social values built into the administrative process.
>
> (1954, p. 31)

This analysis, though sketchy, is striking because for the first time a student of public administration has based organizational design on an interorganizational, political metaphor. It harkens back to the federal design,[25] with a new emphasis on factual checks, not to the classical public administration of Cleveland or Willoughby with their corporate analogies.

Unfortunately, Long's proposed reorientation did not arouse much interest among students of bureaucracy.[26] The theories of interorganizational competition of the classical political economists could not be revived at that time. Thus, public administration continued on its isolated path, undisturbed by the tendency in other areas of American political thought to look to competitive systems. Our patchwork pattern of attitudes about redundancy is thus a legacy of diverse intellectual traditions failing to come to terms with one another. Consequently, neither the absence of empirical support

25. The federalists did not, however, support loyal party opposition; loyal opposition was to be located within the government itself.

26. More influential in stimulating scholars to rethink the matter was empirical work: Arthur Schlesinger's study (1958) of Franklin Roosevelt's bureaucratic strategies and Samuel Huntington's study (1961) of armed services competition. In particular, Schlesinger's description of Roosevelt's use of overlapping assignments and multiple information channels provided a novel way of looking at redundancy in government. By the end of the fifties, the monopolistic model's intellectual hegemony was fading.

nor inconsistency with another major political theory has shaken the hold of the monopolistic ideal on public administration.

The properly suspicious reader will have realized that although I have dwelt on the weaknesses of the argument for monopoly, I have not criticized redundancy theory. This asymmetry is unfair and must be redressed.

Problems in the Theory of Organizational Redundancy

Three major criticisms may be lodged against redundancy theory as presented so far. First, even if we assume that duplication promotes reliability, there are serious questions to be asked concerning the formation and decline of bureaucratic competition. Under what conditions does redundancy originate? Once it appears, is it unstable?

Second, we can raise some doubts concerning the applicability of redundancy theory to organization theory. Reliability engineering, the home field, is a remote technical discipline, and metaphorical transfer is a risky business. Specifically, in hardware systems, duplicate channels must function independently; otherwise the point of the redundancy is lost. How likely are redundant agencies to be independent? Also, hardware examples make analyzing redundancy appear deceptively easy particularly when a hardware redundancy protects against only one kind of error, for example, auto brakes not working when they should. What are redundancy's effects in social situations where there are two kinds of interdependent errors, for example, freeing a guilty man versus punishing an innocent one?

Third, basic normative questions must be faced. In what circumstances is redundancy desirable and how much is desirable? The traditional view that redundancy is never desirable offers an inviting target because in its extreme form it is untenable. The real questions are when? and how much? This is a formidable list of problems. Exploring them in more depth is in order.

The Appearance of Redundancy

The cases of weapons, water, and welfare notwithstanding, the appearance of redundancy in the public sector cannot be regarded as completely unproblematic. Agencies, unlike firms, are not free to compete or enter new fields whenever they wish to: their jurisdictions are legally defined. How then does bureaucratic duplication develop?

1. *Ambiguous boundaries.* Although charter legislation typically attempts to differentiate agencies' boundaries, it may be impossible, as public administration scholars have noted with regret, to assign a problem unambiguously to one agency. The antipoverty case provided an illustration of a policy sector riddled with jurisdictional ambiguity. The fight was, of course, fueled by the desires of agencies for status and budget increases, but the ambiguity itself rested largely on causal uncertainty. Is poverty primarily a matter of inadequate job skills? of poor education? of too little money? Because the answers to these questions were unknown, several departments could claim that their programs were relevant to solving the poverty problem.

In addition to technical uncertainty, the very organization of bureaucracy promotes jurisdictional confusion. We have not settled Luther Gulick's problem: we have not decided whether to organize the executive branches by purpose, process, place, or clientele. This logical ambiguity provides public ammunition for agencies fighting over programs. The logic of classification alone cannot determine where, for example, the program of mine workers' safety should be assigned. Categorized as a mine operation, it falls under the jurisdiction of the Bureau of Mines in the Interior Department; categorized as a workers' problem, it falls under the Department of Labor. But if the life of the law is not logic but experience, the life of bureaucratic structure is not classification but politics. Criterial confusion merely provided the opening wedge for competition in this example; substantive conflict was at the root of the matter. Authority shifted over to the Labor Department because it was believed that the Bureau of Mines was not adequately attending to miners' safety (Grossman, 1973).

Whatever the underlying cause of jurisdictional ambiguity, redundancy more readily develops if it is latent, that is, if, as in this example, the problem activating the latent overlap arises years after the agencies are established. Because no one anticipates the problem that will highlight the jurisdictional ambiguity, no one bothers to differentiate the organizations' boundaries. It is particularly easy to overlook latent redundancies when agencies are established at different times for initially different purposes.

2. *Executive intent.* Nonbureaucrats, such as chief executives, may find it in their interest to instigate competition among subordinates. Franklin Roosevelt's strategy is the best-known example (Schlesinger, 1958). The collective inability of political scientists, however, to detect other cases leads one to believe that the intentional creation of redundancy is quantitatively of small importance when compared with the less dramatic causes such as (1) above.

3. *Vertical Integration.* At the bureau level, an agency may be able to justify expanding its jurisdiction for technical reasons. A bureau's leaders may argue that it is difficult to perform task X without doing task Y as well, even though Y is already assigned to another agency. This branching out is a type of vertical integration, either integrating forward to manage outputs or integrating backward to manage inputs. As James Thompson conjectured: "Vertical integration thus is a major way of expanding organizational domains in order to reduce or eliminate significant contingencies" (1967, p. 41). Though vertical integration is most often studied in industry, public bureaus also engage in it. For example, the Soil Conservation Service argued before Congress that to perform its primary task of soil conservation effectively, it should receive permission to integrate backward into flood prevention. Despite objections from the Army Corps of Engineers, which had dominated this domain, the Soil Conservation Service obtained authorization to build small flood control structures (Simms, 1970, pp. 136–139).[27]

27. Vertical integration does not introduce competition in the public sector when it involves merging two monopolistic bureaus responsible for linked activities. Vertical integration created redundancy only when a bureau develops a new program (linked to its old programs) in a jurisdiction already occupied by another agency.

4.   At the agency level, bureaus can freely negotiate division-of-labor agreements guarding against competition. But these treaties do not prepare for every contingency. New technological opportunities can render agreements obsolete or indecisive. We recall, for example, that the Armed Services Treaty of 1947 (if a weapon moved on or in water, the Navy had jurisdiction; land was reserved for the Army, air for the Air Force) broke down with the advent of Intermediate-Range Ballistic Missiles. Thus, competition flourished despite the existence of a formal restrictive agreement.[28]

In general, a bureau's encroachment on another's domain is more tentative and gradual than analogous market processes. Rapid branching out is inhibited by the budgetary process. Because it is more difficult to obtain funds for new programs, agency spokesmen usually stress program continuity. Also, where agencies' tasks do not fall into natural clusters, gradual encroachment easily follows. If jurisdictions are fine-grained rather than coarse, there are no natural focal points for boundaries; arbitrary boundaries must be set. Division-of-labor treaties may exist in fine-grained cases, but as indicated by the Army's strategy of moving from the short-range Redstone to the intermediate-range Jupiter, such treaties are unstable.

Instability

No organizational arrangement can be both unstable and effective. Though stability is generally a precondition for effectiveness, reformers tend to overlook this property. What factors would make redundancy organizationally unstable?[29]

28. This example illustrates how a common industrial pattern—rhetoric favoring competition combined with behavioral collusion—is reversed in government where rhetoric praising cooperation is often followed by behavioral competition.

29. It may seem odd in a work on redundancy to raise the question of stability, for is it not true that "that which is redundant is, to the extent that it is redundant, stable" (McCulloch, 1960, p. 265)? Neurophysiologists like McCulloch think redundancy is a key source of reliability—hence stability—

1. *Agency-strategic reasons.* When agencies compete over programs, they threaten one another with loss of budget or authority, and potential losers will often be motivated to eliminate competition.[30] This is generally accomplished by negotiating an interagency treaty or memorandum of understanding establishing an acceptable degree of specialization. Because bureaucratic competition is rarely considered legitimate, treaties to reduce competition can be negotiated without the added costs of secrecy or the clumsiness of tacit adjustment. In contrast with colluding private firms, public bureaucracies are urged at every turn to cooperate and resolve their differences. For example, the Armed Services' efforts in 1947 to settle on a nonoverlapping division of labor were made openly and with the administration's blessing.

2. *Executive-stimulated change.* As a structure without an institutional base, bureaucratic redundancy is sensitive to changes in executive leadership. An executive with a taste for freewheeling competition may be replaced by one who abhors chaos. Consolidations may then follow, reducing or eliminating redundancies that had flourished during the previous regime, though, of course, agencies will defend their turf. Unlike changes based upon an agency's strategy, executive reorganizations may be carried out for general ideological reasons, such as conventional notions of efficiency found in campaign rhetoric.

3. *Success.* If one organization's program demonstrates its superiority, other organizations may leave the field, transforming competition into monopoly. For the short run this may be acceptable, for here monopoly results from proven merit. But the short-run gain is likely to become a long-run

---

in organisms. But because these systems have little internal conflict, the question of the *political* stability of a redundant structure is unimportant. In human organizations, however, whether bureaucratic politics permits redundancy to be stable is a significant question.

30. Of course, redundancy is a game that can be played at all organizational levels. An agency head may simultaneously wish to eliminate external competition while maintaining redundant channels below him—just as a firm prefers to sell its goods monopolistically while buying goods from competing sellers.

problem. Changing task environments may render old success ineffective; yet it may be difficult to reintroduce redundancy.

Clearly, redundancy would be a more practical reform if its "death" rate, that is, its instability, were not so great as to require a correspondingly high "birth" rate. Although we can conjecture about probable causes of birth and death, estimating their rates requires empirical investigation.

The Independence Criterion

It is a well-known rule of reliability engineering that to obtain maximum utility from redundancy, channels must be statistically independent of one another.[31] Only if independence is attained can we expect geometric increases in reliability for arithmetic increases in components—and costs (Landau, 1969, p. 350). Clearly, independence is a key attribute of redundant systems. But what does satisfying this criterion entail?

Figure 1 represents the most obvious violation of the independence criterion. Statistical independence requires more, however, than channels that are not directly connected. There is a second kind of violation. Consider the following example. A new weapon system is being designed, and the development of a crucial component is farmed out to three different laboratories. If the probability of any one contractor failing is

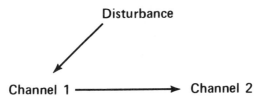

FIGURE 1   *Interdependent Systems*

31. Reducing investment risk via portfolio diversification exemplifies the same principle (Markowitz, 1959, p.102). Achieving safety by diversifying is an exceedingly general strategy.

p, is the probability of all three of them failing p^3? It would be if the labs' performances were statistically independent, but how can that be established? One could scrutinize communication patterns to see whether lab personnel are in contact with one another. One could contract with labs in different firms on the assumption that belonging to the same organization was ipso facto evidence of interdependence. But the problem is more subtle than that. Suppose that the labs' designs, though different in detail, are all based on the same theory. Imagine further that this theory turns out to be either wrong or inapplicable. Initially, at least, all three labs will fail, though not because they communicate with one another or were otherwise directly interdependent. Nonetheless, their failures will not be statistically independent (see Fig. 2). It is not enough that the channels not be directly connected; the disturbances must be uncorrelated.[32]

This fact presents a serious difficulty. Given that complete independence rarely obtains, can we still use redundancy theory to design more reliable bureaucracies? The answer is yes. We shall now show that the independence assumption can be discarded and replaced by a much more plausible postulate.

Consider the following situation. Suppose a boss (a president, a department secretary, etc.) has a choice of assigning a

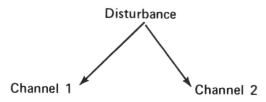

FIGURE 2   *Systems Vulnerable to Common Disturbance*

32. Similar (and erroneous) mind-sets, manifested in assumptions with correlated errors, appear to plague many forecasting models (Ascher, 1978, p.199). An entire generation of models may share the same dubious premises. When this happens, error correction must be sequential rather than simultaneous. Note that redundancies of this kind, in which actors reproduce a particular orientation and every model is similar, are inappropriate when a solution is not known in advance. For more evidence on the problem of correlated judgmental errors, see Felsenthal and Fuchs (1976, p. 475) and references cited therein.

problem to one department or to two departments. To keep the analysis simple, suppose that she has a fixed budget to fund the problem solving effort. If she gives the entire budget to one department, there is enough money for two proposals to be designed; if she allocates the budget to two departments, each can afford to produce one solution.[33]

Department 1	Department 2	Department 1
z_1	z_2	y_1 y_2
Structure Z		Structure Y

Thus, in structure Z the problem-solving efforts are more organizationally separated than they are in the monopolistic structure Y. It is as though two policy analysis units, team 1 and team 2 in structure Y, were located in two different departments in structure Z. For notational convenience, when the teams are both in Department 1, we call them y_1 and y_2; when they are put in different departments, we call them z_1 and z_2.

Let s be any satisfactory level of performance, and let us represent the greater organizational separation of z_1 and z_2 by the following inequality:

$$p(y_2 > s \mid y_1 > s) > p(z_2 > s \mid z_1 > s)$$

In words, the probability that y_2's solution is satisfactory, given that y_1's is satisfactory, is greater than the probability that z_2's is satisfactory, given that z_1's is adequate. This inequality simply formalizes the intuition that because there is more communication within an organization than between organizations, success is more likely to breed success intraorganizationally than interorganizationally. Because the teams are basically the same units with different organizational locations, we assume that the *un*conditional chances of success are equal:

$$p(y_1 > s) = p(y_2 > s) = p(z_1 > s) = p(z_2 > s).$$

33. Here I am making the neutral assumption that there are neither economies nor diseconomies of scale.

Now whichever structure the boss elects to use, she will eventually select the better of the two proposals produced by that structure. So define $Y = \max(y_1, y_2)$ and $Z = \max(z_1, z_2)$, where $\max(y_1, y_2)$ means the better of y_1 and y_2 and similarly for the Z's. Then Appendix 1 (at the end of this chapter) proves the following proposition:

Proposition 1: $p(Z > s) > p(Y > s)$.

The comparatively more independent structure, Z, is more reliable than Y in a strong sense: it is more likely to produce a solution that exceeds *any* arbitrary quality level. Informally, two relatively independent heads are better than two relatively dependent heads.[34] An important corollary follows immediately from this proposition.

Corollary: All decision-makers—satisficers and optimizers alike—prefer structure Z to structure Y.

The corollary states that whether the boss follows the behavioral strategy of satisficing (Simon, 1947) or the economic strategy of optimizing (expected utility maximization) makes no difference: the boss will always prefer the structure that is more likely to exceed every criterion level.[35] Further, the decision-maker's attitude toward risk is irrelevant. Risk-

34. As several readers pointed out, for increasing reliability negative correlation is superior to statistical independence. If two systems are perfectly negatively correlated, then one *always* works when the other is malfunctioning. Hence, perfect negative correlation produces complete reliability. Note that negative correlation is just a special case of the text's assumption that $p(z_2 > s \mid z_1 > s) < p(y_2 > s \mid y_1 > s)$. The Z's could be negatively correlated, and the Y's positively correlated, statistically independent, or less negatively correlated than the Z's. To avoid tedious repetition however, I refer to the Z's as "more independent" and the Y's as "less dependent" rather than using the technically correct phrases of "the Z's are less positively related" and "the Y's are more positively related."

35. For the fact that all expected utility maximizers prefer Z to Y whenever Z stochastically dominates Y, $(p(Z > s) > p(Y > s))$, see Lippman and McCall (1981, p. 216). To prove that satisficers also prefer Z to Y is more difficult since the logic of satisficing choice has not been axiomatized. Nevertheless, it is clear that given a fixed aspiration level, any reasonable satisficer would prefer to discover a satisfactory alternative sooner rather than later, and Proposition 1 establishes that satisfactory options will be encountered more quickly under system Z than Y.

seeking as well as risk-averse bosses prefer the more reliable system.[36]

The proof of Proposition 1 rests on the following reasoning. Since y_1 and y_2 are more dependent on each other than z_1 and z_2 are, they influence each other for both good *and ill* more than z_1 and z_2 do. Since the boss is going to select the better of the two proposals, what counts is to have *at least* one proposal that is satisfactory. Thus, the fact that the more monopolistic structure is more likely to have two bad solutions outweighs the fact that it is more likely to have two good ones.

Note that the proposition does *not* require that teams z_1 and z_2 be statistically independent. The teams may share similar mind sets, have similar beliefs, or be interdependent in a score of undetected ways. All that is required is that they be *less* dependent than y_1 and y_2, that is, less dependent than they would be if they were located in the same department. This is empirically very plausible.[37]

Now the reader may object that the boss is assumed to be infallible because she always chooses max (proposal 1, proposal 2). Surely this is unrealistic. Just as subordinates are fallible, so are superiors. Does the ranking of the two structures change if we assume that the boss sometimes errs and picks an inferior solution? The answer is no. As long as the

36. The following choice defines attitudes toward risk. A person has two alternatives, A and B. These options yield, on average, the same benefits, but A is more likely than B to be extremely good or extremely bad. If the decision-maker prefers A over B, he or she is risk-seeking; if he or she chooses B over A, he or she is risk-averse; if he or she is indifferent, he or she is risk-neutral.

37. It obviously follows from Proposition 1 that if the monopolistic structure Y generates only one proposal, then $p(Z > s) > p(Y > s)$. This more nearly represents the situation that most people have in mind when they compare a redundant structure with a streamlined, nonredundant one: two agencies, each designing one program, versus one agency planning one program. However, this situation is harder to evaluate because it is implausible to assume that costs are equal: creating two programs usually costs more than creating one. Though system Z is more reliable than system Y, it is more expensive. By stipulating that the monopolistic structure designs the same number of programs as the more decentralized one, we can assume that costs are constant, thereby ensuring that the systems' net worth depends only on their reliability. Moreover, showing that organizing two heads in one way is more reliable than organizing those heads another way is more surprising than showing that two heads are better than one.

boss performs equally fallibly in the face of the two structures and she chooses max (proposal 1, proposal 2) at least half the time—which the boss can guarantee by flipping a coin—then we can prove (see Appendix 2 at the end of this chapter) the following proposition:

Proposition 2: $p(\hat{Z} > s) \geq p(\hat{Y} > s)$

(where $\hat{Z}$ and $\hat{Y}$ symbolize structures with faulty evaluations). Thus, the more redundant structure is always *at least* as likely to produce a satisfactory proposal and is strictly more reliable if the the evaluation process works better than chance.

Propositions 1 and 2 reveal that the value of redundant decision-making is enhanced if the redundancy is organized in multiple bureaus. Though it is possible for a single agency to design parallel programs and though this duplication does increase reliability, this is not the best way to organize redundancy. Embedding parallel programs in separate bureaus is a key method for ensuring a diversity of approach, and it is diversity that underlies Propositions 1 and 2.

Type One and Type Two Errors

> *Two hundred years ago David Hume proposed we accept "as a maxim, that, in contriving any system of government, and fixing the several checks and controls of the constitution, every man ought to be supposed to be a* knave, *and to have no other end, in all his actions, than private interest."*
> *(quoted in Niskanen, 1971, p. 128; original emphasis)*

Fearing that knaves may occupy high positions and abuse their authority, the constitutional architects designed a checks-and-balances system that was more reliable than any of its parts. The system was to be reliable, however, in a specific sense: tyrannical acts were to be guarded against.[38] In Hume's words: "A constitution is so far good as it provides

---

38. There was not, however, complete consensus on this point. Alexander Hamilton, among others, was more worried that the central government would be impotent.

against maladministration" (quoted in Wolin, 1960, p. 390). These are errors of commission.[39] Systems may also be reliable with respect to errors of omission, ensuring that a desirable event does occur.

Modern reliability theory distinguishes between a type one error, failing to stop an undesired event, and a type two error, failing to effect a desired one.[40] Organizational redundancy theory has not yet incorporated this point. Landau did not discuss the question in his 1969 essay, and though he subsequently (1973a) discussed redundancy in the context of constitutional design, that a different kind of error is involved was not made explicit.[41] Yet many policy sectors exhibit both types of errors. Recall, for example, that a welfare program may overlook an eligible person (error of omission) or aid an ineligible one (error of commission). A perfect welfare system would be completely reliable in both respects, but there may be trade-offs between these two kinds of reliability. Does guarding against unwanted actions nullify or vitiate efforts to ensure that desired actions occur?

Let us consider a communications system of m parallel units and n units in a series (see Fig. 3). The m parallel units guard against the blocking of an accurate or desired message (a type one error); the more parallel units, the lower the probability that this will occur. The n series units guard against the transmission of an inaccurate or unwanted message (a type two error). Intuitively we see that one could add enough parallel channels so that the increase of type two errors will outweigh the decrease of type one errors. Hence, redundancies can eventually *increase* the total system errors. This supposition is confirmed by Barlow and Proschan's proof

39. For a modern example, consider missile launching from submarines. Two crewmen must independently turn keys: if only one does so, the missile will not fire. This procedure protects against the disaster of an inadvertent launching.

40. If the errors pertain to accepting or rejecting factual premises (hypotheses) rather than taking actions, then the situation is equivalent to the type one–type two problem in statistics.

41. The problem of type one–type two errors resulting from organizational redundancies was, however, noted by Felsenthal and Fuchs (1976, p. 476).

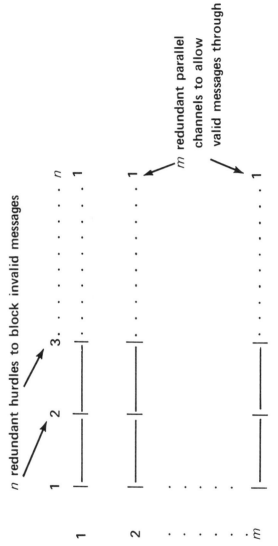

FIGURE 3   m × n *Communications System*

in their *Mathematical Theory of Reliability* (1965, p. 187). This proof constitutes a warning that introducing a particular kind of redundancy, without regard for the kind of error that is already prevalent, can *impair* rather than improve organizational reliability.[42]

Of course, what counts is not merely an error's frequency, but its frequency multiplied by its damage. When there is organizational consensus on the relative importance of the two types of error or when it is agreed that only one is consequential, one kind of redundancy can be increased to reduce total damage even though the total *number* of errors is higher than before. For example, because unnecessarily delaying a NASA launch is a less serious error than launching one that would malfunction, the system is deliberately biased against the former by giving five specialists independent authority to halt a firing.

Redundancy becomes a political issue when there is no agreement on the weighting of the error types. For example, people probably agree that it is preferable to free a guilty man than jail an innocent one but probably disagree over the exact trade-off between the two errors. Redundancy theory alone cannot answer the normative question of which kind of duplication is satisfactory or optimal in such circumstances; normative decision theory is also needed.

We see, therefore, that the existence of two kinds of errors complicates the theory of redundancy either because of trade-offs between the errors or, more politically, because decisionmakers do not agree on their relative importance. Both considerations affect the reasonable allocation of redundancy.

Allocating Redundancy

From its inception, redundancy theory was a normative endeavor. The key normative question of designing organizational reliability is when is duplication de-

---

42. Furthermore, though Barlow and Proschan prove that one can reduce both types of error by adding sufficient amounts of both kinds of redundancy (1965, p. 187), it is doubtful that the attractive property of geometric increases in total reliability for arithmetic increases in cost still obtains.

sirable? An uncritical answer—it is always desirable—is likely to prove untenable, as is the traditional answer that it is *never* desirable.

Because redundancy is chiefly a strategy for reducing and containing failures of various kinds, its usefulness is related to the frequency and significance of failure. Thus, redundancy is desirable (1) the higher the probability of failure in a single channel of action, communication, or decision; and (2) the more critical or costly a failure would be. Because the use of redundancy is complicated when one must worry about the prevalence of both type one and type two errors, redundancy is more desirable (3) when one need not worry about interactions between two types of errors, either because only one kind can occur or because only one is important. Protecting against only one kind of error simplifies applying redundancy.

Because producing innovations is, in the long run, the best way to increase efficiency in government, redundancy is desirable (4) when there is a significant chance that a duplicate agency could discover a more effective way to attain the same results that a monopolistic agency achieves. The more a monopolistic agency is wedded to its current program and the more room there is for significant improvement in the policy area, the more valuable redundancy is.

Finally, although low cost does not of itself make an arrangement more desirable, clearly (5) the *acceptability* of redundancy as a strategy for containing failure is inversely related to its cost.

One limitation of this analysis is that the criteria can conflict. For example, failure may be critical but redundancy expensive.[43] There are inevitably gray areas, but the criteria do indicate what classes of situations would be particularly promising candidates. For example, we shall subsequently argue that it is sensible to deploy competing problem-solving teams primarily in the early stages of an R&D project because uncertainty is highest and cost lowest in the early workings of

---

43. One could superficially handle these inconsistencies by positing a single general rule, such as use redundancy when it creates net benefits. But such rules obscure the fact that there is no single evaluative dimension in the public sector.

such projects. Thus, criteria one and five, two of the most important, point in the same direction concerning the temporal allocation of redundancy within development projects.

The corollary to the fundamental normative question of when redundancy is functional is how *much* redundancy is warranted under different conditions. Because this is a quantitative variant on the first question, the answer depends on the same parameters. For example, the more costly redundancies are, the fewer are warranted, while the more serious an error would be, the more redundancies are functional. Similarly, if type one and type two errors interact, then the number of redundancies needed to suppress one kind of error is constrained by the tendency to produce the second.

In organizational contexts, unlike reliability engineering, it will often be difficult to estimate quantitative values for the relevant parameters, and it will therefore be difficult to answer the how-much-is-enough question precisely. The point suggests a paradox. One of the most important justifications for redundancy is uncertainty—not knowing whether an actor or component will complete a task. But if uncertainty is great, it will be impossible to specify precisely how much redundancy is required to ameliorate the problems caused by uncertainty in the first place. However, this need not counsel despair. It is possible that the theory can provide heuristic rules indicating a general direction without specifying precisely optimal amounts. Engineers may design efficient redundancies, but political scientists will usually have to settle for those that, in Herbert Simon's coinage, "satisfice."

These problems in the theory of redundancy—the organizational stability of competition, the difficulties of metaphorical transfer, and the appropriate allocation of redundancy—are too fundamental to be dispensed with here. They will reappear in subsequent chapters. However, one final problem, hitherto unmentioned, can be resolved.

The concept of redundancy requires some unpacking. Although I have indeed slipped back and forth between "redundancy" and "competition" as if they were synonyms, strictly speaking, they are not. All competitive structures are redundant, but the converse is not true; there are non-competitive types of duplication. This distinction between competitive and noncompetitive redundancies will be used in the following chapters. Now is the time to sharpen it.

Different Types of Redundancies and Their Effects

The general theory of redundancy deemphasizes the adaptability and reliability of single channels, whether represented by individuals or by organizations. It stresses instead the advantages of multiple channels even if each channel individually is unreliable. This implies emphasizing error *absorption,* the ability to function despite the presence of a failed channel, rather than error *correction.* Engineers call systems that operate despite malfunctions *failure-tolerant.* Such systems are not "failsafe," but they are "failsoft." We will refer to this as the backup effect of redundancy, which is produced by a sheer availability of independent alternatives.

The backup effect economizes on diagnostic and corrective resources because the user of redundant channels needs to know neither why one channel failed nor how to restore it. When there are numerous causes of failure, but practical interest focuses on the *consequences* of failure, then a backup redundancy is a sensible design strategy, particularly if the cost of carrying an ineffective, uncorrected channel is not too great.

Competitive Redundancies

The classical theory of redundancy, deriving from the study of nonliving systems, does not analyze strategic interactions between redundant components. Indeed, component interaction is mainly a problem for redundancy theory, as it indicates a disruption of the functional independence essential to the backup effect. If the redundant componets are interdependent, then one channel's failure may disrupt a duplicate.

It is reasonable to assume, however, that if public agencies overlap by providing similar services or by working on similar plans, they will likely be aware of each other's existence. Further, they may fight over "turf." Far from being passive and independent suppliers, the agencies will perceive one another as rivals for an exclusive jurisdiction.

Interdependence, a problem for redundancy theory, can here be seen as an opportunity, particularly if we look through the lenses of economics and see interdependence as rivalry. The independently developed concepts of competition and redundancy conceptually overlap on the backup effect. Like redundancy, competition always connotes alternatives. Competition, however, connotes an additional property of *rivalry* between alternative suppliers for the support of a service's users.[44] Though the backup effect of general redundancy does not require that suppliers of substitute services know about one another, much less conflict, [45] the concept of competitive redundancy connotes a conscious striving of opponents to outdo one another.[46] Hypothetically, a rivalry stimulates suppliers' performance, either preventing decline or stimulating recovery. Competition thus connotes more active error correction than does redundancy.[47]

The property of rivalry is linked to a second difference between competitive and noncompetitive duplication: the organizational location of redundancy. The more competitive

44. In the rest of this work I adhere to a simple pattern of usage. When the attribute of rivalry or conflict is important, only the term *competition* is used. If the significant attribute is duplication, with or without rivalry, the terms are used interchangeably to avoid tedious repetition.

45. In fact, as the Thor-Jupiter history illustrated, creating programmatic duplication is one method of *diminishing* conflict between bureaus. Guaranteeing the stability of redundant programs can remove them from the subset of competitive redundancies by reducing conflict over scarce resources.

46. Conscious rivalry is stressed in competition of the few (oligopoly); in perfect or atomistic competition mutual awareness is inessential (McNulty, 1967).

47. Franklin Roosevelt, well known as a user of bureaucratic redundancy, understood both kinds of effects. Concerning backup, Roosevelt held that if "the obvious channel of action was blocked and it was not worth the political trouble of dynamiting it open, then the emergency agency supplied the means of getting the job done nevertheless. And the new agencies simplified the problem of reversing direction and correcting error" (Schlesinger, 1958, p. 534). As for rivalry: "There is something to be said for having a little conflict between agencies. A little rivalry is stimulating . . . . It keeps everybody going to prove that he is a better fellow than the next man" (ibid., p. 535).

the redundancy, the more likely it is embodied in separate organizations. In competitive redundancies, rivals must be differentially rewarded for their achievements. In addition, they must have discretion over which programs to pursue. The combination of these two elements, discretion over major decisions and differential rewards for results, creates formal or de facto organizational boundaries. In noncompetitive redundancies, where units functionally overlap but do not fight over scarce resources, it is less necessary that redundancy be embedded in separate organizations.[48] For example, a single organization could easily have duplicating communication channels that are not rivals in the competitive sense.

Economists and public choice theorists who have been critical of the monopoly theory in public administration are predisposed to develop alternatives stressing competitive, multiorganizational structures. The two best examples have been the works of Vincent Ostrom and of William Niskanen.

The study by Ostrom, Tiebout, and Warren (1961) is a classic analysis of competitive, polycentric[49] organization in metropolitan areas. Ostrom et al., taking as their empirical base the Lakewood Plan in Southern California, examined cities that by contracting for services expanded the sources of supply open to them. Lakewood cities contracted with Los Angeles County, private organizations, and neighboring cities or sometimes provided the services themselves. This created a quasi-market possessing—the authors asserted— the conventional market virtues of flexibility and responsiveness to client demand.[50] They drew no distinction between the behavior of public and private suppliers; so presumably the mechanism of competition, accompanied by

48. However, for certain types of redundancy, especially redundancy of authority, organizations must be independent.

49. Ostrom et al. (1961) chose not to call their model a pluralist one, and the difference is more than terminological. In pluralist models, few decisionmakers are influential in different policy areas. This property does not, however, preclude a single agency from monopolizing a particular policy area. In a polycentric model, on the other hand, competitive supply is a central property. For some reason the structure of bureaucratic supply was ignored during the pluralist-power elite debates.

50. More recent studies of the Lakewood Plan have questioned whether its effects are as benign as Ostrom et al. (1961) believed (Mehay, 1978; Miller, 1981). Mehay points out that the service contracts are incomplete, specifying

heightened supplier responsiveness owing to threatened or actual loss of customers, applied to all vendors. Ostrom et al. further noted that the chief administrative officer of Lakewood cities behaves like a buyer in a large corporation, bargaining for local consumer preferences instead of being sensitive to production considerations as often happens in American cities. In a follow-up study, Warren (1966) added that the buyer cities' representatives gradually became experts in purchasing services, diminishing informational deficiencies that plague consumers.[51]

Ostrom et al.'s main innovation was not in exploring the process or effects of competition, which were described conventionally, but in transferring them to the context of metropolitan government. They pointed out that by distinguishing production from provision of service, it is possible to introduce competition even though the services ultimately provided are public goods, that is, not packageable for individual consumption.

Niskanen has developed a more formal theory of competitive and monopolistic public bureaucracy. Following profit-maximizing analysis, his 1971 model assumes that bureaucrats attempt to maximize budgets. Under this and other[52] assumptions, Niskanen concludes that a monopolistic bureau is *not* more technically efficient, where technical efficiency means producing at minimum cost, than competitive bu-

---

inputs rather than outputs, a problem that will be taken up in Chapter Seven. Miller contends that households' locational choices reflect differences in wealth far more than differences in tastes. Hence the Lakewood system, rather than helping sort households into efficient communities of homogeneous tastes, helps cities to keep out the poor.

51. Williamson (1975) observes that the experience-based ratings of traders in intermediate goods markets, where exchanges are between firms, are more highly developed than those in final goods markets, where exchanges are between firms and households.

52. In his basic 1971 model, Niskanen also assumes that (1) budgets must at least equal cost of output; (2) bureaus exchange a package of services for a lump sum budget, unlike firms, which exchange units of output for a price; (3) the appropriations committee will not approve a budget if its marginal valuation of the last unit of output is negative; and (4) beyond the weak constraint of three, the legislature plays a passive role. Assumptions two and four have been effectively criticized by Miller and Moe (1983).

reaus.[53] This conclusion contradicts the conventional wisdom that overlapping jurisdictions are wasteful. Indeed, since competing bureaus would give appropriations committees information about sound and unsound programs, thereby eliminating the monopoly of information possessed by a single bureau, the *total* budget of competing bureaus would be less[54] than a single bureau's (1971, p. 160). And although competition would not reduce allocative inefficiency—oversupply of output[55]—competitive bureaus fare no worse on this criterion than monopolistic ones.

In 1975 Niskanen modified his model by relaxing some of the less realistic assumptions, such as the postulate of passive sponsoring committees, and by changing the bureaucrat's goal to maximizing the *discretionary* budget.[56] The major result for monopoly bureaus is that technical inefficiency plagues them more, and allocative inefficiency less, than the 1971 model predicts.[57] Since competition cannot improve the latter condition but can the former, the modifications increase the applicability of competition.[58] Bureaucratic competition reduces some negative implications of the new theory's mana-

53. The 1971 model has two general solutions: a demand-constrained solution, where the marginal value of a bureau's service equaled zero, and a budget-constrained solution, where the amount of service was constrained because total costs had to be covered by the budget. In the latter region, even monopoly bureaus are technically efficient (produce at minimum cost). After Niskanen reformulated his model in 1975, this two-region solution disappears, and with it disappears the conclusion that monopoly bureaus are efficient under budget-constrained conditions.

54. This occurs under demand-constrained conditions.

55. Niskanen defines oversupply as more output than the median voter prefers.

56. The discretionary budget equals the budget received by the bureau minus the minimum budget necessary to produce the output.

57. Specifically, the mix of technical and allocative inefficiencies depends on the value of a parameter that represents how much of the discretionary budget can be appropriated by bureaucrats for personal perquisites. When the parameter's value is zero, then the 1971 solution, high allocative inefficiency (oversupply) combined with technical efficiency, reappears. As the parameter's value increases, allocative efficiency rises but technical efficiency decreases.

58. Since Niskanen discussed only monopolistic bureaus in his 1975 model, I am inferring the effect of competition in the revised theory.

gerial discretion component wherein bureaucrats use a discretionary budget for acquiring perquisites instead of producing output. Competition gives legislative committees more accurate estimates of true minimum cost budgets, thereby reducing the discretionary budget available to bureaucrats.

It is significant that the results of the first sustained, formal examination of competition and monopoly in government are unfavorable, even in terms of cost, to monopoly.[59] The arguments have thus come full circle since Willoughby's day. At that time students of public administration asserted that establishing bureaucratic monopoly was the path to economical government. Now economists themselves are skeptical of this claim. Monopoly's efficiency is doubted; its effectiveness is also challenged. Landau, by showing that a monopoly is equivalent to a nonredundant system, revealed its potential for unreliable performance.

All this is rather abstract. The case studies on urban transit, however, will make plain that redundancy theory has its pragmatic side. But before we discuss the cases, we must translate the general concepts of this chapter into language appropriate to the policy context of urban transit.

59. Though Miller and Moe (1983) provide a telling critique of Niskanen's 1971 model, in particular his representation of legislative-bureau interactions, their model, like his, concludes that bureaucratic competition is superior to monopoly (p. 311).

Appendix 1. Proof of Proposition 1

$$p(z_2 > s) = p(z_2 > s \,|\, z_1 > s) \cdot p(z_1 > s)$$
$$+ \, p(z_2 > s \,|\, z_1 < s) \cdot p(z_1 < s)$$
$$p(y_2 > s) = p(y_2 > s \,|\, y_1 > s) \cdot p(y_1 > s)$$
$$+ \, p(y_2 > s \,|\, y_1 < s) \cdot p(y_1 < s).$$

Since
$$p(z_2 > s) = p(y_2 > s),$$
$$p(z_2 > s \,|\, z_1 > s) \cdot p(z_1 > s) + p(z_2 > s \,|\, z_1 < s) \cdot p(z_1 < s)$$
$$= p(y_2 > s \,|\, y_1 > s) \cdot p(y_1 > s) + p(y_2 > s \,|\, y_1 < s) \cdot p(y_1 < s).$$

Since
$$p(z_2 > s \,|\, z_1 > s) < p(y_2 > s \,|\, y_1 > s),$$
$$p(z_2 > s \,|\, z_1 > s) \cdot p(z_1 > s) < p(y_2 > s \,|\, y_1 > s) \cdot p(y_1 > s).$$

Hence
$$p(z_2 > s \,|\, z_1 < s) \cdot p(z_1 < s) > p(y_2 > s \,|\, y_1 < s) \cdot p(y_1 < s),$$
$$p(z_2 > s \,|\, z_1 < s) > p(y_2 > s \,|\, y_1 < s).$$

Since
$$p(z_2 > s \,|\, z_1 < s) + p(z_2 < s \,|\, z_1 < s) = 1$$
$$p(y_2 > s \,|\, y_1 < s) + p(y_2 < s \,|\, y_1 < s) = 1,$$
$$p(z_2 < s \,|\, z_1 < s) < p(y_2 < s \,|\, y_1 < s)$$

$$p(z_1 < s) \cdot p(z_2 < s \mid z_1 < s) < p(y_2 < s \mid y_1 < s) \cdot p(y_1 < s).$$

Since the boss will take the better of the two solutions in either case, he or she will take

$$Z = \max(z_1, z_2) \quad \text{or} \quad Y = \max(y_1, y_2).$$

$$p(Z > s) = 1 - p(z_1 \text{ and } z_2 < s)$$

$$= 1 - p(z_1 < s) \cdot p(z_2 < s \mid z_1 < s)$$

$$p(Y > s) = 1 - p(y_1 \text{ and } y_2 < s)$$

$$= 1 - p(y_1 < s) \cdot p(y_2 < s \mid y_1 < s).$$

Since

$$p(z_1 < s) \cdot p(z_2 < s \mid z_1 < s) < p(y_2 < s \mid y_1 < s) \cdot p(y_1 < s)$$

$$-p(z_1 < s) \cdot p(z_2 < s \mid z_1 < s) > -p(y_2 < s \mid y_1 < s) \cdot p(y_1 < s)$$

$$1 - p(z_1 < s) \cdot p(z_2 < s \mid z_1 < s) >$$

$$1 - p(y_2 < s \mid y_1 < s) \cdot p(y_1 < s)$$

$$p(Z > s) > p(Y > s).$$

Thus, structure Z is more reliable than structure Y.

Appendix 2. Proof of Proposition 2

Let

$$Z = \max(z_1, z_2)$$
$$E = \min(z_1, z_2)$$
$$Y = \max(y_1, y_2)$$
$$F = \min(y_1, y_2)$$
$$\hat{Z} = \text{final choice of boss, given } (z_1, z_2)$$
$$\hat{Y} = \text{final choice of boss, given } (y_1, y_2)$$

and

$$p = p(\text{boss makes correct choice})$$
$$= p[\text{boss chooses max (proposal 1, proposal 2)}]$$
$$q = p(\text{boss makes incorrect choice})$$
$$= p[\text{boss chooses min (proposal 1, proposal 2)}]$$
$$= 1 - p$$

Step 1. Show that

$$p(\hat{Z} > s) = p(\hat{Y} > s)$$

if $p = q$

$$p(\hat{Z} > s) = p(Z > s) \cdot p + p(E > s) \cdot q$$

$$= \frac{1}{2}[p(Z > s) + p(E > s)]$$

$$= \frac{1}{2}[p(z_1 > s | z_1 > z_2) \cdot p(z_1 > z_2)$$

$$+ p(z_2 > s | z_2 > z_1) \cdot p(z_2 > z_1)$$
$$+ p(z_1 > s | z_1 < z_2) \cdot p(z_1 < z_2)$$
$$+ p(z_2 > s | z_2 < z_1) \cdot p(z_2 < z_1)]$$

$$= \frac{1}{2}[p(z_1 > s | z_1 > z_2) \cdot p(z_1 > z_2) +$$
$$p(z_1 > s | z_1 < z_2) \cdot p(z_1 < z_2)$$
$$+ p(z_2 > s | z_2 > z_1) \cdot p(z_2 > z_1) +$$
$$p(z_2 > s | z_2 < z_1) \cdot p(z_2 < z_1)]$$

$$= \frac{1}{2}[p(z_1 > s) + p(z_2 > s)]$$

$$= \frac{1}{2}[p(y_1 > s) + p(y_2 > s)]$$

$$= \frac{1}{2}[p(Y > s) + p(F > s)]$$

(by substitution of Ys for Zs in above reasoning)

$$= (\hat{Y} > s) \quad \text{when} \quad p = q$$

Step 2. Show that

$$p(\hat{Z} > s) > p(\hat{Y} > s)$$

$$\text{if} \quad p > q$$

Since

$$p(Z > s) + p(E > s) = p(Y > s) + p(F > s) \qquad \text{by Step 1}$$
$$p(Z > s) > p(Y > s),$$
$$p(E > s) < p(F > s)$$
$$p(Z > s) - p(E > s) > p(Y > s) - p(F > s).$$

For $t > 0$,

$$t[p(Z > s) - p(E > s)] > t[p(Y > s) - p(F > s)].$$

Since from Step 1

$$\frac{1}{2} \cdot [p(Z > s) + p(E > s)] = \frac{1}{2}[p(Y > s) + p(F > s)]$$

$$\frac{1}{2} \cdot [p(Z > s) + p(E > s)] + t \cdot [p(Z > s) - p(E > s)]$$

$$> \frac{1}{2} \cdot [p(Y > s) + p(F > s)] + t \cdot [p(Y > s) - p(F > s)]$$

$$p(Z > s) \cdot \left(\frac{1}{2} + t\right) + p(E > s) \cdot \left(\frac{1}{2} - t\right) >$$

$$p(Y > s) \cdot \left(\frac{1}{2} + t\right) + p(F > s) \cdot \left(\frac{1}{2} - t\right)$$

so

$$p(\hat{Z} > s) > p(\hat{Y} > s)$$

$$\text{when} \quad \frac{1}{2} + t = p > q = \frac{1}{2} - t.$$

2

The Policy Context: Urban Transit

Italians of diverse political persuasions recall that one of Mussolini's achievements was to make the trains run on time. This reminiscence reminds us that citizens care greatly about the workaday services that governments provide. The stuff of life for most people is not the grand political adventures, for example, making Italy a world power, but the ordinary services. They want garbage collected, schools administered, and transit run on time. The performance of the bureaucracies providing these services matters to citizens. They care about results and notice deteriorations in quality.

When deterioration occurs, public attention typically focuses first on consequences and works backward to causes. First one observes that Johnny can't read; then one wonders why. Thus there is little public attention on organizational strategies that might work in a broad spectrum of policy sectors; the focus is on a particular sector. This study reverses that sequence of attention. Instead of starting with performance in a particular policy area, our primary topic is an organizational strategy, redundancy, which might be applicable to a wide variety of sectors. But to evaluate the practical payoff of a structural design, it is best to examine it within a particular policy context. And if redundancy is a generally effective structure, it should prove itself in one of those un-glamorous services that affects the daily lives of citizens. A democracy's trains also should run on time. Accordingly, this chapter integrates the general theory of bureaucratic redundancy with the policy focus of urban transit.[1] Thus we hope to join the issues of organizational structure and policy performance, show the pragmatic possibilities of redundancy, and thereby illustrate once again that there is nothing so practical as a good theory.

Redundancy and Urban Transit

In an idealized world of complete certainty, duplication is unnecessary: a transit agency's plans are always accurate, its communication channels noiseless, its service flawless. Such fairy tales need not detain us. The task environments of real transit agencies are never completely free of surprise. Uncertainty is the organizational equivalent of original sin: all bureaucracies are born in it.

Uncertainty, then, is a given in organizational life. And uncertainty, that is, the possibility of failure, is redundancy's raison d'être. The greater the probability that a message will not be delivered or a task completed, the greater a priori justification for duplicate channels of communication and action. It follows, therefore, that the amount of uncertainty confronting a transit agency is an important determinant of the utility of redundancy. Though the task environments of transit organizations admit of many degrees of uncertainty, to keep the analysis simple, we will distinguish between tasks involving only two degrees of uncertainty, between *planning* and *operating* a transit system.

---

1. As often happens, the choice of empirical focus was determined as much by pragmatic considerations as theoretical ones. In this case, a combination of proximity to a clear instance of governmental redundancy—the overlapping services provided by two nearby transit agencies—and research support in this policy area provided the impetus for selecting urban transit as the area of inquiry.

Planning is fundamentally more uncertain than operations. In this stage the basic transit options, a system's technology and configuration, are designed and evaluated. In the course of this design and evaluation, numerous variables must be predicted, and all these projections are subject to error. A transportation planner puts it bluntly:

> Almost all of entities—the unit costs, the travel volumes, the interest rates, the service lines, and the capital and maintenance costs—have to be predicted for the future and therefore fall prey to inaccuracy.
> (Dickey, 1975, p. 326)

To these we can add other technological or supply projections, such as schedule adherence and the equipment's reliability, which may go awry.

Nor is this all. A system may be technologically impeccable, performing according to design specifications but nevertheless useless in its task environment. In defense policy, Jacob Stockfisch (1973) has noted that weapon systems inappropriately designed for their operational environments cause as much grief as those that fail for technical reasons. Regardless of technical achievements in satisfying engineering specifications, if the military user of a weapon is dissatisfied, the weapon cannot be considered an unqualified success. Similarly, a transit system may be technologically satisfactory, but if the system's planners misunderstood which technical features are most important to passengers, the system will carry fewer patrons than had been projected. And predicting which features of a transit system matter the most is not a trivial task. For example, a respected work on urban transit noted one common planning error:

> Numerous studies have found that (reliability) is one of the very few most significant criteria influencing modal choice, yet a recent survey of transit travel forecasting methods found that it was not among the thirteen variables frequently utilized by transportation planning agencies.
> (Altshuler, Womack, Pucher, 1979, p. 115)

In short, between predicting a system's technical capabilities incorrectly and misunderstanding passengers' preferences, transit planners can err in numerous junctures.

In contrast, by the time a transit system has reached the operational stage, uncertainty has been considerably reduced. The first few months of service provide much information about how closely the system will live up to its engineering specifications and how much patronage will be attracted. And the lower the uncertainty, the less needed is duplication. Yet operations never become completely trouble-free, as we shall see when we study the case of BART. And because reliability is a highly prized aspect of transit service, redundancy remains a relevant strategy for operations.

However, just as in public administration in general, so in transit administration in particular the major viewpoint is that duplication is wasteful. Let us now specify in more detail the opposing positions by comparing the hypothesized advantages of redundancy in planning and operations with the conventionally postulated benefits of monopolistic planning and operations.

The Case for Monopolistic Transit Planning

The conventional wisdom presented by the transit planning literature contains two axioms: planning should be comprehensive, and planning should be conducted by only one agency. Thus the conventional wisdom of urban transit planning, as codified in standard textbooks, adheres to a monopolistic model of planning.[2] To be sure, advocates of this model expect that a transit agency will have to submit its design to other decision-makers for approval. Voters must approve bonds and the U.S. Department of Transportation must approve grants. Nevertheless, this is a serial process with virtually every stage in the series monopolized by a single organization.[3]

2. The textbooks legitimize one type of redundancy in this process, but it is a redundancy of iterations on a design-evaluate-design-again loop, over the same group of planners, not over a competing group.
3. See Morlock (1978, p. 16), Dickey (1975, pp. 16–18), and Creighton (1970, p. 136) for examples of urban transportation planning texts that describe the decision process in these terms.

The other idea embraced by conventional wisdom, comprehensive planning, has exhibited two distinct meanings. First, the imperative of comprehensive planning has meant that a planner should search exhaustively through the set of possible transit solutions. Joining this concept of exhaustive search to the notion of a monopoly planner produces the image, familiar to organization theorists, of a single centralized decision-maker engaged in synoptic planning (Lindblom, 1959). In the field of urban transit, the justification for synoptic planning is that only a modally comprehensive transit agency will survey all candidate solutions and choose among them in a rational and unbiased manner. If modally specialized and competing agencies were to advocate their own plans, they would offer partial and unsatisfactory solutions, their vision restricted by technological specialization. Thus, many transportation analysts argued in the sixties and seventies that regions should create unified, integrated transportation agencies. Such organizations, by encompassing both highways and transit, would have jurisdiction over all major modes and could therefore decide on, for example, the relative merits of highway expansion versus public transit investment. Monopolistic control over the entire set of transportation solutions would enable an agency to distribute the modes rationally, thus creating that holy grail, the balanced transportation system.

Comprehensiveness in transit planning has secondarily signified designing systems so that their differentiated and interdependent parts form a functioning whole. Transit systems are composed of complementary components that must fit together in a sensible manner. For example, feeder routes must be appropriately connected to main routes. More widely, this concept of comprehensive planning means ensuring that the premises of a plan are mutually consistent, that, for example, the land-use assumptions are compatible with projections of demand for transit.[4] For supporters of the

4. The transportation texts cited in n. 3 usually restrict the meaning of comprehensive planning of complements to the narrower transit sense. This is sensible because organizing comprehensive transit planning in the wider sense is less feasible politically.

monopoly model, the organizational implications of this second concept of comprehensiveness is to entrust all planning responsibilities to a single bureaucracy. Only an integrated transit agency can ensure that all inputs are in correct proportion to one another; an organizationally fragmented system will produce functionally unintegrated service.

The Argument for Competitive Planning

The conventional wisdom places much faith in the impartiality of a planning agency. To be sure, if transit planners were both unbiased and wise, perhaps entrusting all design responsibilities to a single bureaucracy would be a reasonable strategy. But monopolistic planning is highly vulnerable to the varying amount of search an agency devotes to creating different alternatives. Research in cognitive psychology and artificial intelligence shows that, in any moderately complex task environment, search cannot be exhaustive; it is inevitably selective (Simon and Newell, 1972). Therefore, a monopoly planner will display only the pretense, not the reality, of comprehensiveness. Further, relying on monopolistic planning is vulnerable to games monopolists play with the set of options, such as comparing a favored alternative with ill-conceived strawmen.[5]

The alternative structure of competitive planning assumes neither that any single planning team is free of bias nor that any can attain the objectivity described in planning text-

5. It is curious that despite growing professional awareness of the difficulties in every step of the process, particularly the solution generation phase ("The search for or identification of alternative designs is obviously one of the most important steps in the process, but ironically it is one of the least understood" [Morlock, 1978, p. 11; see also Hutchinson, 1974, p. 20]), recent texts make no attempt to modify the monopolistic model of planning by suggesting devil's advocates or rival planners. Concerning the organization of analysis, the approach is resolutely unredundant. And this has been the central tendency in planning philosophy for quite awhile: changes in the urban planning texts refer to changes in planning techniques, not to the organization of planning.

books.[6] Instead, it is assumed that all planners have pet proposals, blind spots, alternatives they do not take seriously; in short, they have cognitive predispositions that guide their design searches, orienting them toward certain solutions and away from others. But instead of being obstacles to effective planning, these predispositions are essential to providing a healthy diversity of views. Thus a system of redundant planning seeks to transform what are liabilities for the conventional model into sources of strength.

What, then, can we expect from this transformation? First, Propositions 1 and 2 of Chapter One established that a system where planners are more independent is more reliable than one where they are less independent. Because rival planners in different agencies are indeed more likely to generate diverse alternatives than are planners in the same agency, the key assumption of the propositions is satisfied. Hence, the propositions imply that competitive transit planning is more reliable than monopolistic planning.[7] Recall that this involved a strong sense of reliability: regardless of how stringently the

6. This is not to minimize the technical aspect of transit planning; it is a technically informed process, i.e., much depends on the accuracy of factual premises. Nor do I recommend politicizing these technical functions. Rather it is to suggest that the approved version misconstrues the social and organizational bases of rationality in planning. It is not true that a technical process is incompatible with passionate advocacy and even myopia. Indeed, as students of scientific argument have suggested (Popper, 1963; Merton, 1973; Landau, 1972), it is precisely the prevalence of individual myopia and bias, of disregard for negative evidence and competing theories, that increases the need for a redundant system of error detection and theory development. At root, the conventional model of planning confuses the individual and systemic levels: the search for disinterested and infallible planners is doomed to fail; the search for a measure of collective objectivity need not.

7. We must, however, distinguish the narrow-minded search that increases competition from that which reduces it. The fragmented financing of transportation in the fifties and sixties, in particular the earmarked highway trust funds, did *not* promote intermodal competition. Rather it skewed local choice by providing disproportional outside support for the auto-highway alternative. Integrating the financing streams by funneling them through a single metropolitan agency, financially responsible for all transportation investments, could increase intermodal competition by increasing the region's capacity to choose between alternative projects. But integrated financing would be consistent with competitive planning only if the modal advocates were organizationally separated from the financing agency.

proposals would be evaluated, the best proposal of the competitive system is more likely to pass the test than the best proposal of the monopolistic system.

Second, because rival planners have an incentive to discredit contending proposals, options in a competitive system will be scrutinized more intensely and more critically than they would under a monopolistic system.[8] Thus not only will competition enhance reliability in the design of proposals, it will increase reliability in the evaluation stage as well.

Third, competitive planning will shift policymaking power away from bureaucracies and toward representative institutions. In the conventional division of labor, lay decision-makers such as legislators and voters must approve or reject a single option presented by a specialized agency. These screenings come at the end of a lengthy planning process, and because of the momentum built up in such projects, it is often difficult to reject a bureau's alternative. Given a bureaucracy's monopoly of expertise and information, it is awkward justifying a rejection of its final recommendation. Thus, although de jure final authority rests with nonspecialists, under monopolistic conditions specialists are, de facto, extremely influential. Competitive planning, by eliminating an agency's control over information and analysis, gives laymen a basis for reasoned opposition to any alternative.

The last argument for competitive planning is that it combats a pernicious variant of Gresham's Law. Gresham's Law is that programmed activity tends to drive out unprogrammed activity. The variant in transit planning is that discussion of transit equipment, the tangible hardware, tends to drive out discussion of more abstract policy matters.[9] Not only is technology more palpable than, for example, land-use patterns, decision-makers find that focusing attention on transit hardware produces less controversy than does focusing on higher level goals such as whether high-density or low-density land-use patterns should be pursued.

8. The incentives to criticize exist because it is unlikely that all rival plans will be implemented.
9. A similar point is made by scholars studying the relation between weapon system development and defense policy.

Monopolistic planning exacerbates this variant of Gresham's Law. A monopolist prefers to recommend only one option for general consideration. The availability of only a single option on the public agenda fixes attention on hardware details. In contrast, competing planners, by advocating multiple options, will evoke once-latent conflict over higher objectives because the options' differing technologies make different scenarios of the future appear psychologically viable. If, for example, a conflict emerges in a community between advocates of fixed route transit and devotees of flexible route systems, the range of conceivable developmental paths for the region is enhanced because the two technologies obviously have different potentials for influencing land-use patterns. Thus competition will diminish the tendency to let technological decisions drive more important policy choices.

The Argument for Monopolistic Transit Operations

As we move into the stage of operations, the arguments for monopoly become more cogent. Four points are worth noting.

1. A monopolistic transit agency operating a single mode can avoid expensive and unnecessary duplications of investment and effort,[10] that is, it can exploit physical econo-

10. As in the general theory, so with transit we must distinguish the budget-cutting strategy of eliminating service without merging organizations from the consolidation strategy of merging agencies without cutting service. As there are several public transit monopolies in large metropolitan areas (Chicago, London, New York) that have retained parallel intermodal and intramodal routes, it is evident that duplicate service can coexist with monopolistic organization. The consolidation strategy in transit recalls the managerially oriented public administration scholars, who, in the twenties and thirties, wanted to strengthen the presidency; the budget-cutting strategy recalls the old congressional committees on economy and efficiency that tried to reduce programmatic duplication while ignoring organizational merger.

mies of scale.[11] If an organization operates different modes, the dissimilar technologies make physical economies of scale less plentiful. Nevertheless, an agency may still obtain *administrative* economies of scale by, for instance, consolidating two comptroller positions into one.

2. A successful multimodal system requires intermodal coordination of schedules, transfers, and the like. A single organization performs these tasks more effectively because interests are more compatible, communication swifter, and conflict more resolvable within a bureaucracy than between bureaucracies.

3. Service duplication in part of an agency's jurisdiction engenders an opportunity cost: service gaps in other parts of the jurisdiction. Some patrons will have multiple transit alternatives while others have none. This problem is exacerbated if competing agencies behave like profit-oriented private firms. By allocating their resources heavily to lucrative routes, thereby diminishing service on less patronized routes and in off-peak hours, they would injure "captive" riders, the old, the poor, and the handicapped, who lack alternatives to transit. In contrast, a monopolistic transit agency can more easily bear the burden of serving sparsely patronized routes since it is not competing with another organization over the best routes. Thus a monopoly may provide a more equitable distribution of service.

4. An integrated transportation organization, which can set tolls on bridges and highways as well as operate transit, could subsidize one mode by another, for example, by setting bridge tolls high enough to subsidize transit. Cross-subsidizing is rational when transit riding produces exter-

---

11. However, we must inquire again, following Niskanen, whether an integrated transit agency would have an *incentive* to exploit potential economies of scale and, if they were exploited, whether an organization would have an incentive to pass the savings on to users or taxpayers. The idea of integrated transit, particularly as it invokes scale economies, reflects an engineering viewpoint more than an economic one. Economics emphasizes the incentives to exploit technological opportunities as much as the opportunities themselves.

nalities such as reducing traffic congestion and air pollution. This strategy of cross-subsidizing is not feasible for operationally fragmented systems.[12]

The Case for Operational Duplication

It has been argued that as organizations proceed from planning to operations, the utility of redundancy declines. It does not, however, vanish. Indeed, Murphy's Law applies with special force to new systems just starting operations. Unexpected problems inevitably appear, and a second transit system will be valuable as a backup at such times.

Of course one can expect these unanticipated difficulties to become less frequent as a system matures and as a bureaucracy learns how to solve unexpected malfunctions. Thus these developmental uncertainties have a secular pattern: they decline irreversibly. But transit systems also suffer from episodic shocks, such as fires and strikes, that lack a temporal pattern. If a parallel bureaucracy is available to step in when these random shocks disable one mode, passengers will enjoy more reliable service than a single mode would provide. Note, however, that a technological redundancy of modes does not necessarily entail an organizational redundancy. A monopoly may also buffer its clientele from episodic disturbances by keeping in reserve extra trains or buses. It remains, therefore, an empirical question whether the threat of random shocks is solved better by redundant bureaucracies or by a monopoly using internal, technological duplications.

There is, however, another source of uncertainty in transit operations—managerial competence—that does highlight the value of having parallel modes run by separate bureaucracies rather than by one agency. The quality of management affects a transit mode's appeal, for good managers will improve service in scores of small ways that poor managers will overlook. These decisions will show up in a system's performance, in,

12. Whether the American political system would tolerate cross-subsidies if they entailed overt penalties on cars is another question. For a pessimistic assessment, see Altshuler (1977).

most importantly, the number of commuters who regularly ride transit. It is often difficult to predict the managerial competence of a new agency. This uncertainty has implications for the organization of operations. Suppose a boss has a choice of assigning the operation of two transit modes to one agency or to two agencies.

<table>
<tr><td align="center">Agency A</td><td align="center">Agency A</td><td align="center">Agency B</td></tr>
<tr>
<td align="center">Mode y_1 Mode y_2</td>
<td align="center">Mode z_1</td>
<td align="center">Mode z_2</td>
</tr>
<tr><td align="center">Structure Y</td><td align="center" colspan="2">Structure Z</td></tr>
</table>

Though the boss does not know the managerial quality of either agency, she knows that the managers are drawn from the same distribution of ability. Consequently, the boss believes that measured in terms of performance criteria such as patronage or net social benefits, the two modes have the same unconditional (normal) distribution. Furthermore, since management decisions diffuse more within an organization than between organizations, the performances of the modes in structure Y covary more than do the performances of the modes in structure Z. Since the variance of the sum of two random variables equals the sum of their variances plus twice their covariance, Proposition 3 follows immediately.

Proposition 3: if the performance of a transit system is the sum of the performance of its two modes, then structure Z is less risky than structure Y, though their average performance is the same.

Corollary: all risk averse decision-makers prefer structure Z to structure Y (Rothschild and Stiglitz, 1971, p. 66).

Once again, the more integrated organizational structure, Y, increases the chances that both solutions (here, modes) will be either very good or very bad. Thus it is harder to predict how many people system Y will carry than to predict how many Z will carry (see Fig. 4). This greater uncertainty implies that

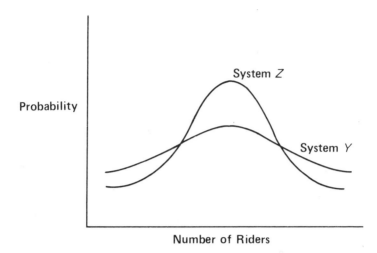

FIGURE 4   *Systems with Equal Means and Differing Riskiness*

decision-makers who dislike risk will always prefer the more independent structure Z.[13]

The redundancy guarding against the first two classes of problems, that is, those plaguing new operations and those striking randomly throughout a system's life, need not involve competition. If two transit agencies duplicate each other only when one is suffering from a breakdown, they are not competing for scarce resources. Far from it. Instead, they are providing mutual assistance. But the third and last hypothesis about the benefit of operational duplication does involve conflict. Following Niskanen and Ostrom, we propose that a monopoly will be insensitive to the preferences of passengers, apt to charge high fares and supply mediocre service, whereas

13. Note that there is an important difference between redundancy in planning and in operations. In competitive planning, we assume that only *one* of the proposals will be implemented. Hence, the boss chooses max (proposal 1, proposal 2). Because Propositions 1 and 2 of Chapter One apply, we know that the more independent organizational structure is preferred by *all* decision-makers, risk-seeking as well as risk-averse. But in the case of operations, we assume that both modes will be used continuously; the boss cannot choose the better of the two but must live with both. Therefore, the somewhat weaker conclusion of Proposition 3 applies: only risk-averse decision-makers prefer the more independent structure. Risk-seekers prefer the more integrated one.

agencies compelled to compete for patrons will offer lower fares and will more readily adjust their service to suit passengers' wishes.[14] Passive duplication would not bring this about; it is the added sting of conflict, the fear of losing riders to a rival, that gives bureaucracies reason to behave flexibly. Table 3 summarizes the arguments for monopoly and for redundancy.

The Case Studies

The logic of Table 3 mandates a research design that compares two kinds of organizational structures, each "photographed" at two periods in the decision process, for a total of four cases. Though pragmatic constraints of time and money precluded four separate situations, the author found three cases that exemplified the four categories of Table 3[15] (see Fig. 5). The category of redundant operations, that is, agencies serving overlapping or identical[16] clientele, is exemplified by two public organizations in the San Francisco Bay Area: the Bay Area Rapid Transit District (BART) and the

14. One sour note intrudes upon this happy vision of competition. Since public transit agencies are supported by taxes as well as by fares, competing agencies could lower fares or improve service without achieving cost reductions, even if lower fares failed to attract enough riders to offset the per rider losses. Lowered revenues could be covered by tax returns, suggesting that operational competition could result in larger tax burdens. A political economist sensitive to the role of incentives might argue that a competitive but tax-supported transit agency would have no reason to investigate cost-saving changes unless its tax revenues were limited. But in these financially hard times, tax revenues *are* limited, so this sour note may seldom play.

15. No attempt was made to establish the representativeness of these cases for a larger population. Instead, they were chosen as instances of categories of theoretical interest. Therefore, the problem of external validity, of generalizing to a larger population, is left unresolved in this study. But in the early stages of probing a theory, finding instances that vary on the relevant dimensions is more important than establishing their representativeness.

16. As transportation planning texts recognize, proposed transit solutions are rarely substitutes for identical populations: usually service areas differ somewhat. For this reason competition inevitably involves more overt conflict in the public sector than in the private, where the consumer is an individual rather than a community.

Alameda-Contra Costa Transit District (AC). BART's trains and AC's buses both carry commuters between the East Bay and San Francisco. The contrasting case of monopolistic operations is illustrated in Figure 5 by the Washington Metropolitan Area Transit Authority (WMATA), which controls bus and rapid rail service in and around the nation's capital.

Because the category of competitive planning is less intuitively clear than the corresponding one of redundant operations, a definitional aside is needed before describing the example of redundant planning. It is clear that two transit agencies provide redundant service when passengers can travel from their origin to their destination via either agency's system. It is the *functional equivalence* of the organization's

TABLE 3   *Summary of Propositions*   (*compare vertically*)

PLANNING	OPERATIONS
Monopoly	*Monopoly*
1. Less expensive	1. Less expensive, avoids waste
2. Avoids conflict, delay	
3. Enables exhaustive search of modal alternatives; creates balanced transportation system	2. Enables more effective coordination of modes
	3. Provides more even service coverage; avoids both gaps and overlaps
4. Facilitates consistency in planning	4. Permits modal cross-subsidizing
Redundancy	*Redundancy*
1. More valid information	1. Increases systemic reliability during:
2. More thorough search of alternatives	a. break-in period in subsystem development
3. More information on alternatives that are generated	
4. Lower probability that decisions on transit hardware will unduly constrain other policy processes	b. episodic disturbances (strikes, etc.)
	2. Competitive redundancy promotes heightened responsiveness to clientele preferences
5. Increases influence of non-specialists in policymaking	

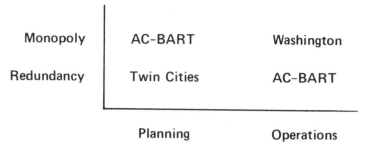

	Planning	Operations
Monopoly	AC–BART	Washington
Redundancy	Twin Cities	AC–BART

FIGURE 5   *The Cases' Categories*

operations that assigns them to the class of redundant bureaucracies.[17] With this in mind, the concept of competitive planning can be easily defined. Two transit agencies are engaged in competitive planning if two conditions are met: first, implementing both proposals would create redundant transit operation, that is, service for overlapping or identical populations; and, second, the agencies are in conflict with each other because they believe that only one of the designs will be realized.

Definitions in hand, we can complete the case description. The category of competitive transit planning is exemplified by a prolonged debate in the early seventies between two regional agencies in Minneapolis-St.Paul, the Metropolitan Council and the Metropolitan Transit Commission. The Transit Commission advocated rapid rail as the solution to the area's transit problems; the council backed buses. The region was not about to fund both proposals; one had to perish during planning. Hence the agencies not only overlapped each other's jurisdictions; they were quite consciously rivals.

17. In the ordinary vernacular, redundancy connotes surplus capacity, but this property is rejected as a defining attribute for three reasons. First, it is difficult to specify what constitutes surplus capacity: what is overabundance for one range of conditions may be inadequate for another. Indeed, a central point of this work is that what on first inspection appears to be surplus capacity will often turn out not to be so. Second, redundant transit service implies offering patrons a choice; the capacity of redundant organizations could be stretched tight even as patrons were shifting back and forth as they discover the alternative they prefer. Thus a key function of redundancy could be fulfilled without an oversupply of capacity. Third, including the property of surplus capacity tends to prejudge the issue of functionality since "surplus" slides quickly into "excess."

The final category of monopolistic planning has no case devoted solely to it; instead, the AC-BART relationship must do double duty. Although AC and BART now have overlapping service areas, and even originated in the same period, they shied away from competing with each other during planning. Their mutual isolation meant that each organization was, in effect, a little island of monopolistic planning, uncontested by a rival. Hence the Bay Area study serves both as an instance of redundant service and of noncompetitive design.

Theory must now yield center stage to evidence as we turn to the first of the case studies.

Appendix 1. Data Sources

The case studies are based on four data sources:

1. I have conducted fifty interviews with AC and BART managers, planners, and operational personnel responsible for interorganizational dealings, as well as with several staffers from the Bay Area's Metropolitan Transportation Commission who participated in interagency meetings; forty-five interviews in Minneapolis-St. Paul with key planners, decision-makers, and observers, particularly in the Metropolitan Transit Commission (MTC), the Metropolitan (Metro) Council, and the state legislature; fifty-one interviews in Washington, D.C., primarily in WMATA and particularly with bus and rail middle executives and their immediate superiors. The interviews were semistructured: I had a list of questions for every interviewee, but the sequence was flexible. Since I was usually eliciting a narrative, the questions were open-ended. Because I have promised my interviewees anonymity, interviews are indicated by number only, for example (#17). Letters accompanying the numbers indicate as follows: C = collective interview; T = telephone interview; G = interview conducted by Harvey Goldman, research associate.

2. The planning controversy in Minneapolis was well covered by newspapers; coverage was most scanty for the AC-BART case.

3. Official government documents were most plentiful and germane for the Twin Cities case; least plentiful and relevant for AC-BART.

4. I was fortunate to gain access to BART memos on AC-BART liaison matters. In Minneapolis one legislator opened his private files to me, and the library of the Metro Council also provided a few (rather formal) letters exchanged between the council and MTC and several intracouncil memos. In Washington I did not discover any informative intraorganizational memos.

In general, data was easiest to gather in Minneapolis-St. Paul while the data sources for the AC-BART and Washington cases were more uneven. Fortunately, the different sources tended to compensate for each other.

In each case, different sources disagreed on several key points. Either the written records contradicted people's memories (which is to be expected, as some events occurred over a decade ago), or people's recollections were inconsistent. When important inconsistencies surfaced, I have indicated them either in the text or in the notes.

3

Redundant Operations in the San Francisco Bay Area

The San Francisco Bay Area Rapid Transit District (BART), if not a household name, is well known in the United States. The first major rapid rail system built in this country since 1950, BART, like many complex new ventures, has suffered from many problems, but anonymity has not been one of them. But anonymity *has* enshrouded several transit agencies whose jurisdictions overlap BART's. BART, which runs along major commute corridors leading into San Francisco from Alameda and Contra Costa counties to the east across the bay and toward suburbs south of San Francisco, is paralleled by a bus agency, the Alameda-Contra Costa Transit Authority (AC), on many transbay routes from the East Bay into San Francisco (see Map 1, p. 86).

This chapter examines the origins, nature, and consequences of the redundant operations provided by BART and AC.

AC-BART Relations During System Planning

As noted earlier, the appearance of competition between public organizations is sufficiently problematic as to

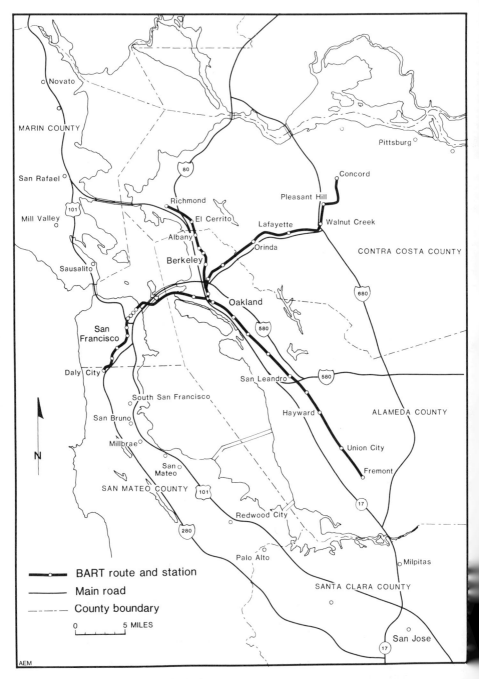

MAP 1   *BART and the Bay Area*

be a question in its own right. Under what conditions does bureaucratic competition appear? This section will address that question by describing the early relations between AC and BART.

This early period produced, in an involved and roundabout way, the service redundancy that now exists. This outcome was not intended. Indeed, there are few clear-cut cases of intentional redundancy in government. Seldom does an executive deliberately instigate competition among subordinates to improve the flow of information or to give him more flexible options—the oft-quoted example of Franklin Roosevelt notwithstanding. Redundancy is more often the by-product of agencies' myopic actions than the result of a reliability-conscious planning. So it was in this case.

Origins

Though one often hears of "*the* metropolitan transportation problem," in the San Francisco Bay Area in the 1950s there was no *single* transportation problem. Certainly no one problem was perceived by the diverse actors who would create AC and BART. In the East Bay, AC's predecessor, the Key System, a private transit organization serving local patrons and transbay commuters by bus and rail, was seen as the primary source of problems. It had been rocked by a seventy-six-day strike in 1953, so disrupting urban life that a public takeover was discussed.[1] (Apparently the possibility of a strike by a public employees' union was not foreseen.) Furthermore, in the early fifties the system had begun the downward spiral that was becoming a nationwide pattern for private transit firms. Patronage fell, costs rose, and service deteriorated. The primary interest in the East Bay, therefore, was to restore subregional transit to a level of service and strikeless tranquility that it had once enjoyed. This interest provided the context for AC's birth.

---

1. In his detailed history of this period, Seymour Adler maintains that the Alameda-Contra Costa Transit Committee "formed as an outgrowth of the seventy-six-day Key System strike" (1978, p. 26).

BART, on the other hand, was originally conceived as a nine-county[2] regional system with San Francisco at its center.[3] This early disparity in scale between the two plans emphasized the systems' differences and deemphasized their overlap.[4] Furthermore, BART was not to be a conservative restoration of an older system but a bold undertaking unprecedented in the region. BART planners wanted to encircle the bay with a completely new rapid transit system that could compete with the auto and reduce traffic congestion. By ensuring a steady flow of commuters into downtown San Francisco, it would help preserve the city's preeminent status as an employment center.[5] Thus it is clear that in the fifties the two embryonic systems could not have been viewed as competing solutions to the same problem, for they faced two different problems.

Finally, the two coalitions that formed to confront these problems were geographically distinct: the coalition backing AC Transit was based largely in Oakland, in Alameda County, whereas BART's coalition was centered across the bay in San Francisco (Adler, 1980). The only significant overlap between the coalitions' memberships was represented by Oakland businessman Sherwood Swan, who was active in the formation of both agencies, and by Clair MacLeod, an early BART board chairman, who sat simultaneously on AC's board. This overlap helped to differentiate the organizations' early plans. Swan and MacLeod agreed that AC should solve local, East Bay transit problems whereas BART addressed

2. The district was created as five counties in 1957; it was reduced to three in the early sixties.

3. The choice of San Francisco as the center of BART further differentiated it from AC, the East Bay system whose center was to be Oakland. The rivalry between the two cities impeded the formation of a more comprehensive, integrated transit authority (Adler, 1978, pp. 18–20).

4. However, some of the earliest plans in the late forties saw BART as an integrated, multimodal agency operating local as well as mainline service (Adler, 1978, p. 20). Had this idea been pursued in the fifties, it would have undoubtedly caused great conflict with AC.

5. It is irrelevant for our purposes whether this plan was created by a tight Bechtel-led cabal (as a San Francisco newspaper, the *Bay Guardian*, claimed) or by a looser coalition of central-city-oriented businessmen who also tapped genuine support for transit among nonelites.

regional issues, and because the two men were leaders of both coalitions in the mid-fifties, they were able to influence their direction. In this period AC and BART assured potential constituents and state legislators that the agencies would not compete with each other but would supply complementary service, and Swan and MacLeod were instrumental in providing these assurances (Adler, 1980, pp. 149, 154–155, 205–206).

Thus, given that there were largely different groups, perceiving distinct problems and conceiving solutions of different scale, innovativeness, and lead time, it is not surprising that the early system planning was noncompetitive.[6]

Of course competition would have been permanently avoided had one of the agencies failed to win the political support necessary for organizational creation. Just as firms face what economists call "barriers to entry" into a new market, so do public organizations seeking to enter a new policy sector. And the higher the entry barriers, the lower the probability of competition. In the public sector, entry barriers may be legal, for example, only one general purpose government at the same level may have jurisdiction over an area, or financial, programs in the policy area being too expensive for new agencies to attempt. In the AC-BART case the institution of the *special district* was essential in permitting the eventual emergence of overlap. Unlike general purpose governments, there is no limit to the number of special purpose agencies that may inhabit a region.[7] Consequently, though AC's two-county district was completely contained in BART's five-county jurisdiction, the state legislature faced no legal barrier to creating AC in 1955 and BART in 1957.

But the state's bills did not by themselves establish viable organizations; both AC and BART had to win bond elections. Each confronted two hurdles: county supervisors had to approve putting the matter to the voters; and more than a majority of voters had to approve the bonds (60 percent for AC, and 66.7 percent for BART). When considering the overlap that

6. Complementarity between the two systems was assumed by BART planners as early as 1956 (Adler, 1978, p. 31).
7. Of course, precisely because special purpose agencies are specialized, territorial overlap does not usually imply functional duplication. A mosquito abatement district and a transit district are not redundant.

exists today, it is wise to remember that these hurdles were high barriers; at the time there was concern that *neither* agency would overcome them. As it was, the Board of Supervisors of one county, San Mateo, withdrew their county from the BART district, and the supervisors of another county, Contra Costa, barely approved putting the BART bond issue on the ballot. The legislature lowered BART's passage hurdle to 60 percent; even so, the bond passed by only 1 percent. AC required yet more help with its bond election, the legislature lowering required approval to 50 percent. This new requirement was still almost too high for AC, as it garnered just over half of the vote in 1959, after having failed in 1958.

During this struggle for organizational existence, both agencies were developing plans for their systems' technologies and routes. There was one critical juncture in the fifties when a clash between AC and BART could have drawn attention to their potentially redundant relation. BART and AC would have been drawn into greater conflict had the two systems' planners decided on identical transit technologies, for the ensuing duplication of equipment would have pointed up their functional similarity. It is difficult for a bureaucracy to pretend that it is free of competitors when another agency is not only fulfilling the same end but using the same means as well. It is therefore pertinent to sketch out how BART and AC arrived at their modal choices.

In neither case did the modal choice process bear much resemblance to current transit planning, for neither organization engaged in an extensive analysis of alternatives.[8] Based on its consultant's report, BART quickly selected rapid rail: "Rapid transit must be a train system. . . . We must, accordingly, search for the Bay Area facilities within the envelope of possible train equipment" (Parsons et al., 1956, p. 49). Buses, which if chosen would have made BART dangerously close to duplicating the Key-AC system, were dismissed

8. Note, however, that a U.S. Office of Technology Assessment report asserts that "it is not appropriate to be critical of BART and its promoters for failing to study alternatives, as many current writers have been. They were not violating planning standards accepted at that time" (U.S. Congress, 1976b, p. 39).

because of their slowness in heavy traffic (ibid., p. 51). After this 1956 report, BART's modal choice was fixed.

There was a greater chance that AC would move toward BART's modal choice than vice versa, for the Key System had run trains across the Bay Bridge between San Francisco and the East Bay for twenty years, and AC considered continuing the practice. In 1957, however, the Key System petitioned the California Public Utilities Commission (PUC) to allow it to abandon the railroad and to use buses instead. The PUC approved the petition. AC's consultant, DeLeuw, Cather, and Company, had "strongly advocated rail rapid transit (possibly pneumatic tires) or some separated right of way reserved for transit alone as absolutely essential to the adequate handling of future growth of transbay traffic" (AC, *Board Minutes*, November 11, 1957, p. 3). Charles DeLeuw personally opposed removing the Key trains.[9] AC, taking the issue to the PUC in 1957, argued that it would take over the Key trains, but the commission let stand its original decision to abandon the tracks. Although AC could have appealed the decision to the State Supreme Court, AC's board voted four to two to abandon the trains. One of the minority, J. Howard Arnold, claimed that the board was giving up the fight prematurely and charged that Clair MacLeod, who had voted to drop the train appeal, was in conflict of interest due to his dual membership on the AC and BART boards. The charge was not implausible. MacLeod was apparently convinced by BART's consultants that the alternative of building an underwater rail tube, though more expensive, would provide faster, more convenient service than would trains on the bridge, and he had supported the consultant's "optimum plan," which included the tube. MacLeod was probably concerned that if AC succeeded in keeping the Key trains intact, the region's voters would not approve the expensive bonds needed to build an underwater tube. Hence, he opposed Arnold's attempts to preserve the Key rail system (Adler, 1980, p. 245). But regardless of the merits of Arnold's accusation that MacLeod's dual

9. Because AC trusted the firm enough to rehire it in 1958 to map out the details of the AC system, we can infer that DeLeuw's recommendations were not taken lightly.

role created a conflict of interest, his charge and call for MacLeod's resignation were futile. The matter was settled: AC would take over only the Key System buses, not its trains.

Had AC followed DeLeuw's recommendation and successfully appealed the PUC decision, BART would have been faced *at the planning stage* with an agency that not only fulfilled part of BART's functions, but did so with a similar technology. A competitive struggle would have been difficult to avoid. But Key proceeded to change to an all-bus system and to tear up the tracks in 1958, and the clash was averted.

Although in this period modal choices were central to the avoidance of early competition, spokesmen on each side also made gestures indicating that a division of labor had been tacitly agreed upon. BART supported AC's bond elections in 1958 and 1959; it would not have done so had it expected AC to become a rival. And AC's *Facts* brochure (1958) promised, possibly in exchange for BART's support, that "when the five-county district begins operation 7–10 years from now and takes over transbay service, the ACCTD [AC] will continue to operate the network of local lines and provide feeder service to rapid transit stations" (quoted in Kennedy, 1971, p. 10).[10] Of course both organizations were then struggling for their existence—AC lost the 1958 bond election and barely won in 1959, while BART was several years away from its bond election—and probably each thought it prudent to concentrate on promoting itself rather than wasting energy attacking the other. It was not obvious then that either district would come into being, much less both. And for AC it was particularly easy to state that its transbay jurisdiction would be only temporary. Its lead time was much shorter than BART's, and for a while that difference alone would protect it from having to cede transbay routes to BART. Besides, "temporary" juris-

10. AC was more cautious about organizational merger (as contrasted with service integration). While testifying before the state Senate, AC attorney Robert Nisbet said that merger should be permitted only if the voters of the two-county district agreed. It is interesting—especially in the light of the Washington Metrobus experience—that Nisbet rejected as inadequate protection a promise that the consolidated agency would maintain service quality in the two counties. He contended that the "level of service is not a point on which you can devise any degree of certainty. It's something the board of the two-county district will have to wrestle with . . ." (quoted in Adler, 1978, p. 39).

dictions have a way of becoming permanent. As an AC director told the author, no one knew whether BART would indeed be built. The interim between AC's beginning and BART's birth could stretch out indefinitely. The reader should remember that in 1956–60 no rapid rail system of this size had been built in the United States for decades; it may have been easy for AC to believe that it would never happen in the Bay Area.

Emergence of Competition

After several years of AC operation, cracks in the informal division-of-labor agreement began to appear. There were several distinct signs of this breakdown in the early and mid-sixties. In 1962 the Alameda County Highway Advisory Commission had DeLeuw, Cather, and Company write a report on the effects of rapid transit on AC. AC provided information about its operations, but BART consultants supplied assumptions concerning future service. The consultants assumed AC would discontinue all transbay service. The study predicted that in 1969, then assumed to be BART's opening date, AC would have a surplus of slightly over $500 million if it monopolized the transbay routes. With BART and no transbay routes, AC would run a deficit of nearly $3 million. AC's general manager, Ken Hensel, quickly observed in AC's newsletter that "these assumptions by BART consultants do not necessarily reflect present or future decisions of policy of this district" (*Transit Times*, July 1962, p. 2).[11] He was supported by a board member at a meeting with Oakland businessmen: "Such policy decisions (the assumptions made by rapid transit engineers and used in the DeLeuw report) cannot be made until a full and complete understanding is reached between the rapid transit district and AC Transit" (*Transit Times*, October 1962, p. 10). This signalled a pulling back from what BART consultants believed, with some justification, to be a commitment.[12] It was, however, not yet a complete repudiation.

11. A copy of Hensel's statement is in BART's "AC liaison" file, but there is no comment on it, nor any other clue as to BART's reaction.
12. Note also that AC did not support BART in its 1962 bond election.

In 1965 the AC board passed a motion that more strongly indicated a shift in their public position. The stimulus for the motion came from

> recent press articles pertaining to future transbay operations of this District, and of the future utilization of the San Francisco Transit Terminal. He [President William Coburn] noted that these accounts appeared to be written from the standpoint of an assumption that AC Transit would terminate its bridge services coincidentally with the commencement of transbay operations by BART. President Coburn felt it incumbent upon the district to correct any misapprehension in this area, observing that such abandonment was not contemplated . . . continuing discussion developed the consensus that the district's transbay service should continue to be performed so long as public convenience and necessity actually require them.   (AC, *Board Minutes*, 1965, p. 14)[13]

The board unanimously passed a motion that BART and the Toll Bridge Authority, which manages the Bay Bridge, be informed of its position.[14]

What happened between 1958 and 1965? Why did AC turn from nearly promising to cede the transbay routes to affirming its right to maintain them? Two explanations are plausible. First, real intentions may have changed less than did public statements. One official recalled that the first general manager's statement that AC would yield the transbay lines was only for public consumption; inside the organization his position was different. Once AC became well established, long-standing hidden preferences emerged. But, second, and less deviously, AC's board had changed. The key linking pin with BART, Clair MacLeod, left in 1958. And those who remained had different facts at their disposal. One former director said that in 1958 the inexperienced AC directors simply had no idea which routes would turn out to be moneymakers. By 1962 they had accumulated enough experience to realize that transbay runs were, by and large, economically the best. Certainly this would have been evident by 1965. East Bay routes

---

13. The vague words, "public convenience and necessity" are a standard phrase from the era of regulation of private transit firms. Generally an organization wishing to supply a new, competing service would have to demonstrate that public convenience or necessity required it.

14. Again, there was no evidence of a BART reaction.

peaked in 1963–64 and declined slowly thereafter; transbay routes climbed steadily from 1960 on.

The Process of Conflict Resolution: Persuasion and Bargaining

We have seen that early agreements on the division of labor showed signs of strain by the mid-sixties. But as argued in Chapter One, agencies can often establish or reestablish nonintervention pacts, even without the aid of an outside mediator, and thereby create monopolized domains. Was this attempted by AC and BART? If so, how and with what success?

The answer to the first question is yes, a most repetitive yes. BART's files reveal that the first serious questions on coordination, that is, eliminating duplication and ensuring complementary service, were raised in 1963, and numerous staff meetings were held in 1964. They would continue to take place off and on for nearly a decade. But as we shall see shortly, the duration of the effort merely indicated the depth of disagreement.

When two public agencies functionally overlap, there are several decision strategies that may effect differentiation: command, bargaining, and persuasion.[15] The simplest is command, where one authority instructs a second to leave the policy field. This presupposes a hierarchical relationship. But back in 1955, East Bay and San Franciscan leaders, during sometimes uneasy negotiations over the future relations of AC and BART, reached a compromise on the organizations' authority relations: neither agency would have authority to direct the other. This nonhierarchical structure was built into legislation (Adler, 1980, p. 150). Both BART and AC are prohibited to

> interfere with or exercise any control over any transit facilities now or hereafter owned and operated wholly or partly within the district by any city or public agency, unless by consent of

15. In fights over organizational jurisdiction, a fourth strategy—threats—is sometimes used, but neither agency was in a position to issue credible threats, and neither tried.

such city or public agency and upon such terms as are mutually agreed upon between the board and such city or public agency. (PUC Code, sections 25803 and 29037; cited in S.F. Bart, 1970b)[16]

In addition to legal safeguards, AC's reputation helped protect its jurisdiction. AC was and is widely regarded in the East Bay as a well-run organization (Zwerling, 1974, p. 108; Viton, 1980, p. 8), making it difficult for BART to use political clout to shunt it aside.

That left persuasion and bargaining. Persuasion involves changing another's perception of the situation by providing new data or new criteria for interpreting data. In bargaining, one takes the other's perceptions as given and instead alters the objective consequence of alternatives by offering incentives. A contract, for example, formalizes a bargain that requires no change of mind by either side. Persuasion is clearly cheaper in terms of money or policy concessions, but its use is restricted to circumstances in which decision-makers disagree less over ends than means.

It is therefore striking that in ten years of AC-BART talks, persuasion completely predominated over bargaining. Regardless of the conflicting organizational goals, public discussion was couched in terms of reaching an agreed-upon goal, such as maximizing the total number of transit riders. This representation of the problem made it appear that persuasion was an appropriate strategy, even though DeLeuw predicted in 1962 that AC's finances would be severely injured by eliminating transbay routes.

We can expect persuasion to eliminate competition when it is in an agency's interest to withdraw from the policy sector but for some reason it has not yet grasped that point. In AC's case this misunderstanding would have resulted either from poor cost and revenue data or from inadequate accounting

16. Of course BART was interested in knowing whether AC could be legally required to coordinate. In 1970, a BART director directed Lawrence Dahms, AC's assistant general manager, to review AC's legislative act, and Dahms replied that he could not "find any reference in the act regarding mandatory coordination with BART. Further, I am advised by [chief counsel] Malcolm Barrett that he is unaware of any such provision."

rules. (Faulty accounting could have overestimated the bridge routes' profitability.) Persuasion would have involved BART's showing AC that this was so. But although AC's data were rough, the differences between most commute and local runs were large enough to provide a substantial margin for error. BART may not have known this in the sixties. One AC director recalls that BART General Manager B. R. Stokes tried to convince AC that they "would get rich feeding BART," and a BART memo states that "our consultants said that rapid transit . . . will have a highly beneficial effect on local feeder bus operation" (S.F. BART, 1964). AC was not persuaded.

Indeed, AC-BART route coordination talks were mutually unpersuasive. As Stokes admitted to his board: "The BART staff has been unable to bring AC staff around to their point of view, and conversely, AC staff has not been very convincing either" (S.F. BART, 1971c). A BART staffer who had long toiled in these fields lamented that "the meetings accomplished nothing, . . . we argued for years." A consultant's report substantiates this point (Voorhees, 1974). That report was still going over the parallel route question that had been raised in meetings since 1964, thoroughly discussed in the report of a previous consultant, Simpson-Curtin, in 1967, and raised again in staff and board meetings between 1967 and 1973.[17]

The use of technical consultants rather than mediators underscored the orientation toward persuasion. Transit consultants gather data and recommend service changes; they are neither trained nor authorized to bargain. Neither Simpson-Curtin nor Voorhees dared venture into the treacherous waters of analyzing how to compensate AC for losing its most lucrative routes. There was, for example, no mention of negotiating an agreement maintaining status quo ante fiscal conditions.[18]

17. The ineffectiveness of the meetings was mentioned in four interviews, in a letter from Stokes to AC chief, Alan Bingham (S.F. BART, 1970a), and in a memo by BART consultant Henry Bain (S.F. BART, 1971a).

18. Just this kind of agreement was negotiated among independent transit agencies in Hamburg, Germany. The agreement was instrumental in bringing about service integration, for it ensured that no organization was made worse off by integrating.

One of BART's consultants, Henry Bain, tried to tackle the problem by convincing AC that it was incorrectly analyzing the comparative strengths of bus and rail. AC's primary criterion for comparing competitive routes was travel time. In their routing proposals AC officials said that transbay routes would be retained where riders could travel faster by bus than by a combination of feeder bus and rail (*Transit Times*, July 1970, p. 3).[19] In a memo distributed at the major AC-BART board meeting early in 1971, Bain argued that this criterion was inappropriate. He proposed several others to take its place: (1) minimizing total travel time (not just vehicle time); (2) maximizing reliability (buses suffer from congestion); and (3) minimizing cost (BART's marginal cost of carrying transbay riders is less than AC's). There is no record of AC's having responded to this proposed change of criteria. This silence suggests that AC's criterion was generated by reasoning backward from conclusions: given an organizational goal of avoiding financial trauma, what criteria will help achieve it?

One should not, however, be completely cynical about the agencies' adherence to publicly stated criteria such as maximizing total transit ridership. Unquestionably there were hidden goals, but the goals in public view were no doubt also held.[20] BART was unable to persuade AC to drop its transbay lines partly because AC officials were skeptical that BART would provide superior service (#3, #8, #22). In the face of relatively certain knowledge that AC would be damaged by withdrawing from transbay competition, BART would have had to demonstrate overwhelming superiority to have been persuasive. This it could not do a priori, thus allowing AC to propose a test of experience—let the rider choose.[21] Using that rule enabled AC to maintain a close relation between what benefited itself and what benefited the transit public. Had AC

19. AC officials have mentioned to me that they thought that AC's no-transfer ride was another advantage, but I have found no documentary evidence mentioning this point during the debates.

20. It is probably accurate to say that the agencies shared the goal, but their preference orderings differed.

21. Several AC officials felt they had more experience in transit than did BART personnel and believed that any abrupt switch from one service to another was a mistake.

used Bain's more complete set of criteria, including cost to taxpayers, it would have been harder to assert that organizational interests and general welfare were identical.

AC's simple trial-and-error approach was consistent not only with its organizational interests but also with its standard operating procedures. These rules, such as increasing a route's frequency when the passenger-to-seat ratio rose and decreasing it when the ratio fell, reflected a predisposition for a reactive decision strategy. BART did not share this orientation. In a memo to BART's assistant general manager Lawrence Dahms, BART's chief of contract administration wrote that AC's secretary

> made it plain that AC . . . is not going to negotiate further the transbay routes question—at least not this time. . . . It is evident he isn't sure *what* AC is going to provide during BART's start in 71/72—saying it *isn't entirely forecastable.* You evidently have a strong feeling that some figure in the "ballpark" of the NCTDP (5 routes) *is* or should be forecastable at this time. It appears to me that this difference between you and [A. E.] Wolf on the one hand, and George Taylor and Sam David [AC] on the other, is the precise point—more so than the number of routes.   (S.F. BART, 1970c; original emphasis)

BART, then, was bucking up against AC's organizational routines as well as preferences. Habit and interest make a powerful combination; it is not surprising that BART's efforts were futile.

Why did BART persist in trying to persuade AC, after years of fruitless effort, instead of buying it off or compensating it in some other manner? The most obvious explanation is that persuasion is the cheaper strategy: it costs only the time that meetings require and the frustration that meetings produce. Then, too, when competing bureaus negotiate division-of-labor agreements, the payoff is often policy rather than money—each agrees not to invade the other's sphere—but this option BART could not pursue. AC had no territory that BART could promise to avoid in exchange for AC's promise to remove duplicate runs. It is hard to conceive of any policy concessions that BART could have offered AC. As for money, the obvious compensation, BART had little to spare. By the time the coordination efforts were most intense, BART's cost overruns had become all too apparent. Furthermore, BART management felt that AC's tax base was stronger. As BART's Stokes pointed out to an AC director who raised the idea of revenue-sharing: "AC has considerable more authority to affect the balance between raising fares and raising taxes than does BART" (S.F. BART, 1971d). Even the *propriety* of compensating AC was disputed by BART. One BART consultant complained to Dahms that AC "is laboring under some serious delusions, such as that BART is a "customer" that might pay AC Transit for service, rather than a public agency that shares responsibility for serving the real customers (S.F. BART, 1971b).

Finally, BART had expected from the very beginning that AC would voluntarily eliminate redundancies. This expectation was partly nourished by AC's own early statements; and these BART did not forget. In BART's files can be found a copy of AC's 1958 *Facts About the ACCTD Plan,* with this key phrase underlined: "When the five-county district begins operation seven to ten years from now and takes over transbay service. . . ." (BART sent AC a copy of similar statements written by a 1958 AC-BART liaison committee, but AC replied that it was an informal conference whose recommendations its board never formally adopted.) And in part BART's expectation may have been sustained by an assumption that AC would have to step aside for the new system (#22). Thus a combination of AC's early commitments and BART's overweening confidence in the centrality of its role led BART to overestimate the likelihood that AC would yield in a gracious, that is, uncompensated, fashion.

If two equals cannot settle a jurisdictional dispute, sometimes hierarchical superiors step in to resolve it by fiat. Did these two agencies have recourse to a common superior? Originally Bay Area transit agencies formed a nonhierarchical organizational system. Before 1971 there was no proximate, superior institution that could or would exert much authority: the California PUC lacked jurisdiction over the routes of public transit organizations, and the issue apparently did not reach the state legislature (#36).

In 1971, however, the legislature established the Metropolitan Transportation Commission in the Bay Area. This agency's major raison d'être was coordinating independent operators, and the issue of overlapping jurisdictions fell solidly within this purview.[22] But the timing of the commission's entry into the fray militated against its playing a vigorous role.[23] The competitive issue peaked in 1971, just as the commission was forming. Its leadership chose—deliberately, it appears—to proceed cautiously in its early years, and it eschewed imperatives (Jones et al., 1974). Furthermore, the Metropolitan Transportation Commission was understaffed (#7). Finally, BART, though it may have *wanted* to use the commission to force AC to withdraw parallel routes, was in no position to influence the commission. By the early seventies BART's political reputation was tarnished. Financial problems were emerging, its construction schedule had slipped, and construction had disrupted several cities.

The result was a low-keyed effort by the commission: it helped organize and finance the last major AC-BART coordination project in 1973[24] but avoided prescribing a solution. The commission has gained new powers since then, but the issue has not yet resurfaced on its crowded agenda.[25]

Unable to persuade, unauthorized to command, unwilling to bargain, BART failed to establish a conventional differentiated division-of-labor with AC. After 1972, *before* BART opened its transbay line, the problem of overlapping func-

22. See Metropolitan Transportation Commission, 1974, Ch. 3, for evidence on this point.

23. Even the commission's formal power does not allow it to decide unilaterally on issues where operators disagree. This authority had been in the commission's original legislation, but the operators objected, and the clause was deleted (Jones et al., 1974).

24. I have been told that the commission served a useful role here because by this time neither AC nor BART trusted each other to lead the project.

25. A commission staffer said that they no longer meet regularly with AC and BART on coordination issues. Rather, the commission intercedes on issues that AC and BART cannot settle themselves *and* on which the staff receives pressure from various interest groups via the commissioners. Apparently the staff would not autonomously put this issue on the agenda, and since the public has essentially ignored it since 1973, it stays off the agenda.

tions receded in importance for BART; the more significant problems of system financing, procurement, and reliability became still more critical. It was not, however, just a matter of a crowded agenda: BART's impaired short-term capacity was making the question of competition moot. BART was encountering so many problems in obtaining reliable cars that in September 1974 the board requested the PUC to *forbid* Greyhound, then serving eastern Contra Costa County commuters, to terminate its routes. BART's capacity problems meant that the demand for combined peak-hour transbay service temporarily exceeded supply,[26] reducing the conflict between the two agencies since they were no longer competing for a scarce resource.

But the issue has never been resolved, merely set aside. The title of this section is therefore a misnomer: there was no conflict resolution in the ordinary sense. BART and AC have "agreed to disagree." Even this odd agreement may be only temporary, for interviews with BART officials indicate that the issue, though quiescent, is not dead. Therefore, the stability of the currently redundant system cannot be considered settled.

The Stability of Competitive Arrangements

Chapter One pointed out that a theoretically untreated (though empirically observed) problem in bureaucratic competition is the question of stability. Are redundant organizations politically stable? Or is redundancy likely to be eradicated by mergers?[27]

26. Assistant General Manager Dahms had warned the board in April 1974 that due to a car shortage there would be many standees during peak hours. In August BART announced there would be twice as many people as seats.

27. Mergers can have an effect more benign than eliminating competition; they can provide economies of scale. But as BART and AC use different technologies, scale economies would be restricted to administration. Since administration is a small proportion of a transit agency's budget, the savings would not amount to much. See the evidence on this question presented in Chapter Five.

Surprisingly, merger proposals have been few and far between in this case. AC, of course, has issued none. But even in BART it has not surfaced often.[28] One director raised the idea in 1969, but his colleagues thought it a long-term question not requiring swift action.[29] At the managerial level, Frank Herringer did say when he started as BART General Manager in 1975 that it was a big mistake not to create one integrated agency, but this remained only an opinion, not a proposal for action. At the planning staff level, interviews reveal more concern with service "rationalization" than organizational merger.

At one time both a preference for organizational autonomy and for financial stability pointed AC in the same direction—to oppose merger. AC's organizational interests promoted competitive stability. But Proposition 13 has ravaged AC's property tax revenues whereas BART is buttressed by the productive sales tax. It is conceivable that AC's precarious financial condition will lessen its resistance to merger. At the same time, however, Proposition 13 probably makes BART leery of merging with an impoverished AC.

A merger plan would encounter legal roadblocks as well as organizational resistance. AC's jurisdiction includes only parts of Alameda and Contra Costa whereas BART's includes all of those counties and San Francisco as well. Merger would thus require charter revisions, a complicated process at best.

Beyond the two operators, little attention has been paid to organizational consolidation. A state senator, John Knox, called for a merger of AC, BART, and San Francisco's transit agency in the early seventies, but there is no indication that his proposal aroused serious consideration, and he dropped the matter.[30] Subsequently in the legislature only one senator, Alfred Alquist, appears to have been interested in the merger

28. This claim is based on office memos and interviews. Of course privately it may have been raised more often.

29. This director did recall, however, that his colleagues favored merger in the long run.

30. We can dismiss the possibility of a three-way merger for the indefinite future. The organizational and political problems are formidable. Because San Francisco's transit agency, Muni, is a city department rather than a special district, a city charter revision would be necessary. Charter revisions occur infrequently. And in any case, it is unlikely that the East Bay counties would want to be saddled with Muni, whose reputation is not the best.

idea (#C1). The Metropolitan Transportation Commission, the other likely source of proposals, has not broached the idea in public although a staffer said that the staff discusses it.

Should AC-BART competition prove unstable, the cause will probably be route reductions rather than merger.[31] Proposition 13 makes AC more financially dependent upon the commission, giving the commission the leverage it needs to realign routes. The commission may indeed seize this opportunity, for route "rationalization," that is, eliminating duplication, has been a long-standing, albeit latent, goal of the commission.

Whether redundant service proves stable will certainly affect the fortunes of the two principal agencies. But what are the consequences of redundancy for those outside the bureaucracy?

What Are the Drawbacks of Redundancy?

No organizational arrangement is free of problems, and redundancy is no exception. What are the disadvantages of duplicative operating agencies? The answers fall into two classes: (1) allocative inefficiency—does redundancy cost too much? and (2) organizational difficulties—has competition between AC and BART weakened their integration of complementary, nonoverlapping services?

Allocative Inefficiency

About twenty years ago the two special districts predicted that they would be financially self-supporting.[32] The predictions badly missed the mark: neither agency is close to being

31. More precisely, though redundant routes are more likely to be eliminated by a merged organization than by a treaty between independent ones, merger itself is improbable.

32. It is well known that BART predicted self-sufficiency; it is not well known that AC did as well.

supported by its riders. Several BART officials acknowledged that one of the most telling criticisms of redundancy in the public sector is that, unlike the private sector, nonusers must support redundant services via taxes.[33] If riders produced a financial surplus for AC and BART, that criticism would be nullified. Though there are no free lunches, duplication is less offensive if only the eater pays.

But obviously both organizations are subsidized, so it seems that nonriding taxpayers pay for duplication. The issue, however, is more complicated. Most transbay runs do well financially, so taxpayers would save little if they were eliminated. The big losers are local routes, but these services are *non*redundant. Then, too, some taxpayers are transbay auto commuters, and that group would suffer from increased auto congestion (of an indeterminate amount)[34] should the transbay bus lines disappear.

An alternative way of assessing redundancy's cost is to argue that for a *fixed* total budget for AC and BART the public could receive better service. Those buses and drivers now serving transbay commuters could be put to better use elsewhere—feeding BART stations, for example. To evaluate this move requires estimating the proportion of AC riders who would switch to BART if there were more feeder buses and no transbay buses. It is difficult to estimate this: a recent AC strike would probably provide a poor approximation. My impression is that insufficient station parking limits access to BART more than feeder service does.[35]

Perhaps we should focus less on transbay commuters—they enjoy the luxury of alternative modes of travel—and more on captive riders in the East Bay. As transportation analyst David Jones has pointed out, people going to work

33. This assertion does not apply to public goods, which by definition are used by all citizens. Chapter Seven will examine the political differences between redundant public and nonpublic goods.

34. Unfortunately it is difficult to estimate how many AC riders would switch to cars, how many to BART, and how many trips would be suppressed.

35. Further, although BART's peak-hour capacity is less strained than it was three years ago, its East Bay Concord line is still crowded. If AC eliminated transbay lines before these capacity constraints of BART can be eased, BART would not benefit during the peak of the rush hour.

usually can choose between redundant modes, but the poor, the handicapped, and the elderly making nonwork trips may not have *any* modes available. And as noted in Chapter One, overlaps in one domain can create gaps elsewhere. Even if more local AC runs would not increase BART commuter patronage, they may help transit-dependent riders whom BART cannot reach. This kind of division of labor, the inverse of redundancy, does make some sense because of the agencies' large technological differences: AC's buses can reach the transit-dependent much more easily than BART's trains can.

Proposition 13, however, makes the last point of academic interest only. AC is much more likely to use a budget-cutting strategy of reducing service than a reallocative strategy of reorienting service.

Organizational Difficulties

Can competition and cooperation coexist? Implicit in many discussions of jurisdictional fights is the proposition that bureaucratic competition in one domain precludes cooperation in domains where coordination is needed because agencies' programs are interdependent.[36] Why might this inverse relation between competition and coordination hold true in this case? First, transit functions may be technically related so that competition in one function necessarily impairs cooperation in another. For example, one type of complementary function—the amount of bus feeder service—is directly constrained by resources devoted to redundant transbay service.[37] Here the inverse connection between competition and cooperation may be quite strong because the more buses used in competitive routes, the fewer remain for feeder routes.

Elsewhere, technical relations between substitutes and complements are rather weak. Consider a second issue of

36. Note that this would be a cost not of redundancy per se but only of conflictual (competitive) redundancy.

37. Some of the feeder disagreements arose, however, because the agencies have in part *different* clientele. Originally BART wanted AC to route more lines to the stations, but AC staffers believed that doing so would inconvenience *local* patrons in some cases. This conflict would have arisen in the absence of redundancy.

coordinating complementary actions: the problem of transfers between modes. This issue did necessitate numerous meetings, prima facie evidence that BART and AC found coordination difficult. But this had little to do with parallel routes. The transfer problem was related to finance (how should free rides be absorbed?) and technology (what kinds of transfers are feasible given BART's automatic fare collection and AC's no-change system?). These issues could easily arise between agencies that do not overlap in the slightest. Similarly, the rail stations' physical designs have presented problems for bus-rail patrons, but these difficulties are not due to AC-BART competition: the stations were designed *before* redundant services became a hot issue. The problems arose apparently because BART contractors neglected to design the stations with bus requirements in mind (#22, #C3). Again, this problem is typical of relations between differentiated, interdependent agencies; redundancy need not be present for such difficulties to arise.

Second, competition and cooperation may be inversely related because when different functions are closely tied *organizationally*, antagonisms may spill over from the domain where rivalry festers to other functions. Thus, the key here is the degree of organizational, rather than technical, linkage between domains.[38] In BART and AC the spheres of competition and cooperation were poorly insulated from each other. The staffers who met to quarrel over transfers, feeders, and physical connections were the same people who met to argue about parallel routes. The same board committees met to discuss questions of complementary and competitive service. The general managers, Bingham and Stokes, were likewise involved in both matters. Thus a negative spillover could have occurred: agency officials, disgruntled by their failure to reach agreement on redundant routes, may have been loath to cooperate on other issues. The data, however, show no clear pattern. Several BART and AC officials indicated that personal antagonism between certain agency personnel may have interfered with coordination. How much of the antago-

---

38. In many private firms that both compete and contract with each other, separate divisions handle the different tasks. AC and BART are too small to have such independent divisions.

nism, however, was due *specifically* to the agencies having redundant functions is uncertain. And on the other side of the ledger, the relations between several officials can best be described as instances of friendly rivalry: they were playing a competitive game, but one which did not inflict deep wounds.

Most importantly, external constraints prevented ill will from having serious effects. Several inter- and intra-organizational memos showed an awareness that if the agencies failed to cooperate on obvious links such as feeders and transfers, "the newspapers will crucify us." One BART official wrote bluntly: "If our inability to 'bend the will' of AC on transbay routes holds up virtually all other progress much longer, it appears to me that both BART and AC are in an untenable position with respect to the public—not to mention our own management" (S.F. BART, 1970c).[39] Neither agency could afford an extensive spillover of antagonism from the parallel route conflict to other issues.

Officials who discuss overlapping and those who focus on complementary functions are more organizationally separated today than they were during the major coordination drives of a decade ago. The organization of the Bay Area's major transit agencies, the Regional Transit Association, encompasses six functional committees, and the issue of redundancy is addressed in only one, the services and tariffs committee.[40] Interviews with BART and AC representatives on four other committees did not reveal any negative spillovers.[41] Indeed, some of AC's and BART's functions, for example, procurement, are so dissimilar that they can neither affect each other nor act jointly, so the problem of antagonistic spillover cannot arise.

39. A commission staffer, discussing his organization's passive role, stated that had AC done something "really atrocious," the commission would have intervened.

40. However, the advertising committee could become entangled in questions of competition via the issue of mutual advertising. (Why advertise for another organization that supplies competing service?) And initially there were some conflicts (S.F. BART, 1972). In the last few years, relations seem much improved. Both sides think that the general managers were largely responsible for the progress.

41. In four of the ten cases, the agency representatives are relatively new and were not working for the agencies when the early seventies' talks were taking place.

Hierarchically, there is now sufficient differentiation so that the old policy disagreements at the top do not seem to affect supervisors responsible for routine coordination (#11, #G2, #G3). Routines insulate operations from conflicts elsewhere.

In summary, the evidence does not support a *strong* version of the competition-cooperation thesis, that is, the former precludes the latter. The data are sufficiently inconclusive, however, so that we cannot dismiss the weaker thesis that competition impaired cooperation. Nevertheless, we cannot attribute the bulk of coordination difficulties to rivalry.

What Are the Advantages of Redundancy?

The drawbacks of redundancy are well known; the benefits, less so. Five kinds of benefits, unevenly realized in this case study, are worthy of consideration.

BART's Developmental Uncertainties

All complex new systems require a period of debugging: BART required one but did not have one. Owing to a combination of schedule slips and political pressure to get the system operating quickly, the scheduled testing period was squeezed out. BART started operations while still debugging; the result was, and to a lesser extent still is, an unreliable system. Assuming that a shared goal of BART and AC is to entice commuters out of their cars, to have only one means of public transit across the bay while the trains were still unreliable would have been exceedingly risky. How many patrons would have become frustrated and gone back to their autos had they been forced off reliable buses and onto unreliable trains in 1974? Though that figure cannot be precisely estimated, a thorough review of consumer attitudes toward transit stressed that patrons cherish schedule reliability (see Altshuler, Womack, and Pucher, 1979, p. 115), so we can infer that the number would have been significant.

Furthermore, because of a variety of problems, including a strike at a manufacturing plant and difficulties with car brakes, BART opened with far fewer cars than they had anticipated. These problems worsened the load factors (ratio of people to seats): in June 1975 the ratio during the rush hour on the East Bay's Concord line was 1.77. Because of these unexpected troubles, BART, particularly during the first two years of transbay operation, carried fewer people than it had expected. Consequently, bus routes paralleling BART were not a posteriori redundant, in the pejorative sense of superfluity, since there was no excess capacity. It is important to remember that during planning BART expected that rapid transit would have sufficient capacity to make parallel bus routes superfluous. What was thought in the early, optimistic stages of BART development to be excess turned out to be barely adequate. Of course, had there been no problems with the automatic train control system, the cars' brakes or motors, car procurement, or central computer design, perhaps the planned ninety-second headway would have been attained in 1974, and duplicate bus routes might then have constituted excess capacity.

This, however, is not how affairs turned out because all those above problems did develop and because BART's design is sensitive to failure. Indeed, as former general manager Frank Herringer commented: "When they built BART, they did not really anticipate that things would fail, and they did not allow for the system to continue operating when something went wrong" (*Washington Star*, January 25, 1978). His statement captures the central irony of the AC-BART experience. On the one hand, BART's hardware was intentionally built "with the assumption that nothing would ever fail—the inverse of Murphy's Law" (Herringer, Commonwealth Club, S.F., July 28, 1978). Thus, at the technological level BART's designers did not exorcise Murphy's Law with the shade of von Neumann; indeed, they thought it unnecessary to do so because each component of the system would function reliably. This design philosophy courted trouble.

But, on the other hand, the unwarranted optimism of the BART planners was counteracted by the undesigned redundancy of parallel routes, a redundancy built not by a reliability engineer but as the by-product of organizational interests. Thus, the interorganizational system behaved as if it believed in Murphy's Law, and designed technological fragility was compensated by undesigned organizational redundancy. The sharpness of this irony, however, may soften with time. Development problems, unlike episodic disturbances, have a temporal direction. BART has become less failure-prone and less failure-sensitive, and this trend will probably continue, suggesting that future transbay transit will need less redundancy to compensate for development mishaps.

Episodic Shocks

These, by definition, can occur at any time. Since they have no developmental component, they do not subside as a system ages. Nor are they restricted to one mode: both AC and BART are vulnerable to random shocks.

Strikes

During this study's research, there was only one major strike when both BART and AC had transbay service, so we have only this instance in which to examine their roles as mutual backups. BART's transbay patronage jumped immediately following the beginning of AC's strike on November 21, 1977. In late November, weekday transbay lines increased an average of 36 percent, and two lines gained better than 70 percent. December exceeded the strikeless previous December by 56 percent, and its forecast, which had not anticipated the strike, by 40 percent (S.F. BART, 1977).

Due to BART and carpool increases, auto traffic increased only marginally. December 1977 was only 2 percent higher than November, and 4 percent higher than December 1976. Though a California Department of Transportation official told the author that "strangely, the strike had very little impact on congestion," it should not have been surprising. Operational redundancies reduce the disturbance caused by any one channel's breakdown.

We can compare this episode with the AC strike of July-August 1974, *before* BART's transbay start. Auto traffic increased in July by 9.4 percent over June, and by almost 11 percent over July of the previous year (California Department of Transportation, 1968–79). Because these increases were probably concentrated in the peak hours, the absence of a transit backup was still more significant than the raw figures indicate.

One-day technical breakdowns

These are not purely episodic shocks since we can expect their frequency to decrease as BART troubleshooting proceeds. But one cannot expect them to disappear. Even AC, which has operated transbay runs for twenty years and is certainly not in a developmental phase, has prepared emergency plans with BART if the Bay Bridge is closed by fire or other disasters. So far AC has not had to avail itself of BART's help, but BART has used AC twelve times from 1973 to 1978. This redundancy has been routinized to the point of codification, and bus substitutions have worked smoothly.[42]

Redundancy and Organizational Independence

Riders can be shielded from a new mode's developmental problems and from certain episodic shocks as long as a second mode provides parallel service. The parallel modes need not be operated by separate organizations; in principle, a single agency could run both. Have transit patrons in the Bay Area benefited because modal redundancy was embodied in distinct organizations? Put negatively, would they have been hurt had BART taken over AC in the late fifties?

It is clear that AC is a well-managed agency. Philip Viton, a transportation economist, observes that "the district has gained a reputation for cost efficiency, a reputation which is confirmed by comparing its operating costs to those of other

42. This evaluation is based on letters from BART to AC, thanking the latter for competently executed substitute service.

bus transit properties" (1980, p. 8). Given this high standing, it is unlikely that merger, and ensuing dominance by BART's managers, would have resulted in better bus service than AC has provided. Indeed, since AC's management has been so well above average, it seems quite likely that a BART takeover would have resulted in a bus system inferior to the existing one. This assessment is gained with the aid of hindsight: we *know* how AC and BART have performed over the years. But could one have *predicted*, in the late fifties, before much was known about the agencies' abilities, that lodging redundant operations in separate organizations would be a superior strategy to creating a single, integrated agency? Proposition 3 gives us a basis for such predictions. Suppose one must decide whether to merge transit organizations A and B, with the understanding that B's managers would be in control. If nothing is known about the competence of A and B's managers except that they are drawn from the same probability distribution, then Proposition 3 tells us that merger is a riskier strategy than is maintaining separate organizations. On average, the integrated agency will do as well as the parallel organizations, but because its performance is less predictable, a risk-averse decision-maker would prefer to keep the agencies apart. Thus, one need not have known or predicted that AC's managers would turn out to be unusually competent in order to have concluded in the late fifties that a BART takeover was unwise.

Demand Uncertainty, Redundancy, and Diversified Service

What features of a transit system are especially important to passengers? This question could not have been answered with much precision when AC and BART were planned in the 1950s, for little was then known about the service attributes riders wanted. More precisely, the correct *weighting* of preferred attributes was unknown; obviously speed, reliability, and safety were known to be "Good Things." But because building a system always entails assigning weights to and making trade-offs between service attributes, there was considerable demand uncertainty in the fifties.

Not only did the systems' planners have to make decisions about service in the face of much uncertainty, had they guessed wrong about what riders like—if they, for example, overemphasized speed at the expense of reliability—those choices would be hard to undo once the system was built. Because the kind of service a transit system, especially rapid rail, can deliver is constrained by the system's physical plant, mistakes in service strategy are frozen into the system's design.

Faced with a choice both uncertain and irreversible, a wise central planner might hedge his bet by designing multiple systems with diverse service characteristics. In the Bay Area that wisdom was mimicked by a decentralized process. AC's and BART's modal choices created a mix of service packages: notice that in Table 4 trains are described by the attributes of column A and buses by those of column B. The organizations' uncoordinated modal decisions produced a diversity that could well have been beneficial given how little was known about passenger preferences.

This assessment is theoretically plausible, but actually measuring the payoff of diversified service strategies is difficult. One measure, ridership, indicates that each system's set of attributes has appeal: AC and BART are still roughly splitting peak transbay ridership. Neither set of design trade-offs has proven clearly superior. But this revealed preference approach is contaminated by price differentials and BART's short-term reliability problems. A second measure, survey data, might more directly reveal how patrons view the systems' attributes. Surprisingly, one study of potential transit commuters in the Bay Area indicated that BART and AC scored much the same on dimensions such as travel time, waiting time, and dependability.[43] The difference between

43. One study has concluded that both riders and taxpayers would be better off if BART differentiated its service more by sharply reducing the waiting time for trains and by supplying its own feeder buses (Viton, 1980, p. 4). Viton argues convincingly that there are enough affluent commuters who would pay much higher fares for this premium service so that BART could cover its operating costs without levying taxes.

TABLE 4   *Design Trade-offs*

SELECTED QUALITIES (A)	SACRIFICED OR COMPROMISED QUALITIES (B)
1. High average speed between stations; therefore, widely spaced stations	1. Closely spaced stations; therefore, ease of access to stations
2. Mainline system serving major traffic corridors	2. Network of transit lines serving subareas of the region; ability to complete trip in a single vehicle without having to transfer to and from feeder system
3. Batch-type transport mode: cars in trains carrying many passengers	3. Flow-type transport mode: smaller vehicles carrying comparable numbers of passengers at shorter headways, with branching local distribution at origin and destination
4. Fixed rail on exclusive grade-separated right of way	4. Flexible routing in response to changing travel patterns. Economy of construction; right of way usable by other vehicles; disabled vehicles do not disrupt operation of entire line
5. Limited number of access points into system to encourage clustered urban development	5. Compatibility with foot-loose trends and low-density settlement patterns
6. Frequent service with stops at all stations	6. Differentiated service with both "local" and "express" operations
7. High aesthetic and comfort standards	7. Economy of construction
8. Regional long-haul design	8. Local trip-making capability

SOURCE: Webber, 1976, p. 100.

cars and the two public modes was generally larger than the differences between the transit alternatives (Johnson, 1975, p. 4). Note, however, that this study sampled *potential* commuters; whether actual riders perceive larger differences between AC and BART remains unknown.

These limitations of the data mean that we should remain empirically agnostic as to whether commuters sense a significant difference between the services of AC and BART. But even if future research detects only delicate distinctions, we should remember that because most service characteristics are durable features of transit systems, whatever variations that are perceived will last a long time. And the value of small but durable differences cumulates over time. Thus, because of its permanence, even a modest amount of service diversity may justify a continuing redundancy.

The Rivalry Effect

Chapter One predicted that *competitive* redundancies, in which organizations fight over scarce resources, would have effects beyond those of redundancy in general. An agency might use rival organizations as reference points, consciously striving to best them via service improvements or price cuts. There is little evidence of a rivalry effect in the AC-BART relationship. AC's primary points of comparison were initially the Key System and subsequently itself. Historical self-evaluation appears more important than cross-organizational comparison. Though during the 1970–72 transbay discussions AC frequently referred to comparative route times, there is no evidence that AC tried to *improve* its position vis-à-vis BART. The basic transbay lines, including self-feeding express buses, were established well before BART became a rival. As for BART, during its design phase the competitive standards were set by the auto, not by the other transit agency (Parsons et al., 1956). During BART's early operation, internal problems such as reliability and safety provided sufficient room for improvement. Progress could be measured by changes in the gap between system design and system performance; an external performance standard such as AC was not needed. In both agencies, then, internal history swamped inter-organizational comparisons, so rivalry had little effect on performance.

Future Uncertainties

The long-range function of redundant organizations is to hedge against future problems that are but dimly perceived in the present. A major long-run uncertainty in Bay Area transit is future travel patterns. Although there are stable corridors (East Bay commuters funneling into downtown San Francisco), in several decades new employment centers may appear elsewhere. Both BART and AC have rigidities that inhibit adaptation to unpredictable origin-destination changes. But so long as these rigidities are not correlated, the two together retain some flexibility. Although AC currently makes only one stop in San Francisco, at its downtown terminal, it is *technologically* able to shift with travel pattern changes. The buses of the Golden Gate Bridge, Highway, and Transit District, an agency serving counties north of San Francisco, drop off and pick up commuters at several San Francisco locations; AC could do likewise. There are, however, institutional and fiscal constraints. The city of San Francisco was reluctant to let the Golden Gate Bridge District's buses on its streets, and a similar reluctance would confront an AC request. And AC lacks Golden Gate's political leverage in San Francisco.[44] In addition, AC, especially after Proposition 13, is reluctant to get on congested city streets and increase turn-around time for their peak-hour buses (#3). BART, on the other hand, would incur formidable construction costs if it extended to new employment centers—its technology is less flexible than AC's—but institutional constraints would be less binding.

Thus, taken together, AC and BART form a more flexible response to long-term problems than does either one taken separately, just as jointly they constitute a more reliable solution to short-term difficulties than does either by itself.

44. Golden Gate's board has representatives from San Francisco; AC's has none. Consequently, deals between counties north of the Golden Gate Bridge and San Francisco can be arranged more easily than can agreements between the East Bay and San Francisco.

Conclusion

When it runs, BART is a pleasure—quiet, smooth, clean. Unfortunately, it does not always run. Problems, particularly in BART's early years, plagued it: equipment, brakes, motors, and control systems were not up to snuff. Moreover, BART's overall design made the system too sensitive to its mechanical failures. The lack of side tracks for disabled trains is only one illustration of BART's internal fragility, of its reliance on every component working to perfection, of its unredundant design.

Fortunately for commuters in the Bay Area, the organizational system of public transit was not designed in the same risky, unredundant way that BART's physical system was planned. Indeed, the organizational system was not designed at all. Instead, the transit agencies engaged in rather messy bureaucratic politics, fighting over their jurisdictions for years. The central irony of this story is that this messy, unplanned, and seemingly irrational organizational politics produced a valuable redundancy that had been deliberately removed from BART's technology.

4

Competitive Planning in Minneapolis-St. Paul

Institutional and Policy Contest

Minnesotans take planning seriously. Many residents of the Twin Cities area also take regionalism seriously. It should, therefore, come as no surprise that Minneapolis–St. Paul established its Metropolitan Planning Commission well before most urban areas in the United States began regional planning. The commission, created in 1957, was a bold experiment in regional governments. One of its assignments was to investigate and report on the transit situation.

This region had once boasted a fine network of streetcar lines. In several dubious transactions[1] during the fifties, the streetcars were sold and replaced by buses. As the streetcar network steadily contracted through the sixties, the buses did not fill the gaps. Indeed, Twin Cities Lines, by far the largest firm,[2] cut back on bus routes. Although the system was reasonably well managed (#23), service deletions and aging equipment accelerated the classic downward spiral of urban transit. Bulking larger than this trend was the region's auto-

1. These transactions ultimately led to prosecution.
2. It carried about 97 percent of the region's transit riders.

and-highway-based growth following World War II. Unlike older Eastern cities, this metropolis experienced its greatest growth in the auto era: the population rose from 940,000 in 1949 to 1,874,000 in 1970. The auto's impact on development is revealed by growth dispersion. The central cities stabilized following World War II, and the suburbs picked up nearly all the 900,000-person increase. Employment centers likewise scattered.

The region's geography facilitated this dispersed development. The Twin Cities are in the Great Plains: wide-open land stretches in every direction as far as the eye can see. Because there are no natural barriers to development, there are no natural traffic corridors. Hence, though some people do commute into downtown Minneapolis and St. Paul, the densities do not match those of most eastern cities. Obviously, transit suffered in this environment, the proportion of work trips carried by transit falling considerably.

The Planning Commission, charged with investigating the problem, collaborated with the Minnesota Highway Department in a set of studies (the Joint Program) of both land-use and transit possibilities. The Joint Program produced three alternate development scenarios: (1) classical central city with radial corridors; (2) "spread city," a dispersed pattern; and (3) "constellation cities," with growth outside the central cities clustered in activity centers. Constellation cities received the most political support (#12) and was duly adopted by the Planning Commission in 1967.

Transit, which was supposed to be consistent with the recommended development pattern, had proved more troublesome. The Joint Program had hired DeLeuw, Cather, and Company in 1964 to advise on long-range transit possibilities, within the set of conventional (rapid rail and bus) alternatives. To forecast patronage, DeLeuw used data from a 1958 Highway Department study, modifying those data by assuming the radial corridors plan would be in effect. The consultants concluded that, even assuming the downtown-oriented corridors plan, travel demand would be too light to warrant rapid rail. (The estimated maximum peak-hour load in the year 2000 was 4,200 passengers.) DeLeuw recommended an express bus system as more compatible with the Twin Cities' density and travel demands.

The Joint Program did not adopt the report. Although the program agreed that the area lacked the density to support rapid rail, it found buses' fixed routes, slow speeds, and high operating costs unappealing (Joint Program, 1967). There was considerable interest in innovative, advanced technology systems, and the Joint Program formalized its interest in Policy 8 of its *Metropolitan Development Guide*: "Encourage the development of a new form of rapid transit system more specifically tailored to the needs of the Twin City area than conventional bus or rail rapid transit systems" (Metropolitan Council, 1971, p. 26).

But the Planning Commission could not realize either its chosen development or transit options. It was a voluntary federation having neither implementing nor financial authority. Its legacy to its successor was plans and personnel, not policies in force.

Although the state legislature could have created a more authoritative public organization for solving transit problems, concern for these issues was low in the mid-sixties. Apart from one or two influential legislators, the legislature was more concerned with another regional issue, sewers. That was an awkward political problem, involving hot questions of finance, location, and timing, and legislators were eager to be rid of it. In 1967 the legislature established a regional council and empowered it to deal with the sewer problem. Although the Metropolitan (Metro) Council was created as a multi-purpose agency, all participants understood that its first responsibility was to solve the sewerage issue (#24).

At the same session, backers of a public takeover of urban transit had written a bill that would create a single-purpose regional agency, the Metropolitan Transit Commission (MTC). Passing the bill would authorize the commission to do both short-term and long-term planning. The bill's key section, despite its ambiguous division of labor, does indicate that the commission was obliged to create a long-range plan:

> The commission, with the cooperation of the Twin Cities Metropolitan Planning Commission or its successor in authority and the department of highways, shall develop a plan for a complete, integrated mass transit system . . . so designed as in the judgment of the commission to best fit the needs of the area.   (State of Minnesota, 1967, p. 1901, statute 473A.06)

It was not certain in 1967 that either bill would be approved; it was conceivable that the legislature would create *neither*[3] a council nor a Transit Commission.[4] It was probably at this point that a latent redundancy of authority was built into the charter legislation of the two regional bodies. Public transit advocates, fearing the Transit Commission bill would fail, may have helped draft the council's bill to authorize it to conduct overall transportation and transit planning.

> The Metropolitan Council shall prepare and adopt . . . a comprehensive development guide for the metropolitan area. It shall consist of a compilation of policy statements, goals, standards, programs, and maps prescribing guides for an orderly and economic development, public and private, of the metropolitan area. The comprehensive development guide shall recognize and encompass those future developments which will have an impact on the entire area including but not limited to such matters as land use . . . the necessity for and location of airports, highways, transit facilities. . . .
> (ibid., p. 1928, statute 473B.06)

Exactly what a "compilation of policy statements, goals, standards, programs, and maps prescribing guides" meant the legislature did not specify. In particular, it was unclear how much the council could constrain the selection of a transit mode by enumerating goals, programs, and the necessity for and location of transit facilities. As the legitimate scope of the council's transportation planning was inexact, so the legislature's intended relation between MTC and council planning was uncertain. The ambiguous relationship became more than an academic point when, to the surprise of many legislative observers, both bills became law.

Although the division of planning responsibilities was fuzzy, it *was* clear that the legislature intended the two new agencies to be hierarchically related. The 1967 law authorized the council to review all long-term comprehensive plans of the specialized commissions and to direct that a plan be "indefinitely suspended" (ibid.). (The commissions could appeal a decision before the entire council. If agreement could not be reached, the matter would be brought before the legis-

3. A similar problem affected AC and BART's formations.
4. A bill to create an MTC had failed in the 1963 and 1965 legislatures.

lature. This arbitration clause proved significant.)[5] In the confident words of a founding councillor: "There was no doubt that we were the system planners" (#24). As a multi-functional agency charged with overseeing special purpose ones—the Airports Commission, the Waste Commission, and the Parks and Open Space Commission, in addition to the Transit Commission—the council was supposed to coordinate regional activities in accord with its *Metropolitan Development Guide*. The law required that the special purpose agencies make decisions that were consistent with the guide. Unlike AC and BART's relation, the Transit Commission-Metro Council relation possessed a definite hierarchical component. That at least was the legal theory; it is well known that many regional coordinating authorities have real authority over little and coordinate less.[6] The council's legal powers represented only a potential; it had to prove itself in the late sixties by handling its first assigned problem. (As we shall see shortly, the hierarchical arrangement could have enabled a conventional, nonredundant relation to evolve between the council and the MTC, the latter generating proposals and the former reviewing them.[7] Differentiation is ordinarily conceived of horizontally, but hierarchy is a division of labor as well.)

The Quiet Years: 1968–70

The latent overlap between the council and MTC was not activated for the first four years of the agencies' lives.

5. Apparently, however, the legislature did not establish the arbitration rule with the deliberate intent of deciding between competing plans. The rule was simply a procedure for resolving conflict between two differentiated agencies.

6. Many significant regional organizations were created in this period, and the entire organizational ecology of the region was in ferment. The council was jockeying for position not only with single-purpose commissions but also with the Minnesota Highway Department and local governments. (In particular the central cities' planning staffs felt capable of long-range planning [#35].)

7. In retrospect, the possibility of this conventional evolution makes the overlap that did appear still more improbable: it depended not only on the virtually simultaneous passing of two ambiguous bills but also on avoiding the conventional evolution of division of labor.

The tranquility was due to a de facto division of labor and attention. This differentiation was not based on an agreement, not even a tacit one. Rather, the council, preoccupied with sewers, gave transportation low priority (#12), while the more specialized MTC began short-range bus improvement studies in 1968 and long-range system planning in 1969. Although council staff was involved—to what degree is unclear—in consultant selection and sat in on MTC's planning sessions, the council seemed content to let MTC lead the way in system planning. With no pressure from councillors, their staff played a passive role.

Regarding jurisdictional relations, the MTC's legal position was strengthened in 1969 through specification of its enabling legislation:

> The commission shall have the power to plan, engineer, construct, equip, and operate transit systems, transit projects, or any parts thereof, including transit lanes or rights of way . . . and any other facilities useful for or related to any public transit system.   (State of Minnesota, 1969, p. 1072, statute 473.405)

These are broad and general powers. In the same session, however, the council secured greater authority over the commission by receiving the right to approve the latter's capital expense budget. So though the ambiguity of overlap persisted, the relation's hierarchical component was clarified.

Substantively, the model choice process was murky. Transit planning in this region was not an easy task. MTC and council staffs shared a belief that the region, though crisscrossed by highways, needed some kind of mass transit (#36). But *which* kind of transit was appropriate for the Twin Cities' moderate density? To answer the question, MTC hired Voorhees as its first long-range planning consultant. The Voorhees group, after evaluating numerous alternatives,[8] recommended fixed rail or conventional technology over both buses and the advanced technology fixed guideway systems suggested by the Joint Program. The recommendation was not lightly made: the Voorhees report was the least optimistic of MTC's long-range plans and recounted soberly the

8. Several interviewees believed this was the fairest MTC study (#4, #26).

difficulties that any kind of transit would have in the Twin Cities area (1969, pp. 43-55). Although its patronage predictions exceeded DeLeuw's, it nevertheless predicted that only on five major corridors would volumes exceed 5,000 passengers hourly by 1985 (ibid., p. 128). Its claims about the impact of rail on variables such as air pollution, reducing the need for new highways, and shaping development were modest (ibid., pp. 43, 54, 60).

The report recommended that the region construct the system in stages because corridor densities differed so greatly. This proposal, a reflection of the report's political naïveté (#12), evoked considerable antagonism: the newspapers and city of St. Paul were especially critical of the staging sequence (*St. Paul Dispatch*, January 9, 1970; *Minneapolis Star*, March 3, 1970). John Jamieson, head of long-range planning, replied that the agency would reassess the staging sequence (*St. Paul Dispatch*, January 28, 1970), and Chairman Lester Bolstad tried to soothe the critics by noting that it was only an engineering report.

Following the Voorhees report, disagreements surfaced *inside* MTC. The arguments concerned not staging but technology. Although no one was thinking of an express bus as a long-term choice (#23, #37)—express buses were seen as strictly a short-term solution—the commissioners backed different kinds of fixed guideway systems. The chairman and several colleagues favored relatively conventional rapid rail. Two others had been contacted by Edward Anderson, a University of Minnesota engineering professor who had been investigating new forms of transit. Anderson recommended trying Personal Rapid Transit (PRT), an experimental mode that combined features of trains and automobiles. Like trains, PRT would run on rails; like cars, the vehicles were small units designed for individual riders, and they would be activated by patrons rather than run on a fixed schedule. The two commissioners were sufficiently impressed to advocate that alternative, despite the Voorhees report's warning that such systems were insufficiently operational to be a current option. The divisions within MTC were so great that the executive director, John Doolittle, resigned in June 1970 amid speculations that the agency's indecisiveness hastened his resignation

(*Minneapolis Star,* June 6, 1970). Doolittle's departure was followed by that of a senior long-range planner, Manuel Padron, who cited similar reasons (*Minneapolis Tribune,* June 11, 1970).

The board was divided; the staff, unified. The preferred mode in the long-range planning section was conventional, though automated and scaled-down, rapid rail. The section's head, Jamieson, had told the *St. Paul Dispatch,* over a year before joining MTC, that subways should provide the backbone for mass transit (December 20, 1967), and it seems that his vision never wavered. (It is uncertain whether there was consensus among the long-range planners or whether only Jamieson's opinion counted. Outsiders, such as council staff, were acquainted mainly with Jamieson's views [#53]. If there were any disagreements within that section, they failed to reach even MTC's board, much less outsiders.)

Tension prevailed between Jamieson and the commissioners interested in advanced technology. The commissioners believed that PRT was not receiving a fair hearing and that they were being presented with a *fait accompli* rather than with a choice. But there was little they could do. Their primary source of information was the long-range planning staff and consultants who worked, by all accounts, closely with staff. This internal monopoly of information tied the hands of the dissenting commissioners.

Potentially, the most natural bus advocates in the MTC were the short-range planners who were improving the bus system. But a clear division of labor was maintained between short-term and long-term planners. The planners and their products were considered complements, not substitutes, which no doubt reduced intraorganizational conflict. There is no evidence that the short-term planners ever intervened in long-term planning as bus advocates.

At this time MTC's internal modal divisions were more pronounced than interagency disagreement. As mentioned above, council staff was not yet taking an active role. In addition, the head of the council's transportation staff, despite a background in highway planning, was not unfavorably inclined to a fixed guideway alternative (#36), as was the council's chief planner (#9, #12).

The basis for the agencies' consensus in the late sixties was twofold. First, council staff believed that if transit were to shape development, rather than merely respond to it, then the choice had to be a fixed guideway system; buses were clearly inadequate (#35). On this the agencies agreed. And at this time the region's population was projected to grow sufficiently in the next three decades to provide the demographic raw material for shaping development.[9] Second, it is likely, although such points are hard to pin down, that the *image* of a mass transit system connoted fixed guideways to both staffs and excluded an expanded bus system as a long-term alternative (#35). This implicit preconception might have guided the early, fundamental choices.

Consensus between the agencies reached its peak in a February 1970 report. The *Joint MTC-Metro Council Staff Conclusion* asserted that the long-range transit system should be based on a "family-of-vehicles" concept. Precisely what this concept implied—and therefore what the agencies were committing themselves to—was interpreted differently by different decision-makers and staffers.

One interpretation was quite specific: urban transit performs the functions of collection, long haul, and distribution, and different vehicles are appropriate for different functions. Further, for the long-haul function in congested corridors, fixed guideway is needed. This interpretation is supported by the following statement from the document:

> Four subsystems will be necessary. . . . The subsystems include:
>
> 1. Rapid transit operating on exclusive right of way to provide a highly automated backbone to the system for schedule reliability and rapid movement.
>
> 2. Express bus fills the continuing need to provide rapid service on low-volume trunklines. . . .
>
> (Metropolitan Council, 1970, p. 2)

It seems clear that (1) and (2) eliminated an all-bus option. By specializing vehicles to transit function (rapid transit for long

9. The Joint Program's estimate had been 4,000,000 by the year 2000.

haul, other vehicles for collection and distribution), council staff was agreeing to eliminate any advanced technology vehicle, for example, a fine-grain PRT that served all functions (ibid., p. 5). It is, therefore, fair to conclude that at this time the family-of-vehicles concept was rather specific and did constitute a fundamental choice among technologies.

The second interpretation was that the family-of-vehicles proposal was, as one interviewee said, "a classic copout" that merely listed the variety of functions performed by metropolitan transit but left the choice of hardware unresolved. This interpretation means that the family-of-vehicles idea finessed the fundamental choices. Indeed, several officials believed that the concept's ambiguity was essential to creating the *appearance* of agreement despite underlying differences (#12, #22). This interpretation, of course, would have committed the council to very little.

The above quotations from the *Joint . . . Conclusion* do not bear out this interpretation. As we shall see shortly, however, the agreement incorporated into the council's *Metropolitan Development Guide* was vaguer and somewhat closer to the second interpretation.

It is well to bear in mind that regardless of how definitive an agreement the joint staff conclusion was, it concerned only substantive matters. It did not address the question of jurisdictional overlap, thus leaving the door open for the council to become more involved in system planning.

Complementary Planning

Throughout the early seventies the potential for a non-overlapping division of labor lay in the relation between land-use and transit planning. The council had exclusive authority to conduct land-use planning. Had it adopted a definite land-use plan, it could have required MTC's transit plan to be consistent with it. This would have produced conventional, hierarchical specialization: the subordinate generates alternatives that the superior reviews. Council staff, however, disagreed over how much influence a land-use plan would have exerted. The former chief planner thought it would have constrained transit planning, but a former chief of transportation planning held:

> In a heated, long-term process, that strategy becomes very difficult. A guy comes back with a consultant who says, yes, this alternative is consistent with the development plan. It becomes wishy-washy, the facts in no way clear for decision-makers. Then no one wants to talk about land-use decisions, and it will become a question of one guy saying, build the system and another guy saying, like hell. (#14)

Regardless of who was right, the council would not agree on a land-use plan definite enough to constrain transit policy. The legacy of the old Metropolitan Planning Commission was the constellation cities approach, but the council was not bound to accept that as its own. While constellation cities (renamed major diversified centers) did find its way into the council's 1971 *Development Guide*, the council was insufficiently committed to it to implement it. Instead, a majority of the councillors were content to let diversified centers emerge as the by-product of locational decisions of companies and households. Because they disagreed over the desirability of alternative development paths, it was easiest to adopt a path requiring little action. And as the major diversified centers were a compromise between the extremes of "spread city" and "radial city," their relation to transit plans was hazier than those of the other two. Spread city would clearly have entailed a commitment to highways, radial city to rail. But which transit mode followed from a constellation cities plan was unclear.[10]

The lack of a clear signal from the council constituted a problem for MTC. Because its long-range plan was required to be consistent with the council's development assumptions, MTC, of necessity, had to use some land-use assumptions as decision premises. It was therefore reasonable that the authors of the first two long-range transit plans assumed that

10. An MTC staffer reported at a board meeting that council staff was uncertain whether a fixed guideway plan was consistent with constellation cities. Commissioner James Martineau said that he tended to agree with the council (*Minneapolis Star*, April 9, 1970), but the staffer replied that they needed more information from the council on details of the constellation cities plan before consistency could be judged.

the constellation cities approach was a firm council decision; there was little else to go on. Despite occasional intra-MTC grumblings, it was easy to argue that a transit system with a fixed guideway as its backbone was consistent with the land-use assumption. Transit stations could cluster growth around major diversified centers, and the fast link guideway provided access between centers (Daniel et al., 1971, p. 17).

The agencies' formal hierarchical relation was confused by the perceived relations between land-use patterns and transit. As far back as the old Metropolitan Planning Commission, Twin Cities planners had posited a reciprocal causality between land use and transportation (Joint Program, 1968, p. 6). Land use affected demand for transportation; transportation in turn affected land values and use. A hierarchy of authority, on the other hand, presupposes a recursive or one-way causality wherein goals determine means. In this relation one adapts means to ends. But reciprocal causation specifies no causal ordering: one could make decisions about either transportation or land use and require the second policy to be consistent with determinations made on the first. If, as seems to be true in this case, land-use planning is "softer" than transportation planning, then transportation planners will argue that land-use decisions should follow their choices. And this is technically reasonable because of the postulated causal reciprocity.

The Second Round of Transit Planning

Though the council had not criticized the Voorhees plan, it was sufficiently attacked, externally and internally, to warrant a new plan and new consultants. MTC hired Daniel, Mann, Johnson, and Mendenhall (DMJM) in 1970, instructing them to reanalyze advanced technology fixed guideways as well as rapid rail. Furthermore, the consultants were not to recommend technology for the trunkline (*Minneapolis Tribune*, May 14, 1970).

DMJM, following the instructions, maintained that "no vehicle system selection is intended or implied in this report" (Daniel et al., 1971, Report 1, p. 25). Such *conclusions*, however, could be easily inferred from their modal *evaluations*. Bus systems fared badly against technologically unspecified fixed guideway systems in the cost-benefit analysis (ibid., Report 7). Within the class of fixed guideway systems, the report was more cautious. It did, however, point out that Personal Rapid Transit (PRT) systems would require major expenditures by the federal government and the private sector to be made feasible (ibid., p. 20)—a point verified by subsequent investigations. In contrast, the report noted that approaches such as developing a scaled-down BART system, using an existing medium-capacity system, or organizing a joint effort of several cities to develop a standard system for medium-size urban areas were practical at that time.

1971: Year of Transition

1971 Legislative Session

As intended, the DMJM report was completed in time for the 1971 legislative session. Chairman Bolstad and his staff had originally wished to recommend a detailed long-range plan to the legislature and to receive preliminary engineering approval. But numerous obstacles blocked this course of action. First, the MTC board was itself too deeply divided to recommend a technology. Second, several legislators had become interested in advanced technologies. (A small PRT study would be financed in this session.) Third, although the council was still acceding to the family-of-vehicles concept, its meaning had been diluted in the transportation chapter of the *Metropolitan Development Guide* adopted by the council in February 1971. The chapter did not mention fixed guideways, but only "fast-link high-speed transit supported by local and feeder lines." This phrase provided a wedge for advanced technologies. Further, the chapter added that "this new transit service may run on its exclusive right of way, but opportunity to use existing transportation routes such as highways with exclusive bus routes or operational priority should also be examined and adopted if they improve transit service" (Metropolitan Council, 1971, p. 14). This phrasing provided a wedge for buses.

In this climate of opinion it was impossible for the chairman to tell the legislature that MTC had selected a specific mode. In its January 1971 booklet that was used for lobbying, MTC finessed the technological issue: "It is the intent of the commission to utilize the latest technology available. The transit planning accomplished to date by the commission does not preclude the use of small vehicles in fast-link corridors" (Metropolitan Transit Commission, 1971, p. 18). Bolstad reluctantly decided to emphasize the short-range bus-improvement plan (MTC had taken over the private bus firm in 1970) and merely maintain long-range momentum by getting funds for detailed planning rather than for preliminary engineering. The staff chafed under the slow progress, as still another high official left in May, citing reasons similar to Padron's (*St. Paul Dispatch*, May 19, 1971). Yet it is doubtful more could have been obtained. The time was not yet right, as one official put it, to "talk about steel wheels on steel rails" (#23).

Governor Wendell Anderson's election in 1970 had set the stage for the transition year of 1971. He appointed new chairmen of the council and MTC, Albert Hofstede and Douglas Kelm, respectively, and several new councillors. More than personnel was changing: the council's agenda was shifting. The council, having successfully brokered the sewer problem in 1969-70, was turning its attention to new, large-investment issues, particularly airport and transit. Even before Hofstede took the chair, his predecessor, James Hetland, and several allies in an influential local group, the Citizens' League,[11] had voiced concern that the council was losing its role as development shaper, that development was becoming a byproduct of decisions made by special purpose commissions such as the Airport Commission and the Transit Commission.

Accordingly, the council sought to bind MTC more tightly to it, following what was called the Sewer Board model. (The council appointed Sewer Board members and approved its

11. The Citizen's League, an important political group, had advocated creating the Metro Council and tended to support it. The two organizations enjoyed many close informal ties.

annual budget.) The council secured legislation directing that

> the Metropolitan Transit Commission shall implement the
> transit elements of the transportation development program as
> adopted by the Metropolitan Council as a part of its devel-
> opment guide. . . . No portion of the public or mass transit
> system shall be acquired, constructed, or reconstructed in the
> metropolitan area except in accordance with the council's plan.
>
> (State of Minnesota, 1971, p. 1595, statute 473.065)

This once again strengthened the council's authority without distinguishing what was to be in the MTC's plan from what was to be in the council's transportation development program.

The jurisdictional overlap and dispute that began the following year might have been avoided had the council obtained its entire 1971 legislative package because that package included power to appoint MTC commissioners. The council could then have appointed commissioners sympathetic to the transit views of its Development Guide Committee (see below, p. 155). This power, however, was denied by the legislature.[12]

Concern that the council was being "preempted" continued in the new council. Its institutional position was still insecure, its authority again seen to rest on its ability to make lasting decisions on major upcoming issues (#4). Hofstede's assignment of the important Development Guide Committee chairmanship to new councilor David Graven, a man known for his energy, signaled late in 1971 that the council was shedding its passive role in transit planning. The personnel turnover further freed the council's hand. Whatever the January 1971 joint staff conclusion meant, it had not been written during Graven's tenure, and he felt it did not bind the council. But it appears that the council had no strong modal predilections in 1971. Institutional concerns of council leaders, rather

---

12. At this time some people in the region feared that the council was becoming dangerously powerful, and enough legislators shared this view to weaken the council bill (*Minneapolis Star*, April 28, 1971). Ironically, the new MTC chairman, Douglas Kelm, described himself "as a fan of the Metro Council" and publicly supported efforts to increase its powers in order to shape regional growth (*Minneapolis Tribune*, November 11, 1971).

than technical concerns of council staffers, were the driving reasons for involvement in transit planning.[13]

Just when Graven was taking over the Development Guide Committee, an equally energetic official, Douglas Kelm, was assuming MTC's chairmanship. Kelm was regarded by others—and by himself—as too much of an activist to be content merely with taking over a bus company. Though, unlike the planning chief Jamieson, Kelm had not evinced early partiality toward any transit mode, he had been involved in transportation controversies before, having led one of the earliest antifreeway fights in St. Paul. The need to rely less on autos and more on transit had become part of his credo. Further, he was concerned about land-use development, having been a planning and research committee chairman of the Metro Planning Commission in the sixties.[14] Kelm's interest in shaping development nicely complemented Jamieson's advocacy of rapid rail; the chairman and his chief planner worked well together. Given that relationship, given that MTC had already completed two lengthy studies directly or indirectly recommending rail, given that Kelm felt that "the time for planning is over; it is time for action," it is not surprising that he became a rail supporter. He had no outstanding reason to doubt the conclusions of reports supervised by his more knowledgeable colleague. Moreover, the conclusions prepared the way for the greater activity of the preliminary engineering stage.

When Kelm joined MTC, it was still divided between advanced technology (PRT) and conventional rail advocates. The resignation of the two strongest PRT advocates in 1971 gave Kelm the opportunity to pull the board together. And as Kelm was made full-time chairman in 1972, all other commissioners being part time, his influence over modal choice in-

13. An MTC official gave the author an extreme version of this interpretation, arguing that the council's need to assert authority in this policy area dictated that it back a different alternative than MTC's. But I doubt that the council's modal choice was so closely tied to its stimulus for becoming involved.

14. Indeed, one sympathetic participant-observer remarked that he thought that Kelm was basically trying to implement a land-use plan via his new job as MTC chairman.

creased. For the critical next four years, internal MTC conflicts receded, and we can treat the organization as a unified agency.[15]

1972: Competitive Planning

Though Graven had said in late 1971 that there was a leadership vacuum in transit planning, that MTC was too divided to reach a decision, by January 1972, he was more concerned that MTC was moving too rapidly and was prematurely discarding options. Graven, believing that "Ed Anderson had polarized the issue between fuddy duddies and new technology," was dissatisfied because he thought the PRT "was not going to make it." That by elimination would have narrowed the choice to MTC's fixed guideway system.[16] The council would then have been forced to decide without thinking through the choice's implications, thus weakening its authority.

Therefore, in order to slow down MTC's planning, the Development Guide Committee directed MTC to include a busway (freeways with fixed bus-only lanes) alternative in its third long-range plan before going to the 1973 legislature for preliminary engineering approval. MTC agreed reluctantly, arguing that that option had been studied in the second plan and found wanting. MTC leaders felt this was an unwarranted interference in their technical domain (#3, #5). As a shrewd observer remarked: "The council couldn't really expect MTC to just sweep all those plans, time, etc., into the wastebasket. That's not how things work" (#1). Nevertheless, by March MTC had fulfilled the council's request by

15. Several interviewees (#33, #28) believed that board members grew less independent in this period, and it is true that the chairman was more dominating in 1972–75 than 1968–71 and that the views of other commissioners were less reported by the press.

16. MTC was seeking not final system approval in the following year's legislative session but only preliminary engineering approval. But the council activists probably believed that preliminary engineering approval would be a nearly irreversible decision and that the battle would be fought as though final approval were at stake. This belief would explain the priority the Development Guide Committee accorded transit that year.

instructing its new consultants, the firm of Simpson-Curtin, to examine the busway alternative.

Meanwhile, council staff was drafting a new transportation chapter of the *Metropolitan Development Guide*. Transit was made a top priority in the chapter (Metropolitan Council, 1972a). The heart of the emerging planning overlap lay in this preparation of the transportation chapter. Transportation planning necessarily included transit planning, but at what level of specificity the councillors themselves did not know. One councillor told the author: "It was not clear whether we were supposed to do transportation planning . . . what the hell, [we'd] try it and see if anyone salutes. We started doing it, and people believed we *were* doing it, so we were doing it" (#4).

At this time some council staffers were still sympathetic to the family-of-vehicles idea (ibid., p. 3). However, their list of major alternatives for the Guide Committee's consideration resembled the range of options that MTC and Voorhees had already analyzed in 1969: there were five kinds of bus systems and four kinds of fixed guideway alternatives ranging from "reduced rail" to Personal Rapid Transit. This choice set indicates that the staff was instructed to take neither the earlier MTC studies nor the joint agency staff statement as starting places. This point was reinforced by a Guide Committee memo to the whole council in late January. The memo posed two questions: "(1) What did we commit ourselves to? (2) Whatever we committed ourselves to in July, do we still want it in January?"[17]

Graven hoped the answers would emerge by addressing a set of questions drafted in February. The questions were intended to represent a generalist's interest in transit functions rather than a specialist's interest in transit hardware. Thus the committee, or at least Graven, did not see itself as doing redundant planning; it was asking questions appropriate to a general purpose agency, including many questions MTC was believed to be skirting. But even at this point councillors and staff started probing into questions of technology and sub-

17. The committee noted that the council's February 1971 statement referred to the more ambiguous "fast-link" transit whereas the council-approved *Transit in Transportation* referred to fixed guideways.

stantive alternatives, and not only a generalist's concern with function. All through this and the succeeding year the council's stance of a generalist asking policy questions co-existed uneasily with its advocacy of a specific modal alternative.

Probably to avoid being dependent upon MTC, the Guide Committee sought outside sources of information as it moved through the staff's schedule of questions. In addition to hearing scholars such as Alan Altshuler and Anthony Downs,[18] the committee decided it needed its own consultants and hired Barton-Aschman Associates. The consultants produced the final plan in the spring of 1972. It was not clear whether their report, *Feasibility of a Low-Risk, Incremental Investment Strategy*, was a guide to transit investment, hence within a generalist agency's jurisdiction, or whether it was a modal (busways) plan. MTC officials saw it as a substantive plan (#3, #5)—and a poor one at that. Newspapers also tended to regard it as a specific modal alternative to MTC's selection. But a former Barton-Aschman consultant argued:

> Our contract with the council was not to design busways; it never was. We were in to the contract three-quarters of the way, [and] the council said, we understand the concept, but we got to have something . . . how are we going to go over to the legislature with a theory? [We] can't go up there with a concept against a fixed rail plan. (#18)

The strategy, as he saw it, was to delay the technological choice by avoiding commitment to large sunk investments (Barton-Aschman, 1972, p. i). The strategy's justification was that since "substantial technological advances" were anticipated in transit in the next several years, it was premature to make a decision.[19] Practically, however, that rationale *did* imply a modal choice because a bus system was the only option with the desired property of low sunk costs. (This did not necessarily imply buses on busways since ordinary express buses or buses on metered freeways would have had even

18. These Kelm said were "carefully selected," presumably to present a case against fixed guideway systems. I found no pro-fixed guideway speakers invited.

19. This was partly for external consumption, as most council staffers and several councillors were privately skeptical about advanced technologies.

lower capital costs.)[20] Furthermore, the six questions that the council asked Barton-Aschman, whose answers consumed nearly the whole report, referred exclusively to buses, not to an incremental investment strategy. Confusion about the report persisted because it was *both* a general strategy and a modal choice. This confusion paralleled the ambiguity surrounding the council's role.

At any rate, Barton-Aschman contributed most to the Guide Committee's planning by convincing the committee that a lower capital alternative was feasible. This persuasion mattered because by the spring of 1972 many committee members were beginning to believe that the region lacked the density to support a rail system, that capital costs would be prohibitive, and that labor savings from an automated rail system would be less than MTC expected (#4, #24). With the Barton-Aschman plan in hand, the committee could *favor* some kind of transit as well as oppose MTC's alternative. In late July, the committee voted 6-0-1 to recommend a busways-plus-freeways alternative to the council as the transportation chapter of the *Metropolitan Development Guide*.[21]

MTC's plan, though it did not specify a vehicle, included two crucial choices that distinguished it from the alternatives of the council and the PRT group. First, it retained the family-of-vehicles concept with a fixed guideway backbone. This distinguished it from the council, which by this time had abandoned the family-of-vehicles idea and was easing away from fixed guideways. Second, one of MTC's policies was to use the "best available technology," thereby differentiating it from the PRT coalition.

The reactions to the council's alternative were swift and sometimes intense. The city governments of Minneapolis and St. Paul were displeased, as both favored rail. (Indeed, the Minneapolis staff had even created its own subway plan.) Other groups opposed the number of freeway miles in the

20. Apparently one would use busways only as a measure of last resort on parts of routes where buses would otherwise become bogged down in traffic (#18).

21. The other end of the spectrum, advanced technologies, had been devastated by the visit of several councillors to a disappointing exhibit on new transit technologies and by the subsequent circulation of a memo on that subject by the influential Donald Dayton.

plan (Metropolitan Council, 1972b). The conflicts were, in part, due to the council's increasing pessimism about what transit could do for the region. The council was not claiming that its transit selection would significantly affect congestion, pollution, or development; it denied that *any* alternative could have such impacts.

The exchanges between the council and MTC in August reveal their major agreements and disagreements at this time. They agreed, as usual, on the short-range plan to expand and improve the bus system. This agreement extended beyond the agencies and reached their allies; bus improvement was uncontroversial then. During the year both sides had tried to stress the plans' similarities and to minimize the differences, but the disagreements were too large to gloss over. MTC criticized the council's plan for not addressing: (1) the operating costs of busways, (2) how busways would function in winter, and (3) how to distribute additional buses downtown. These were not trifles; all were later acknowledged to be severe problems by one of the council's consultants (#18). One drawback of such a cheap plan was its failure to detail how the plan could be realized.[22]

For its part, the council levied three criticisms against MTC's plan. (1) The region's moderate density meant that even the heaviest corridor's patronage, as estimated by MTC's consultants,[23] would be only 16,000 passengers per hour.[24] (2) Capital costs were excessive, especially given other large investments the region was considering. (3) The first two points jointly implied that the region would pay too much for too little: rail was not cost-effective. The council argued that a billion dollars was too much to pay for increasing transit's proportion of trips from 4 percent to 8 percent.[25] MTC's service strategy was mistaken. To compete with the

22. According to one official, the council had a chronic problem of forever "playing catch-up" with the plans of its special purpose agencies (#18).

23. This was DMJM's estimate for 1995; Voorhees's for 1985 was 8,000.

24. The rule of thumb of council planners was that a corridor should generate 30,000 passengers per hour to justify rail. MTC retorted that the successful Lidenwold line in Pennsylvania showed that more moderate densities sufficed.

25. MTC retorted that its plan would boost transit's proportion of *peak-hour* trips to the central cities from 40 percent to 60 percent.

auto, MTC should offer a similar transfer-free ride. The family-of-vehicles idea, if it connoted a different vehicle for every function, implied multiple transfers. These were the fundamental criticisms that would be exchanged in the next year and a half.[26]

Conflict Resolution

As in the AC-BART case, each side tried to persuade the other to change. Bargaining or logrolling across unrelated issues did not occur. Compromise, seeking a middle ground between proposals, would have been hampered by the technologies' discreteness and was not tried. Persuasion was no more successful here than in the Bay Area. From the summer of 1972 through the following years, at meetings on the council's transportation chapter, at Citizens' League gatherings, and at other interest groups' debates, representatives of the two agencies met and argued without diminishing the differences between them. As one council staffer noted: "We were like two battleships firing at each other, traveling on parallel courses" (#17).

Why did these efforts produce so little convergence?

1.   Lines were hardening. Each side was convinced, by late 1972, that its transit mode was superior; consequently, each tended to retain planning estimates supporting its position. For example, a council staffer observed about arguments over projected inflation of bus drivers' wages that "it was patently obvious if we used their technical inputs, they'd win, and vice versa" (#17).

2.   There was objective uncertainty surrounding several key projections, such as patronage estimates, the cost inflation of construction, rail's labor requirements, and how much transit could shape land use. Other important magnitudes—for example, the amount of air pollution a rail system would eliminate—partly depended on uncertain variables in the first set (patronage, land use). These uncertainties made it easy for

26. Newspaper reports and interviewees' memories concur on this point.

advocates to maintain their positions. And because these planning disagreements were not transformed into experimental competition, unlike the parallel development of missiles by the Army and Air Force, the uncertainties were not resolved empirically.[27] The disagreements remained on paper.

3. There were no established rules for resolving disagreements over factual estimates, not even an agreement that disputants should stick to one point until it was hammered out. As one official remarked, and as a legislator would later complain, the agencies often talked past each other. If one side made a telling point, the other side raised a new issue rather than replying (#10). There was no referee[28] to ensure that the game was played reasonably, and the conflict was insufficiently institutionalized and involved too high stakes for internal norms to constrain behavior. Indeed, far from being an institutionalized conflict, MTC leaders were angry that competitive planning had occurred at all. One MTC official told the author that the commission was unpleasantly surprised to hear of the council's alternative plan (#5), implying the conflict was unexpected as well as uninstitutionalized. And whether or not MTC was actually surprised,[29] clearly the leaders were angry. They believed that not only was the council overstepping its jurisdiction; it was reversing its commitment to a family-of-vehicles concept.[30] Strong words were exchanged in private (#4, #5). MTC officials questioned the motives of councillors and staff, suggesting that the highway lobby was behind the opposition to MTC's rail plan. Councillors resented that charge (#10, #4).

27. Of course some of the disagreements in principle could not be resolved empirically. Most important of these was the council's argument that a rail system's patronage under a rail system was insufficient to warrant the cost.

28. Even when there were referees (the legislators the following year), they found it difficult to regulate the process.

29. Several council officials doubted that the MTC was unaware that the council was preparing a counterplan, as the agencies then occupied the same building (#22).

30. The MTC reminded the council several times that year of commitments made in 1971.

On the other side, some councillors said harsh things about MTC's consultants and top staff, alleging that the former reported only what the latter wanted to hear. [31] These accusations enflamed MTC's leaders.

This personalizing of the conflict hardened the positions and impeded conflict resolution. In public, the officials were more restrained but equally stubborn. Kelm urged the council to adhere to a differentiated role as plan reviewer rather than a redundant role as plan generator:

> The review and approval function performed by the Metropolitan Council is a vital one, and it is important that it be conducted by a staff and a council that did not participate in the specialized planning process. Otherwise, the review function could be merely a self-serving justification of a prior decision by that same body.
>
> (Kelm, 1973, p. 2)

I think that Kelm, an early supporter of the council (see n. 14), was sincerely advocating his conception of the proper interorganizational relations. It was not only that the council had opposed MTC's plan; it had done so in a manner Kelm and Jamieson considered illegitimate and that amplified the conflict. Moreover, the staffs were less insulated from this top-level acrimony than were the staffs in the AC-BART case. It was unlikely, given these circumstances, that the agencies could have persuaded each other on technical grounds.

Perhaps the conflict would have been less intense had the council eschewed redundant planning and criticized the rail plan on a complementary basis, that is, on the basis of its land-use policy. But in 1972 the council still did not have a land-use policy. The board was still uneasy about controlling development (*St. Paul Dispatch*, January 21, 1972), and staff drafts of the transportation chapter, which mentioned coordi-

31. We must tread cautiously on this point because of its sensitivity and because we lack hard evidence, having only hearsay and unconfirmed suspicions. And opinions ranged widely on this matter: some council staffers thought MTC's consultants highly competent (#35, #14), while some MTC commissioners were more than a little suspicious of the staff-consultant relationship (#37, #25, #23). Regardless of who was right, the distrust that developed is an important datum that cannot be ignored in any study of bureaucratic competition.

nating "compact development . . . with transportation," were expressing a pious wish, not a guiding rule. The only element of land-use planning that did have an effect in 1972 was not a decision but an estimate: population projections were revised sharply downward.

Other Decision Forums

Large public meetings are poor settings for resolving interorganizational differences; the desire to save face is too strong. But the agencies' heads were members of the same political party, and several had known each other before (#4). There was, therefore, ample opportunity for informal persuasion, which if successful would have averted the embarrassment of exposing intraparty disagreements before the 1973 legislative session. Informal channels did not work, however. The Democratic party in Minnesota is diverse and loosely connected; common membership rarely overcomes firmly held policy differences. One serious attempt was made to resolve the problems informally, but the get-together was a disaster that exacerbated the conflict (#4).

The Urban Mass Transit Administration (UMTA) of the U.S. Department of Transportation might have played an informal mediating role by indicating which alternative it favored. UMTA, however, stayed out of the contest. It consistently held that the region's governments must make the choice.

Finally, there was an alternative formal forum, the Transportation Planning Program (TPP), composed of regional and state transportation agencies and local jurisdictions. Since the TPP was established to coordinate its members' activities and to make recommendations on the council's transportation chapter of its *Metropolitan Development Guide*, formally it appeared a natural forum. But the TPP, a weak institution, had not won the respect of any of its key members. Consequently, when it criticized an earlier draft of the council's transportation chapter, the latter ignored the criticism. It was increasingly evident that the issue would have to go to the legislature in the upcoming session.

Jurisdictional Perspectives in 1972

The legislation of 1967, 1969, and 1971 could neither prevent nor resolve the jurisdictional dispute over which agency
was authorized to conduct long-range transit planning. Both
sides found legal advice supporting their positions. The lawyer consulted by MTC advised that the 1971 amendments
requiring the commission to implement the council's transportation development program only "conditioned the
exercise" of MTC's authority to plan a transit system; they did
not remove that authority. He further argued that not only
did MTC have planning authority, but *no other body* had jurisdiction, that is, there was no overlap (Doty, 1972, p. 4). But
whereas the lawyer could easily cite the legal precedent
demonstrating that MTC was a legitimate planner, he did not
even try to demonstrate that the council had not been similarly authorized.[32]

The council had refused to review MTC's plan since "the
MTC is legally directed to implement the council's *Metropolitan Development Guide*, thereby precluding the need and
authority to produce an independent long-range 'transit
development' program" (Graven, quoted in *Minneapolis Tribune*, February 2, 1973). In January 1973, its legal counsel
advised that the council could first review MTC's program "to
determine what portions of it are outside the authority of the
MTC and come within the planning authority of the Metro
Council under section 473A.065" (Hay, 1973, p. 1). Only then
was the council obliged to review the remainder of the plan to
check for consistency with the development guide. The counsel submitted that, by virtue of Minnesota statutes 473A.065
and 473A.05, subdivision 10, only the council could legiti-
mately prepare a long-term plan on transportation and transit. By implication, therefore, the council could deny substantive review. This counsel's reasoning concerning overlap
appears similar to MTC's (see n. 33 below): if the council
possesses long-term planning authority, then it *must* follow

32. A presumption of exclusive or monopolistic authority may have been
made: if one can show that the MTC clearly has authority to plan, then it
automatically follows that no other agency could have such authority.

that no other agency could as well. This reasoning presumes the illegitimacy of competitive planning.

The 1973 Legislative Session

The course of the 1973 session was influenced by three significant conditions. First, the attitude toward mass transit was more positive than it had been in 1971. Many new liberal assemblymen, elected in 1972, were positively disposed toward transit, and there was a diffuse feeling that "something had to be done" about metropolitan transit (#19). In a 1972 poll, transit was rated the leading issue, deserving highest priority and money. The time was ripe for legislative action on a transit bill. Second, the legislature was not facing an ordinary yea-or-nay choice on a single alternative proposed by a single agency. That, given the diffuse positive disposition, would have been the simplest situation for the legislature to handle. Instead, it confronted an interagency conflict on two levels, substantive and jurisdictional. In addition, complicating the picture, a group of University of Minnesota academics had completed a legislatively financed PRT study in time for the 1973 session.

Third, the 1967 metro bills included a contingency plan for dealing with this type of problem. The legislature had designated itself the arbitrator should regional agencies fail to reach agreement. Organizationally, however, the legislature was ill-equipped to manage the dispute. Transit was a relatively new issue, and the legislature had not developed the small core of specialists that had developed in more repetitive domains such as taxes. Further, staff support was limited.

The legislature was at liberty to address either or both the substantive and jurisdictional questions. Because the agencies disagreed so sharply, it was evident that a jurisdictional settlement favoring the council would automatically determine a substantive choice whereas a jurisdictional settlement favoring MTC, recognizing its right to submit a long-range plan to the council, would not necessarily imply a substantive selection.

Moving procedurally would have enabled the legislature to avoid entanglement in transit technicalities for which it was ill-prepared, but there was considerable internal interest in dealing directly with the substantive question.

The Substantive Debate

Both sides now acknowledge that MTC's lobbying was better organized and generally better received, particularly in the state House of Representatives (#18, #19). The MTC, reaching beyond the transit subcommittee of the House's Metropolitan Affairs Committee, tried to contact all of the committee's members whereas the less well-organized council failed to find a receptive audience for either its hardware (busways) or overall strategy (incremental investment).[33]

The House moved swiftly to pass MTC's bill, so swiftly, in fact, that there was little debate (#15, #16, #19). One well-located representative [34] told me that though the bill's author learned more about transit policy than any other representatives, even he knew relatively little by the time of passage. Though one cannot be certain of how much the assemblymen knew when they voted, it is likely that the decision was made without careful scrutiny.

In the state Senate the debate was more prolonged (#16, #19). This did not lead to a preference for the council's plan: the committee chairman objected to busways quite early on (*Minneapolis Tribune*, March 21, 1973), and there is no evidence of any support for an all-bus system at this time. Nevertheless, interviewees on all sides agreed that had the council

33. I have not discussed the activities of interest groups such as business firms or labor unions, in part because of the theoretical focus on bureaucratic redundancy and in part because their role was apparently minor (#20, #19). The business community was divided between support for MTC's plan and opposition based on fiscal grounds; the disagreement precluded great influence. In addition, because several highly respected businessmen sat on the council, business probably felt adequately represented. Regarding labor, although it solidly backed the MTC, at least after 1973 it seems to have had little effect. Legislators who became transit specialists apparently discounted labor's support for the construction alternative since its position was so predictable.

34. I cannot reveal his identity, but he was in a position to know.

not presented a plan,[35] MTC's bill would have passed both chambers. How can we explain this seeming inconsistency between the negative reaction to the council's plan and its perceived impact?

First, we must remember that there were *three* proposals before the state Senate—the two agencies' plus the Personal Rapid Transit plan. The latter drew the support of certain powerful Senate committee members, who believed the PRT offered a set of service attributes that could compete with the auto (*Minneapolis Star*, November 2, 1973). But the PRT option alone would probably not have sufficed to delay the legislature's decision on preliminary engineering. By 1973 PRT had little support inside the council. Therefore, if the council had not produced its own alternative, it would not have advocated PRT. Rather, it would have gone before the legislature with only weak ammunition in its rhetorical arsenal, that is, with the procedural claim that MTC should not have prepared a long-range plan. Given the widespread feeling that something had to be done about transit, there would have been strong pressure to approve the only governmentally backed alternative—MTC's solution. Even if the council had been able to criticize MTC's plan incisively, a "what-do-you-offer-instead?" rebuttal would have been most telling in that year.

The council's option and the PRT alternative were individually necessary and jointly sufficient to prevent immediate approval of MTC's plan. The former, by creating a conflict that could not be ignored, established the framework of the legislature as arbitrator and as selector of substantive alternatives. The latter sufficiently impressed senators so that they could say that they supported transit but did not yet favor MTC's plan.

The council and PRT alternatives were jointly powerful because they bracketed MTC's plan: PRT offered better service, busways lower fixed cost. Combined, they raised the aspirations of state Senate decision-makers.[36] MTC's proposal

35. Unlike MTC, the council presented only a plan rather than a bill.

36. However, the aspirations created by PRT in 1973 were unrealistic. The Senate subcommittee's report, which instructed the MTC to investigate an advanced technology system, enumerated a set of design properties that proved to be a wish list, infeasible in the medium-range future.

simply looked less attractive than it would have had it been presented by itself. The two plans combined in yet another way. They were more compatible with each other than either was with MTC's plan and would become still more so after the council discarded the fixed guideway element of its busway plan. Personal Rapid Transit advocates backed the council's plan (#26) because it would not preclude developing an innovative fixed guideway system whereas MTC's fixed guideway probably would have. The council did not overlook this point and argued that an advantage of its plan was that it would not foreclose to-be-developed options such as PRT.

Finally, the council's plan fulfilled a "sleeper" function: it provided an easily modified backup alternative when the disappointing news about PRT started trickling in. But this is getting ahead of the story.

It should be noted that the conflicting plans affected specialized and nonspecialized legislators differently. The conflict seemed to confuse representatives involved in other policy sectors (#8). But legislative transit specialists used the agencies' disagreements to locate questionable premises and estimates. (They did not use the conflict to produce their own estimates, e.g., by averaging.) The most thorough example of this cross-checking was a report written by Representative John Tomlinson and Senator John Milton, two MTC supporters, who systematically compared the two agencies' responses to twenty-six questions. As redundancy theory leads us to expect, their analysis revealed that neither agency's position was free of distortion. The council, for example, took consultants' statements out of context, and MTC's density argument was suspect. The important point is that *at least* the involved legislators were aware of significant distortions, for it is unlikely that either adversary had overlooked a premise in its rival's argument that was both vital and dubious.

After several weeks of intense discussion, the state Senate committee decided not to decide. Personal Rapid Transit appeared too promising to ignore but too risky to propose without further investigation. Accordingly, the committee decided to conduct a postsession tour of cities to meet with transit experts who understood both conventional and advanced technology and then to write a report for the 1974 session.[37] Leaders of the state House and Senate committees met to resolve their differences, but despite common membership in the Democratic Party they were unable to do so.[38]

Jurisdictional Activity

The belief that something must be done about metropolitan transit was matched by a belief that something must be done about the messy metropolitan organizational structure.[39] Indeed, opinion was probably more unified on the organizational issue. For example, Representative John Salchert, a staunch MTC ally, cosponsored a bill establishing a metropolitan Transportation Board, with council-appointed members. The board would have supplanted MTC. Salchert stressed, however, that though the council should control subordinate agencies, the legislature should make a substantive transit decision in that session: "This has been studied to death. Let's do the job." The House leadership had managed to partition the substantive and jurisdictional questions and agreed to vote on both.

The Senate committee preferred to postpone the substantive choice while pushing to resolve the jurisdictional conflict. Senator John Chenoweth's bill would have given the council appointive powers, placed the MTC directly under the council, and given the long-range transportation planning function to the council.[40] He declared his intent to make the council "the system planner," indicating a more pro-council position than the House bill exhibited. This difference was highlighted when the Senate's jurisdictional dispute spilled over into the substantive debate. MTC spokesmen argued that Cheno-

37. The legislature started annual sessions that year.
38. One interviewee hinted that cool relations between the two chairmen hindered the effort (#5).
39. Legislators generally conceded that there was no way to decide, on the basis of the pre-1974 statutes, which agency had stronger jurisdictional claims (#19). Consequently, there was widespread agreement that a reorganization bill of some sort was required.
40. He criticized the existing structure as "a patchwork . . . in which the council's planning role and its authority overlap and conflict with those of the cities, other metropolitan agencies, and the state" (*Minneapolis Tribune*, March 21, 1973).

weth's bill would involve the council too deeply in operations. Senator Milton, MTC's strongest supporter in the committee, pointedly inquired: "How specific and how detailed does [the bill] give the Metro Council the power to plan a transportation program?" (*Minneapolis Tribune*, April 26, 1973). Milton feared the bill would eliminate the advocacy function of the specialized agencies.

Extended debates between metropolitan agencies and internal committee differences prevented the Senate committee from (narrowly) recommending passage until late April. The bill stalled on the Senate floor, whereupon Chenoweth withdrew it late in the session. The 1973 session ended with neither substantive resolution nor jurisdictional clarification.

The 1973-74 Interim

The initiative had now shifted from the agencies to the state legislature. The interim enabled a few legislators to delve into the details of fixed guideway alternatives. Their information sources broadened; one remarked that during the session his informational diet had been restricted to MTC, but during the interim he became omnivorous.

Following the tour, the Senate subcommittee submitted a report in November 1973, which, though rejecting "pure," fine-grained PRT networks, recommended that MTC, under general council direction, develop a plan "for an automated small vehicle fixed guideway system for consideration by the legislature." The system would have PRT's properties of demand-activation with origin-to-destination service (i.e., transfers would be unnecessary). The report recommended other measures, including accelerating the bus improvement program and promoting low-cost options such as carpools, but it was clear that the subcommittee's major interest was the small vehicle study.

The Low-Capital Coalition

The impressive capacity of the Twin Cities region to generate alternatives was not yet exhausted. While the Senate subcommittee was investigating advanced technology personal transit, three other organizations, the Citizens' League, the council, and eventually (in 1975) the House, were groping toward an alternative far removed from Personal Rapid Transit in the technological spectrum—low-capital, manually operated small vehicles.

The Citizens' League was the first major group to advocate the idea that the region needed more effective management of existing transit capacity instead of additional capacity. In its March 1973 report, *Building Incentives for Drivers to Ride*, the league proposed a novel definition of transit: instead of signifying hardware, transit "should mean riding with others, rather than driving alone, regardless of the type of vehicle" (1973, p. 2). Carpools, for example, would be considered transit. The report argued that regarding regional goals, such as decreasing air pollution or reducing the need for more freeways, one should be indifferent between a former car driver riding in a public bus or in a private auto. The report seems to have influenced few people in 1973, but in January 1974, the Citizens' League issued another report that pursued the same theme.[41] By this time changes in the council's direction reinforced the league.

The council was aware that though the busways plan was unpopular, a plan to expand the bus system, without the capital-intensive busways structure, elicited much approval. Consequently, the council mentioned an expensive, exclusive right of way for buses less frequently: "It just fell by the wayside" (#15). The easy abandonment of that component indicated how peripheral it had been to their approach. Council strategy increasingly focused more on making do with the region's existing capacity than on hardware.

In addition, the council's transportation staff was developing the new idea that the route structures of both MTC's and the council's first plan were excessively downtown-oriented (#17). Origin-destination studies emphasized that only 15 percent of the work trips were bound for the two central business districts and only 25 percent for the central cities (Transportation Planning Program, 1974, p. 64), yet

41. It also advocated diminishing the demand for transportation by enacting land-use policies that encouraged living near work places, another point on which the Citizens' League and the council would agree.

both plans were designed to serve this small clientele. Gradually, stimulated by the appointment of a new transportation director in late 1973, the council moved away from a capital-intensive, downtown-oriented busways plan toward a much less capital-intensive, subregional[42] bus system.

The 1974 Legislative Session

Substantive Issues

At the start of the 1974 session the chambers' leaders were still at loggerheads. Nothing had occurred in the interim to reduce the differences. Because either chamber could block any bill, a compromise package was proposed. MTC would be charged with investigating several small vehicle systems and comparing the results of that study with MTC's alternative. After the second evaluation MTC would recommend the preferred alternative to the legislature. Simultaneously, the ten-year bus improvement program would be telescoped into three years. The short-range bus improvement plank was, once again, uncontroversial. The oil shortage of 1973-74 had prepared the way for faster spending on transit, and rapid improvement of the bus system was consistent with *all* of the long-range plans. Though bus improvement would prove to be the most dangerous alternative to MTC's fixed guideway plans, it also greatly increased that organization's budget. MTC accepted it as second best.

The first plank was naturally more difficult. MTC leaders, believing they had already analyzed PRT systems adequately, were not keen on doing it again. Moreover, by this time a good deal of personal animosity had arisen between MTC chairman Kelm and the primary PRT expert, Professor Ed Anderson (#25). Several key Senators, on the other hand, came back from their tour convinced that "the MTC proposal is dead" and were presumably uninterested in letting MTC

---

42. Council planners, then beginning to draw maps of trip clusters, found higher clusters of subregional trips than they had expected (#17).

compare the preferred small vehicle system with its conventional rail. But as the two sides needed each other to pass any bill, the compromise was effected and the bill passed in March.

Because MTC's credibility about PRT had worn thin, the bill assigned the council to serve in a general oversight capacity. The assignment did not necessarily indicate that the council's credibility in general was held in higher regard by legislators; rather, on the specific issue of PRT it was considered less biased. Kelm had fervently opposed advanced technology; the council, though unenthusiastic, had not vehemently opposed it.

Jurisdictional Decisions

In the Senate, Chenoweth won over the last session's opposition by concessions that do not concern us. Within two months, the joint conference committee agreed on a compromise authorizing the council to appoint the eight MTC commissioners and the governor to appoint the chairman. The bill sailed through both chambers, and after the governor signed it, the Metropolitan Reorganization Act became law. Legislators hailed the act as a great step in clarifying the planning relationship between the council and MTC, but when one inspects the bill, one is hard-pressed to find roles more clearly differentiated than those in the 1971 statutes.

The 1971 amendments had directed the MTC to "implement the transit elements of the transportation development program as adopted by the metropolitan council." This was changed to read:

> The commission shall prepare and submit . . . a transportation development program, providing for the implementation of the policy plan adopted by the council. . . . The transportation development program shall also contain a description of the type of right of way or routes required; the type of transit service to be provided in each portion of the system; designation of transit mode. . . .
>
> (State of Minnesota, 1974, p. 872, statute 473.411)

The 1971 law had already established a means-end relation between the two agencies: the council was to provide general goals and criteria, and MTC was to supply the means. The ambiguity derived from the failure to agree on how specific the criteria could be or, equivalently, what point on the means-end chain marked the boundary between the organizations. The new law did not solve this problem. True, it specified more clearly what constituted a transportation development program and a policy plan, but even this was insufficient. Compare the above definition of MTC's development program with the following elements of the council's policy plan:

(b) A general description of the physical facilities and services to be developed by the metropolitan commission. . . .

(c) A statement as to the general location of physical facilities and service areas.

(d) A general statement of timing and priorities in the development by the metropolitan commission of those physical facilities. . . .

(e) A general statement on the level of public expenditure both capital and operating appropriate to the facilities and a statement of the relationship of the policy plan to other policy plans and chapters of the metropolitan development guide.

(ibid., p. 857–858, statute 475.146)

Section (b)—and possibly also (c), (d), and (e)—is quite elastic and could easily spill over into tasks included under MTC's development program. Precisely this overlap occurred, despite bitter but ineffectual protests of the Transit Commission.

Three changes, however, not merely in wording but in substance, did convey specific legislative intent. First, commission revenue bonds had to receive council approval. This fiscal power added teeth to the still vague language describing the policymaking and implementing relation between the two bodies. Second, the legislative arbitration proviso was removed. Henceforth, if the council rejected a plan, the special purpose agency would have to revise it. No formal[43] clause

43. Removing the arbitration clause probably rested at least as much on

encouraged by-passing the council.[44] Third, the council would appoint all commissioners except MTC's chairman, a change considered the "ultimate signal" of legislative intent by one veteran observer (#33). Taken jointly, these three changes communicated the legislature's desire to strengthen the council.

The Reorganization Act did not, however, immediately affect transit planning in 1974-75. The reasons were twofold. First, all MTC commissioners, including Kelm's supporters, had several years to go. In 1977 the legislature would indicate continued displeasure with the rail faction by abruptly shortening the terms of four commissioners, allowing the council to appoint four new ones of its own liking.[45] But in 1974, when the policy controversy was more intense, this penultimate sign from the legislature was still several years away. Second, MTC's primary task in the 1974-75 interim was to conduct a small vehicle study, compare the selected small vehicle with its more conventional rapid rail, and recommend a final selection to the legislature. This process was legally prescribed, but the governing law was not the Reorganization Act. Thus, the drama came to an end in the 1975 session without the act's having a significant impact, save one: the council was doubtlessly heartened by the bill's enactment. It encouraged the councillors to take a tough public stand against MTC's last report. Given the act's passage, the council could expect that its opinions would be heard.

The Reorganization Act was the last important rearrangement of interagency relations in the period studied here (1967-75), for the 1975 legislative session considered no new bills on this topic.

---

the legislature's desire to have done with metropolitan quarrels as upon a desire to strengthen the council. A major reason for establishing the council in the first place was to remove a nasty problem from the legislators' shoulders; the arbitration clause opened the way for such problems to return to them.

44. According to a veteran observer of regional politics, by-passing still occurs (#33).

45. Apparently the council used, as a criterion of selection, loyalty to itself (#4).

The 1974-75 Interim

By August 1974, the council finally produced a land-use policy.[46] In brief, it involved drawing a "Municipal Services Area" line around the suburbs and attempting to slow growth beyond that line to avoid the cost of extending urban services deeper into the hinterlands. As Kelm quickly pointed out, this policy, by implication, deemphasized clustering development *within* the suburban rings. This clustering had been the focus of the older major diversified centers concept.[47] As one veteran planner put it: "The council took the earlier strategy and turned it upside down: before, there was a definite regional center with fuzzy edges; now, there is a definite edge but no definite insides" (#12). The significance of the shift for transit planning was obvious. Whereas before MTC could argue that its rail option would promote the major diversified centers plan, rail was irrelevant to the new development policy, which not only lacked corridors but also minimized subregional activity centers. A key justification for a rail system was eliminated—and Kelm knew it.[48]

We should note here the difference between the stability of MTC's land-use assumptions and the council's instability. MTC's land-use premises had the virtue of consistency— many people had criticized the council's indecisiveness in this matter—but once the council took a definite position, it became evident that MTC had been planning on premises of sand.

Had this land-use policy crystallized just two years earlier, the council could have used it as a criterion to evaluate MTC's transit plan. The council could have reviewed the plan and declared it inconsistent with its land-use policy, and it had the authority to insist that transit adjust to development plans and not vice versa. A conventional, differentiated relation

46. It was not approved by the whole council until March 1975.

47. One council staffer maintained (correctly) that the two ideas were not inconsistent (#10).

48. Kelm undoubtedly would have liked to challenge the council's development policy, but the MTC lacked the requisite expertise and legal authority. A "reverse redundancy" of MTC's becoming involved in land-use planning did not occur.

would have evolved. The problem was timing: the council had not been within shouting distance of a firm land-use policy in 1972.

The 1975 Legislative Session

By the time the 1975 session began, the Citizens' League and the council were in agreement that whatever mode would be selected, it must not require a huge amount of capital. The stage was set for the last of the trio, the state's House of Representatives. Between 1974 and 1975 House transit specialists had changed. Salchert, the committee chairman, had not run in the fall of 1974 and was replaced by Thomas Berg, who had voted with tepid enthusiasm for the 1973 MTC bill. Berg named Peter Petrafesso as transit subcommittee chairman, and together they dominated transit policymaking in the House.[49] Their May report (1975) emphatically rejected all fixed guideway solutions, both conventional and advanced. A new *Zeitgeist*, emphasizing paratransit (carpools and vanpools) and managing available transit capacity, was appearing in the urban transit literature, and the Berg-Petrafesso report took its cue from this literature.

An older conventional wisdom once exerted a strong hold on decision-makers' minds. As recently as 1968, council and MTC planners thought automatically of fixed guideway systems when designing transit. Only seven years later a new image had appeared. The conflict between the council and MTC gave the new ideas the *gestation time* they needed to become more coherent and to receive institutional expression. In 1973, when MTC was seeking preliminary engineering approval, the low-capital idea was just emerging. The council's busways plan still bore the capital-intensive imprint of the MTC plan that had influenced it, and the Citizens' League had just proposed its first low-capital transit solution. By 1975, the ideas had percolated into the state legislature where

49. This turnover created temporary organizational amnesia, for what the former top House specialist had learned about transit alternatives in eighteen months of work, Petrafesso now had to rediscover.

the council's 1975 policy plan served as a rallying point for low-capital advocates. Shorn of busways and eighty-three miles of freeway, the council's 1975 plan cut millions of dollars from its 1973 predecessor, magnifying the difference between it and MTC's fixed guideway alternatives.

While the low-capital coalition was taking shape, MTC encountered problems. Officially, MTC's main activity in the 1974-75 interim was its small vehicle study. But unofficially the controversy took a new turn that transformed the debate. During the interim, MTC unwisely engaged in intemperate lobbying, wherein senators opposing MTC's proposal were disparaged. (Ironically, the low-capital advocates, who eventually won the contest, were not targets.) It was a grievous tactical mistake. The senators held Kelm responsible, and the affair became more personalized. The Senate subcommittee voted 10-3 not to reconfirm Kelm as MTC's chairman; veteran legislative observers said this had not happened in twenty-five years. Kelm had allies, including the governor, and to avoid an intraparty confrontation, the question was tabled. But the damage was done. Senatorial attention focused, with hostility, on Kelm's person rather than on Kelm's proposal, and in the brouhaha the proposal "just faded away."

The personalizing of disagreements was not the only crippler of MTC's bid in the Senate. The key senators had been primarily interested in advanced technologies, and when it became apparent in January 1975 that the technology was less developed than once thought, their interest in fixed guideways declined (#11). The negative assessments of advanced technology were reinforced by a report from the U.S. Office of Technology Assessment (OTA) with similarly pessimistic findings.[50] The bad news must have dampened interest in the matter, for considering the amount of attention devoted to the problem just months before, surprisingly little interest was generated by MTC's final report. Only a few senators attended, and even they seemed disinterested (#11).

In its report MTC avoided making a final recommendation

50. One MTC official felt that the Senate "was ready to jump all over us" for its small vehicle study and that only the independent corroboration of the OTA report prevented that. But memos from a legislator's files indicate that though the senators were indeed suspicious, they thought the study was conducted fairly.

between conventional and advanced technology, a maneuver that displeased the senators, particularly Chairman Chenoweth. (The indecision probably irritated them less than did the lack of support for an advanced technology. The senators would not have been pleased had MTC recommended its conventional technology.) Two months earlier, Chenoweth had announced to the press that MTC could begin preliminary engineering on a small vehicle fixed guideway as early as June of that year (*Minneapolis Star*, February 14, 1975). Certain participants viewed this as a compromise (#13): MTC would receive support for a fixed guideway system that was a hybrid of pure PRT and its own more conventional vehicle; the Senate would get some of the service attributes it desired. But MTC never responded, losing its only opportunity in three years to form a larger coalition with other decisionmakers.

It is likely that MTC's leaders believed they *were* compromising by skirting a final recommendation[51] and by advocating further evaluation of PRT and conventional rail. But by this time legislators had had their fill of transit studies and were not about to fund another. In fact, following a council suggestion, the legislature imposed a moratorium on fixed guideway studies in this session.

As the fixed guideway efforts wound down in a peculiar, anticlimactic way in the Senate, the initiative swung back to the House, where in May the low-capital advocates found expression in the Berg-Petrafesso report. The Senate's disillusionment with advanced technology and MTC's indecisive recommendation contrasted sharply with the House report's confident outline of the direction the region should take. Though the majority of the members of the subcommittee were critical, the report probably reflected increasingly common sentiments among legislators specializing in other policy sectors. It called for an end to transit planning and to elaborate technical studies, which fatigued most legislators, and advo-

51. For the MTC to make a simple recommendation was probably difficult, as the evaluation of intermediate capacity rapid transit (ICRT) and group rapid transit (GRT) turned out to be close—neither system dominated across all dimensions. And as Senate leaders had insisted that the weighting of evaluative criteria be left up to legislators, the consultants did not sum the systems' scores across dimensions.

cated a noncapital-intensive solution that avoided the politically dangerous step of raising taxes.

Although no poll was taken of state legislators, it is probable that mass transit had toppled from its 1972 position as a top priority issue. It is equally likely that taxes had risen in priority. The Berg-Petrafesso report reflected these issue cycles, and the steps it outlined—no new capital outlays for transit, increased emphasis on paratransit—guided the legislature for the next two years (Todd, 1977).

Conclusion

Competitive planning in the Twin Cities exhibited both vices and virtues; the relevant question is which of the two predominated. Of this, more shortly. But if, as we shall argue below, the process had, in net, benign effects, the process itself was not particularly robust. Indeed, redundancy in the region's transit planning was doomed from the beginning. The council regarded the jurisdictional situation as unsatisfactory almost from the start, and attempts were made to rectify it as early as 1971.

The Reorganization Act, which differentiated the planning and implementing roles, did not reduce the overlap as much as did the council's new appointment powers and fiscal authority. Even had Kelm not erred by using impolitic tactics, the council would have eventually appointed commissioners supportive of its views. (Curiously, although partisans on both sides appreciated the role that competitive planning can play (#1, #4, #5), all were eager to eliminate it. The substantive outcome was more important than an abstractly valued decision process.)

One can argue that since selecting a transit system is a one-shot choice, planning competition—though unstable—lasted long enough. Ongoing competition in such situations is undesirable. Indeed, Burton Klein's model (1962) of redundancy in development projects *requires* that parallel paths be pruned. This view has merit. But transit planning is a more continuous process than the weapons systems Klein studied.

As specific corridors become congested and oil prices rise, rail may yet prove desirable, as several antirail partisans acknowledge (#24). But a strong organizational advocate for rail no longer exists: MTC is now clearly subordinate to the council. It is therefore premature to conclude that the instability of redundancy is exactly appropriate to the lumpiness of the decision.

Of course this instability was not due solely to a formal restructuring of powers. By 1975, MTC's leaders had become a nuisance to the legislature as well as to the council. Eventually, legislators decided to treat the problem as if it were a one-shot choice, to close the books for a while on trunklike rail. This decision resulted from informal feuds as much as from legal prescriptions. Risky solutions require energetic leaders to sponsor them—the legislature commended Kelm in 1973 for doing just that—but such leadership can be its own undoing. It will take a new generation of political elites to forget old battles and reconsider rail.

Dysfunctions of Redundant Planning

This brings us to the negative side of the ledger.

1.   One may dismiss the personalized politicization of the issues as an idiosyncrasy of this case. In part, it was, but only in part, for one variable that increases the likelihood of agency competition, vigorous leadership, also increases the probability that fights will become acrimonious and personal. Strong leaders do not take setbacks calmly or opponents lightly. There are situations where people with intensely held beliefs clash without a frequent *ad hominem*, for example, scientists arguing over the validity of theories. But the institution of science has been evolving for three hundred years, ample time for the growth of powerful norms proscribing personal attacks. American public administration has no equivalent tradition. Indeed, the anticompetitive tradition has made less likely the emergence of norms regulating conduct in the face of "loyal opposition." (One must add that the Twin Cities' political culture's emphasis of policy and program over party

and person makes it all the more striking that this conflict became personalized. If it can happen in Minneapolis-St. Paul, it can happen anywhere.)

The tendency to personalize disagreements was strengthened by the weak empiricism of planning competition. In Klein's model, rival solutions are developed until a significant amount of uncertainty can be resolved empirically. Once one has several prototypes in hand, one can estimate more confidently how closely alternatives will approach their performance specifications. Although this procedure does not eliminate personal conflicts, it reduces their importance. But in this case several key uncertainties, such as patronage, could not be resolved in this incremental fashion. Because the conflict remained on paper, whether or not legislators personally trusted the modal advocates became more significant. Hence the mutual deprecation of staffs and consultants, which slid easily into invective.

We must take care, however, not to exaggerate the effects of personalizing. Although relations between the two agencies became unpleasant, as in the AC-BART case, external incentives induced cooperation in other areas. An UMTA official commented: "Believe it or not, the council has good relations with the MTC in terms of getting work out" (*Minneapolis Tribune*, March 6, 1974). The negative by-product of conflict was more an enduring negative posture toward rail than a crippling of the staffs' ability to work together on other problems.

2.   The financial costs of redundant planning were trivial. The council paid Barton-Aschman only $12,000 for its 1972 report. However, if the ultimate selection had been MTC's system in, say, the 1975 legislative session, duplicate planning's financial costs would have been much greater since the two-year delay would have inflated final construction costs. (If MTC's bill had passed both chambers in 1973, then competition would not have increased construction costs.)

3.   The time spent by councillors and staff was not included in financial costs. Time, as an opportunity cost, was more important than money. Several issues, such as land use and

regional finance, could be handled only by the council; if it did not work on these, no other agency would. This is therefore an instance of the gap-overlap trade-off discussed in Chapter One: by initiating transit planning, the council created a temporary planning gap in another issue area.

But could the council's Development Committee have profitably spent its time on another problem? The most important candidate for the committee's attention was land use. The council did not start serious work on a land-use plan until the new Physical Development Committee was created in 1973;[52] the council did not officially accept the plan until 1975. Is it possible that had the Development Guide Committee spent less time on transit from 1971 to 1973, (1) it could have produced a land-use plan earlier, which (2) could have been used to evaluate MTC's transit plan, thereby avoiding the acrimony of duplicate planning?[53] Statement (1) is probably correct; (2)'s accuracy is less certain. The Physical Development Committee required, despite its concentration on land use, nearly two years to develop a plan acceptable to the whole council. It is doubtful that its predecessor, the Development Guide Committee, could have completed the intricate technical and political process in time for the 1973 legislative session, which would have been necessary for the council to have used a differentiated rather than a redundant check on MTC.

4.   Vertical redundancies of the sort studied here typically involve organizations with unequal resources. A specialized, subordinate agency has less authority but greater expertise and more time to analyze alternatives in detail. A hierarchically superior organization is forced to play catch-up, and its staff is rarely as technically up-to-date as the specialist's. For this reason one council planning official made it a rule never to transform his generalist staff into transportation specialists: they would become outdated too quickly (#12). Although Chairman Graven's committee, staff, and

52. The council reorganized its committee structure that year.
53. It would have reduced some of the acrimony anyway; the agencies doubtless would have quarreled even if the council had challenged the MTC in a differentiated manner.

consultants covered much ground in six months of intensive work, their report was far less detailed than MTC's third plan. They had ignored crucial issues, and these omissions became glaringly apparent in the debates.[54]

5.   One could argue that advocates of different transit systems devoted so much time fighting one another that they lost the opportunity to coalesce, agree on a strong transit alternative, and promote that against the highway coalition. By fighting one another, they weakened the transit coalition and achieved only the lowest level option, an all-bus system lacking exclusive lanes. As a result, the area must still rely on its auto-highway system.

This assertion is partly correct. It is fair to say that the council's transportation plan for 1990 emphasizes highways. The plan, estimated to cost $5.8 billion by 1990, apportions $4.5 billion to highways (although most highway construction will be outside the urban ring). But the assertion assumes what should be proven, namely, whether there was a strong transit alternative in the early seventies. Much of the controversy focuses on just this point, for all participants recognized that the Twin Cities are not the classic high-density, strong transit case. It was not, and is not, obvious that any of the options were strong candidates. Different groups were differentially optimistic, MTC about rapid rail, Ed Anderson et al. about PRT, the Citizens' League about paratransit, and, to a lesser degree, the council about buses. Summing up each group's deflating criticisms of the others' options produces a pessimistic picture. The operating costs of buses *have* risen quickly, riders have *not* swarmed into carpools, PRT still *does* have numerous technical problems, and it is uncertain whether rapid rail would have been worth the price given modest corridor volumes. The diffuse optimism of 1972-73 that one of the alternatives would be highly effective has dissipated. The region was nurtured by the car, and it is unclear how to wean it.

54. Similarly, the Senate subcommittee and staff, although they boned up quickly on transit information, pursued an alternative—advanced technology transit—that proved to be unpromising for at least the medium term. And that conclusion, reached in 1975, had been reached *six years earlier* by MTC's first consultant on long-term planning.

Functions of Redundant Planning

1. The council, by producing a positive alternative to MTC's plan rather than by merely criticizing it, focused an enormous amount of newspaper coverage and public attention on the issue. Thus, there was little danger that a large investment could have been foisted upon an ignorant electorate.

2. As dangerous as an uninformed electorate is an uninformed legislature. In 1973, when virtually all legislators were uninformed, having three alternatives before the Senate helped legislators resist pressure to vote immediately, giving them time to obtain more information in the next two years. It may be asked whether the legislators' increased knowledge was beneficial. This is not easily answered, but it should be pointed out that the legitimacy of the regional planning *process*, if not the effectiveness of its *product*, may rest on the belief that when a higher authority approves a plan, it is doing more than rubber-stamping. It can do little other than rubber-stamp if its members are ignorant.

3. The delay caused by competitive planning allowed changing regional trends, in particular declining population projections, to become more evident and to work their way into planning.[55]

4. The delay facilitated the maturation of an idea—defining transit as riding rather than as public vehicles—which *may* prove the most important policy shift of all. Unfortunately, it is too early to tell. But if the associated strategy of increasing vehicle occupancy works, it will be a very inexpensive success.

5. The big question, of course, is whether the correct decision was made. An unequivocal yes or no would be the most satisfying pronouncement, but such a bald judgment is unwarranted for two reasons. First, it is difficult to know how the discarded options, in particular rapid rail, would have worked out.[56] Although we can compare, for example, bus

55. For example, the patronage estimates in MTC's final report were based on the most recent population forecasts provided by the council.

56. Building a single corridor of rail in the most densely traveled section would have reduced these uncertainties, but, as indicated by the angry reac-

operating costs with the council's projections, we cannot contrast rail's actual patronage with consultants' projections. Second, as some officials on both sides acknowledge, whether choosing buses over rail was wise depends partly on exogenous variables, such as the price of oil in 1990, which they can neither control nor accurately predict.

Nevertheless, I provisionally conclude that a sensible decision was made. The main consideration is the greater flexibility of the bus alternative. This flexibility was demonstrated in 1977 when the legislature, alarmed by skyrocketing operating deficits, established fiscal criteria for routes. Decisions based on these criteria reduced the system's size. Had rail been caught in an inflationary spiral during construction, there would have been essentially no option but to continue building. Second, because the council has not adopted a land-use policy that complements a rail system and because the population is not increasing quickly, it is unlikely that rail by itself would have significantly shaped development. MTC's hoped-for circular causation, in which rail creates development corridors that in turn sustain rail, would not have occurred. Finally, rail could not have substituted for freeways, as it probably has in Washington, D.C. (see Chapter Five) since the council's 1990 transportation plan does not recommend building any long freeways that would have been rendered superfluous by a rail system.

---

tions to Voorhees's staging recommendations, trying that in 1970 would have provoked a controversy. Today that sequential strategy is probably not feasible.

5

Metro: Monopoly in Washington, D.C.

The Washington Metro,[1] a system of nonoverlapping bus and rail service managed by one organization, is an ideal case to compare with the AC-BART structure of independent parallel service, for Metro's structure is precisely the preferred form of the conventional wisdom. Hence, this chapter concentrates on the advantages and disadvantages of integrated, nonredundant service. The introductory section describes premerger relations between private bus companies and the Washington Metropolitan Area Transit Authority (WMATA) and how merger was accomplished. The first section is not a general history of Metro planning. That has already been done (Murin, 1971; Hamer, 1976). Rather, it focuses on bus-rail relations.

Premerger Bus-Rail Relations

The illusion of inevitability often plagues hindsight. Mindful of that tendency, we must take care not to interpret the history of premerger relations between the bus

1. The organization's official title is the Washington Metropolitan Area Transit Authority (WMATA); Washingtonians call it Metro.

companies and Metro backward from time of merger. Bus-rail integration did not result from a methodical planning that led inexorably to a public takeover. Indeed, in the sixties it appeared that if integration were to occur, it would be under the auspices of the largest bus company, D.C. Transit, rather than a public takeover of private organizations.

When mass transit planning started in the late fifties, the four Washington metropolitan area bus companies were profitable concerns. They had not yet experienced the downward spiral of declining patronage, increased fares, and further patronage loss that had already ruined many transit firms. This is not to imply that they were in uniformly good shape. In particular, D.C. Transit may have already been suffering from undercapitalization (*Washington Post*, April 6, 1972). After Roy Chalk, the last owner, bought the franchise in 1956 from Louis Wolfson, a financier who had plundered the property, D.C. Transit needed improvements. Chalk, however, invested little in it. Although he enjoyed a few years of good relations with Washingtonians[2] (after Wolfson he was an improvement), by the mid-sixties D.C. Transit's reputation was again slumping. Although precise comparisons are impossible, it is a reasonable inference that D.C. Transit, during Metro's planning years, was a less satisfactory operation than AC was at a comparable time during BART planning.[3] Buses in Washington were from the start weaker competition.[4]

The bus firms, though mediocre transit competitors, were adept at political opposition. And unlike AC and BART, there was never any pretense in Washington that rail and bus were going to coexist peacefully. When Metro's predecessor, the National Capital Transportation Agency (NCTA), unveiled its plan in 1962 for eighty-three miles of rail,[5] the bus companies

2. For example, Senator Wayne Morse said that Chalk was living up to promises he had made to Congress (*Washington Star*, October 10, 1963).

3. Of course, AC had the advantage of nonfarebox revenues.

4. Alexandria, Barcroft, and Washington (AB&W), a much smaller company that served several Virginia suburbs and ran commuter lines into D.C., had an excellent reputation, comparable with AC's (#8, #12; U.S. Congress, House of Representatives, 1963).

5. There were also fifteen miles of improved commuter rail, fifty-two miles of express bus routes, and fifty miles of freeway.

responded quickly, meeting in summer 1962 to discuss the common threat. Since the bus firms' service areas barely overlapped, there was little intramodel competition. Consequently, forming a coalition was not difficult, and they agreed to meet the challenge collectively.[6] Monopolistic transit had a long tradition in the region, dating back to streetcar days, and the owners intended to maintain it.

NCTA planners tried to persuade the bus firms, particularly the suburban lines, that introducing rail would help them by eliminating the most congested parts of the bus commute routes (approaches to D.C. and downtown) and by generating a great demand for feeder service to stations. Although there was no study of rail's financial impact on buses, such as the gloomy 1962 DeLeuw report done for BART, the bus owners were unmoved by NCTA's argument.[7] At the 1963 congressional hearings, the general manager of Alexandria, Barcroft, and Washington (AB&W), a Virginia company, protested that rail would "cream" AB&W by taking the through riders and leaving the burden of local lines: "It is a known fact in the business that the through routes are the backbone of the business" (U.S. Congress, House of Representatives, 1963, p. 2).[8] The testimony of NCTA's chief, Darwin Stolzenbach, only partly reassured them. Though he did not propose eliminating Virginia-D.C. bus lines entirely, as

6. NCTA and D.C. Transit originally appeared to have been on fairly cordial terms. This amicability evaporated after several months, with each side accusing the other of misconduct. NCTA's chief Darwin Stolzenbach stated that after his organization displayed little interest in Chalk's idea of a monorail, Chalk cut off contact. The bus companies countercharged that NCTA did not try to contact them.

7. See Chalk's skeptical testimony on the profitability of reorienting routes (U.S. Congress, House of Representatives, 1963, p. 265).

8. The different financial assessments may have been partly due to different expectations of the highway program. NCTA at that time was strongly antihighway, and its planners probably assumed that if Congress passed its bill, the D.C. highway program would not be approved. This would mean worsening traffic for the buses, and as one NCTA planner put it: "The most serious threat to financial stability of the bus companies isn't rail but increasing downtown congestion" (U.S. Congress, House of Representatives, 1963, p. 14). The bus owners were relying on the highway program to relieve congestion.

long as there was sufficient traffic, he was "sure that the putting in place of a large rapid transit system is going to require vast rescheduling of local bus operations throughout the whole region" (ibid., p. 85). But even if long-haul buses were not *forced* to turn back, the owners were displeased with the prospect of competing with rail for commute patrons (ibid., p. 265). Chalk advised the committee that his franchise gave him monopoly rights over all public transit in Washington. In fact the 1963 bill did not designate who would operate the system, but it was evident that Chalk feared the government would. And if rail were going to be built, he wanted to run it.

Beyond the issue of operational control, the bus firms and their ally, the Washington Metropolitan Area Transit Commission (WMATC), argued that rail was not needed for the area's projected densities. Buses could do the job for less money.[9] Here Chalk relied heavily on a report by transportation analyst Martin Wohl.[10] This report, like the well-known Meyer, Kain, and Wohl book (1965) then circulating among Washington planners, argued that corridor flows of greater than 30,000 people per hour were needed to justify, on financial grounds, investing in rail.[11] In less heavily traveled corridors express buses would suffice. On narrow cost-effectiveness grounds this position had merit, and subsequently transit specialists critical of Metro's planning would point to this period as the time when Washington missed its best opportunity to avoid the burden of a massively expensive, capital-intensive project (Hamer, 1976, pp. 139-143; Roth, 1977). But this argument had one serious flaw: a misunderstanding of the historical context. An earlier plan, the 1959 Mass Transportation Survey, had evoked a storm of reac-

9. WMATC leaders may have genuinely believed that buses were the superior alternative, but there was the added factor of organizational interest. A regulatory commission is only as important as its domain, and WMATC's would have contracted with the birth of the public rail agency.

10. Although the Wohl report was never officially released by Commerce, it was widely circulated informally (*Washington Star*, July 21, 1963; *Washington Post*, July 28, 1963). In his analysis of transit planning in Washington, Andrew Hamer (1976) overstated how buried the report was. Given the informal circulation, official release would have had little additional effect.

11. Wohl assumed that transit was to be financially self-supporting.

tion from early antihighway groups. The proposed 148 miles of highway threatened Washington's distinctive physical character and would displace between 28,000 and 75,000 people, mainly blacks in inner D.C., from their homes. NCTA's plan, in large measure a reaction to the 1959 plan, offered rapid rail as a *substitute* for new highways.

This issue was the Achilles heel of the bus proposals. When Chalk and his allies were arguing for express buses as an alternative to rail, they were also endorsing the freeway program—explicitly so (U.S. Congress, House of Representatives, 1963, p. 263). Congestion on bridges leading from Virginia and southeast Washington was hurting the suburban bus companies; congestion on D.C. streets was hurting D.C. Transit. Consequently all four companies endorsed building new freeways in inner D.C. and from D.C. west to Virginia, northwest along the Potomac River, and north to Maryland. Hence an express bus system necessitated a highway program, and with the highways came their destructive side effects of displacing residents and removing property from the tax rolls.[12] These implications were underscored by Representative Basil Whitener during the District of Columbia hearings on "The Transit Program for the National Capital Region" (ibid., p. 330), and the D.C. Transit Commission's director then testifying had no answer to the criticisms. Washington was quite unlike Minneapolis where selecting the bus alternative did not imply much highway construction in densely populated areas.

Although the bus firms opposed NCTA's plan, the debate before and during the 1963 hearings failed to reach the level of competitive planning of the Twin Cities' agencies. The bus companies had not developed detailed alternative plans, claiming that they could not finance the consultants needed to study the matter. When Whitener rebuked the Transit Commission for criticizing NCTA while unable themselves to answer specific questions about an express bus system, the commission director replied that they could produce answers if

12. Thus rail and bus were on equal footing since both required capital-intensive construction projects. At that time—1962—the idea of using ramp metering with preferential access for buses had not been broached.

they had more money. Whitener, however, retorted: "Yes, but you would be duplicating the same studies that the taxpayers have already paid for one time" (ibid., p. 325). Planning money never materialized.

The organization of transit planning in Washington was relatively monopolistic;[13] there was criticism and opposition but not counterplanning. In part, this derived from a conventional division of labor. NCTA was authorized to conduct transit planning whereas the Transit Commission, the natural governmental spokesman for bus firms, was a regulatory agency without planning responsibilities.[14] Furthermore, NCTA and the Transit Commission reached a reconciliation in March 1964 when they agreed "not to criticize each other in public anymore" (*Washington Post*, March 5, 1964). This agreement ended an argument, which, though lacking the specificity of competitive planning, at least engaged agencies with a vested interest in different solutions.

In addition, the bus companies were not particularly interested in counterplanning. The 1963 testimonies clearly showed that they concentrated more on reducing the financial threat of rail to their properties than on generating alternatives. In this endeavor they were not alone. In the early sixties rail's prospects in Congress were poor. Transit labor union locals had joined the powerful highway lobby in opposing it, and support for local financing was problematic (Murin, 1971). The bus firms' executives may well have believed that *opposition without developing options* would suffice. Thus, they were sluggish in giving congressional committees even sketchy plans. Subsequently, in May 1964, Representative Carlton Sickles would berate the bus companies for taking so long with their financial plans (*Washington Star*, May 23, 1964). But though the bus firms failed to persuade the subcommittees that they had a viable alternative, they successfully

13. The D.C. Highway Department had expressed interest in bus-on-freeways as "a key part of mass transit" as early as 1961 (*Washington Post*, March 12, 1961), but it had neither the authority nor the expertise to do combined highway–mass transit planning.

14. WMATC's planning resources were meager at this time: the position of Urban Transit Planner was unfilled until 1969.

argued that a government-run[15] system would unfairly compete with private enterprise by creaming the commute routes and leaving the less profitable lines. While today government ownership and operation of transit are taken for granted, both were hot issues in 1963-65. Furthermore, the bus companies, particularly AB&W and D.C. Transit, had powerful friends on the Hill.[16] (The bus companies' contacts in Congress were better than their relations with highway agencies.[17] That reinforced their tendency to use a strategy of protecting their property rights rather than specifying an express bus system plan, for the latter would have required collaboration with highway agencies.)

These powerful friends, solicitous of the bus companies' particular interests, joined with congressmen doubtful of rail's financial solvency (Murin, 1971, p. 58) to defeat NCTA. NCTA's first, eighty-three-mile plan never made it out of committee; instead, the committee recommended a "bobtailed" version of twenty-two miles. This was basically a D.C. subway with short spurs across the Potomac River. Even this the bus companies opposed,[18] arguing that letting commuters ride buses almost to D.C. only to transfer for a short rail ride made no sense. NCTA replied that "a major asset of 8929 [the bobtailed system] was the location of proposed rapid transit terminals outside the congested area" (U.S. Congress, House of Representatives, 1963, p. 14), so commuters could by-pass the worst traffic. Once again, underlying this disagreement were different preferences for and expectations of new highways leading into D.C. If these were not going to be built, NCTA's reply may have been valid.

15. The 1963 bill did not say who would operate the system, but the bus owners claimed that it implied a governmental agency would.

16. These friends included Judge Howard Smith of Virginia (#17).

17. This was particularly true in Virginia, where the road people had little truck with buses (#14). In general the highway-bus relation was asymmetric: the latter needed the former but not vice versa. Consequently, the bus systems were in the worst of all possible political worlds: they made enemies by being associated with the controversial highway coalition, yet belonging to the coalition yielded few benefits because highway agencies were not interested in transit.

18. AB&W dissented by not opposing a purely intra-D.C. system.

The bus companies must also have been worried that big systems can grow from little ones. This concern was articulated by their ally, the Transit Commission. The commission urged that if rail were to be built at all, the construction should be staged not by constructing a scaled-down version of a big system but by erecting *single* lines in the most favorable, high-density corridors. Though this satisfied technical transit criteria, it was politically naïve because it ignored financing and fair-share[19] problems, as well as Congress's expressed interest in a downtown subway.

Even the scaled-down Whitener plan was sent back to committee by the House. NCTA's attempt to develop a transit plan that would substitute for highway plans, rather than conciliate the highway coalition by producing a "balanced"[20] transportation plan, stimulated animosity toward NCTA, its plan, and its chief. In addition the bill threatened labor unions and bus companies. The next director of NCTA, Walter Mc-Carter, would take care to avoid such mistakes.

Not only was NCTA's second plan rejected; the agency was stripped of its highway planning powers. This loss ensured that it would thereafter be concerned only with rail because improving the bus system required augmenting roads and highways, and such changes after 1963 were outside NCTA's jurisdiction. It would henceforth be identified as a modally specialized organization.

Not so the bus companies, however. During the next congressional hearings in 1965, Chalk still displayed interest in operating the rail system. In fact, he pushed more forcefully for an integrated transit system than did McCarter. The latter was content to say that though he was for private, possibly contract, management, "the areawide transportation system does not necessarily have to have a unified management. It is good if it does but it does not have to have it. . . . Coordination of service can be achieved by agreement, and through the local transit regulatory commission [WMATC]" (U.S.

19. Deen (1974) points out that where recent large systems needed voter approval, they were not proposed incrementally by corridors.

20. *Balanced* is a code term familiar to students of weapons systems: a balanced weapons system is one with something for all the rival armed services.

Congress, Senate, 1965, pp. 76, 273). To further placate bus opposition, a clause proposing that "unnecessary duplicating service be eliminated" was itself eliminated. McCarter claimed that "there is no intent that privately owned companies would be forced to discontinue a service merely because it was paralleled by, or was competitive with, rapid rail service" (ibid., p. 47).

Chalk, worried that the region could not sustain two competing transit systems, argued that his company should operate both under a franchise arrangement. His strategy[21] had changed from simple opposition to seeking organizational consolidation. Why Chalk modified his approach is unknown.[22] It is possible that the bus firms were informed by their close congressional contacts that after certain financial changes were made in the 1963 bobtailed version, Congress was likely to approve it and that the most the bus firms could get was a guarantee that rail be privately managed.[23] This guarantee was written into the bill passed by Congress in 1965. The bus companies—more precisely, D.C. Transit—had won a victory in securing the private management clause, but they could not prevent congressional legitimation of rail. Thus, by 1965 the scanty degree of transit planning competition came to an end.

During the late sixties bus-rail relations diminished in importance. Congress had given NCTA a mandate, and there was little the bus companies could do about it. NCTA's biggest problem by far was Representative William Natcher's effort to block funds, an obstacle dwarfing other concerns. The modes' only major contact in this period was a formal meeting between McCarter and the bus firms' heads in 1966 in which the participants agreed to cooperate on an origin-destination survey of bus passengers. Relations between D.C. Transit and NCTA remained strained—the former refused to

21. The other bus company owners did not make presentations at this hearing.
22. One veteran of this period described the second strategy as Chalk's fallback position (#17).
23. What tack the other bus companies were taking at this time I do not know. D.C. Transit was the only one making a strong pitch for managing the rail system.

let the latter study its records—but the Transit Commission had the information that NCTA needed to plan bus-rail coordination, and its books were open.

In 1968 Metro[24] completed its first detailed finance and services plan, which required making assumptions about the organizational status and service characteristics of buses for the next decade. The study assumed private ownership, for it was expected that, given fare increases commensurate with rising costs, the bus companies would remain solvent. But Metro had set aside McCarter's laissez-faire position of 1965.[25] There was to be "no inefficient competition":[26] duplicate routes would be eliminated,[27] and the bus systems reoriented toward feeders. To promote combined bus and rail rides, there would be free transfers in both directions. Although the report did not mention a detailed revenue-sharing procedure, it recognized that some kind of revenue-sharing was required to keep the bus companies in the black and recommended a simple fifty-fifty split.

These were Metro's expectations, not the bus firms'. The author heard conflicting opinions about the bus firms' strategies, in particular, whether or not they were going to cooperate with Metro's plan for a differentiated and interdependent relationship. A former D.C. Transit manager said his firm probably would have discarded parallel lines and reoriented toward a complementary relation (#9); a former AB&W executive and two former suburban bus staffers indicated the contrary (#6, #5, #14). The deciding factor probably would have been the revenue-sharing arrangement. Presumably the bus owners were disinterested in competition per se, and a reasonable profit margin would have induced them to reorient. Of course, the organizations might have been unable to nego-

24. With the passing of the interstate compact in 1967, NCTA dissolved and WMATA began. There was complete staff continuity.

25. Undoubtedly a greater political security and legitimacy were potent factors in producing the shift from 1965 to 1968.

26. There had been a "declaration of policy" against "unnecessary duplicating service" a year earlier in the 1967 WMATA Compact (WMATA, 1976b, p. 2), but the modifier *unnecessary* rendered the expression toothless.

27. The planners added the caveat that "complementary radial service" would be maintained (WMATA, 1968, p. 13). The definition of this service was a trifle vague.

tiate a settlement, but here the situation differed markedly from the Bay Area. In California until the Metropolitan Transportation Commission matured, no organization was both able and willing to broker AC-BART revenue and transfer problems. In Washington there was the Transit Commission, and it was expected (#6) that if the bus companies and Metro failed to agree on a revenue-sharing and transfer scheme, then the commission would step in. Though it lacked jurisdiction over Metro, it had authority to direct the private carriers to coordinate schedules, joint fares, and routes with Metro (WMATA, 1976, p. 28). The Washington area was institutionally equipped to handle interorganizational disputes.

Toward the end of the sixties, however, these issues became increasingly moot. D.C. Transit entered the red permanently in 1967, and by 1968 all but AB&W were losing money. The 1968 riots following Martin Luther King's assassination merely accelerated the decline: the bus companies belatedly started the downward spiral that had already ruined most major private transit systems. AB&W, which provided excellent service, including express buses on exclusive highway lanes, was least affected, D.C. Transit most affected. As one former Metro official put it, D.C. Transit started "to devour its own corpus" (#17): maintenance men were laid off, service cut, equipment deteriorated. Washingtonians considered the bus system a public disaster and held Chalk responsible. Far from being an alternative to rail, the major bus system was bungling the tasks it already had.

By 1971-72 it was obvious that a public takeover was imminent. Congress, exasperated by Chalk, was urging such a step. But Metro, immersed in rail construction and financing, was far from enthusiastic (#7, #22, #39). Several top officials believed that the timing was poor and that they should wait several years to complete construction before assuming a new responsibility.

While Metro was moving slowly, the Northern Virginia Transit Commission (NVTC), urged on by AB&W management, was contemplating taking over the two Virginia lines. Publicly the NVTC said it would do so only as an interim measure, but some participants and observers believed that several northern Virginia officials and politicians, opposed to a Metro takeover, wanted a permanent arrangement (#17).[28] The NVTC was the only organizational alternative to Metro, but it lacked the latter's political clout in Congress, and Metro leaders had decided they would accept the charge that Congress was urging upon them. Hence Metro, without difficulty, turned aside the NVTC challenge and in 1972 received authority to acquire the bus systems.

Given Metro's reluctance and the pressure of some opposition, why did the buses land in their laps? The answer is simple. It was widely held[29] that the four interstate bus systems should be unified, and Metro was the only interstate organization with operational transit responsibilities.[30] Thus Metro was the only candidate. Composing the 1967 WMATA Compact had been quite a political feat, and creating another interstate authority was thought a waste of energy. That Metro would suffice was the opinion of Congress, Department of Transportation Secretary John Volpe, and every participant and observer with the exception of the NVTC and a few others.[31] It was not a controversial decision, for virtually no one anticipated the difficulties that Metro would encounter.

It must be emphasized that although speakers at the takeover hearing anticipated that merger would produce the benefits of ensuring complementary service (U.S. Congress, Senate, 1972, pp. 8, 43, 47) and eliminating overlaps,[32] the takeover was not a calculated attempt to realize these ends. It was a rescue operation, with Metro as the reluctant rescuer.

28. The Fairfax County, Virginia, executive director was eventually fired for going against official county policy for a regional system by lobbying in Congress for a Virginia takeover. I believe that the county board of supervisors was divided over this issue.

29. Newspaper discussions and hearings indicate that most participants took for granted that a unified transit system would be beneficial.

30. WMATC had always been purely a regulatory body, and there is no evidence that it ever sought or was ever considered as a candidate to operate the buses.

31. A transit consultant, Stephen Swain, warned that the bus systems required many improvements going far beyond coordinating with Metrorail (U.S. Congress, Senate, 1972, p. 170).

32. No one mentioned economies of scale.

Postmerger Modal Relations

Though more accidental than planned, the merger nevertheless provides an opportunity to compare the effects of organizationally integrated, nonredundant service with the organizationally separated, redundant service of AC and BART. We must take care to disentangle the effects of two distinct, though related, causes: (1) the effects of integrating the administration of two modes within one organization and (2) the effects of changing the bus route network in order to create service monopoly;[33] see Figure 6, which indicates that although integration increases the probability that service redundancy will be eliminated, an integrated organization could have retained service redundancies.[34]

We will first describe the advantages of integration and follow that with an analysis of the benefits of nonredundancy.

Advantages of Integration

It is a cliché in public administration that coordination is desirable. When things go awry, a call goes forth for more coordination. And coordinating the operation of two modes *is*

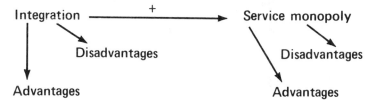

FIGURE 6   *Relation of Integration and Monopoly*

33. There was yet another change: from private to public ownership. This shift produced its own set of consequences; the most obvious benefit was the injection of nonfarebox monies.

34. The converse proposition, that separate bus and rail organizations would have agreed to eliminate parallel routes, is less probable. It is unlikely that a bus agency would have unconditionally pulled off all duplicate routes; instead, it would have employed a load or revenue criterion and eliminated runs that were faring badly.

important: patrons want to transfer smoothly, cheaply, and reliably between modes of transportation. Moreover, as we have seen in the AC-BART case, it takes no little effort to provide this linkage. Metro, as an integrated organization, proved to have an advantage here. There were two indications of this.

1.   Metro financial staffers devoted considerable effort to reducing the expense and awkwardness of the bus-to-rail transfer. At the same time they could proceed with confidence, knowing that any proposed solution would have to be accepted only by a single (albeit federated) organization that treated intermodal financing as an internal accounting matter rather than as interorganizational negotiation. The Metro staff first proposed an arrangement that was equivalent to AC-BART's, but their work did not end there. Methods more acceptable to riders were sought, and a decision was reached in 1978 to sell "flashpasses," which could be used in Metro rail's fare gates and flashed to bus drivers.[35] It seems that the integrated structure increased aspiration levels for meshing complementary modes, in turn increasing the problem-solving effort.

2.   Intermodal transfers create numerous problems of timing, for example, buses leaving just before a train arrived. These problems tended to fall in the cracks between AC and BART;[36] in Metro, fairly substantial resources were devoted to smooth things out at stations (#20). Rail supervisors can hold up the buses when trains run late (#45), and bus supervisors are instructed to monitor bus drivers' behavior.[37] There is no doubt that Metro tried harder to solve interface problems than AC and BART did.[38]

35. Some Metro officials were concerned that the poorer riders would not often buy the flashpasses (#4), but that does not seem to be a major problem (#43). However, it is still too early to assess the effects of the passes.

36. But this "slip 'twixt the lip and the cup" did not happen to the express buses that BART contracted for with AC in eastern Contra Costa County.

37. This problem was unanticipated and proved to be a drain on the supervisorial resources of the bus office (#20). But because a single organization was in charge of ensuring that the change to a bus-rail system went smoothly, the bus section could be ordered to attend to the problem.

38. Note, however, that Amtrak and Conrail have similar arrangements on an interorganizational level with Metro (#45).

One might think that a third indicator of Metro's integrative superiority was the convenience of the physical layout of its rail system, Metrorail, stations for patrons using rail and bus (e.g., parking spaces for buses, busbays, were well located). But Metro staffers drew the designs in the late sixties *before* the organizations merged and even before it was obvious that merger was imminent. Consequently, the superior physical interface cannot be attributed to organizational integration; rather, it probably resulted from Metro's expectation that buses would be the key access mode to rail.[39]

Economies of Scale

Although potential economies of scale were not discussed during the takeover hearings, it is often expected in governmental reorganizations that merging like functions will produce such benefits. Before plunging further into this matter, one qualification must be mentioned. It is quite possible that several of the bus firms, particularly the smallest, were below optimal size in terms of inventories or garages and that merger with other bus companies would have permitted better use of these factors. These benefits constitute plant economies of scale, alluded to in Chapter One; they result from merging organizations with common technologies (buses) rather than like functions (transit). A bus-rail union would not be required to realize these.

Scale economies resulting from bus-rail mergers are administrative rather than plant savings. Unfortunately, because Metro does not keep historical records on the proportion of the budget devoted to administration, we cannot directly establish whether or not Metro saved money as a result of the 1973 merger. However, because the U.S. Department of Transportation now requires that all public transit agencies compile this information, we can indirectly probe the question by analyzing whether larger transit agencies spend a smaller portion of their operating budgets on adminis-

39. In the sixties it was expected that 70 percent of the morning rail patrons would arrive at the stations by bus.

tration.[40] The answer is they do not (U.S. Department of Transportation, 1982, chap. 8, pp. 39–43). Regressing the percentage of operating costs allocated to administration on the organization's size (measured by number of buses) yields the following equation:

$$\frac{\text{admin. costs}}{\text{total operating costs}} = 16.2 \text{ percent} - 0.0003 \text{ size.}$$

The R^2 is a paltry 0.3 percent. For agencies operating between 250 and 4500 buses, size appears to have no systematic effect on administrative costs.

Because managing a rail system and managing buses are not administratively identical, one is more likely to find administrative economies of scale by studying, as we have, the effects of size on bus-only agencies and the bus divisions of multimodal organizations than by examining bus-rail mergers. The fact that there are no administrative economies even in bus organizations implies that it is highly unlikely that the 1973 merger of Metro's rail system with the four bus companies generated economies of scale.

Advantages of Monopoly Service

The primary advantage of nonredundant transit service is either budget reductions or maintaining the budget and reallocating redundant resources. Metro has adopted a mix of the two courses. Some buses and drivers have been eliminated, and some buses that previously carried commuters downtown now drop their patrons at rail stations and turn back for more runs. Instead of the single peak-hour trip they once made, they now make two. The integrated organization can exploit the different modal technologies, allocating each to tasks for which they are suited—the bus, with its greater ability to collect and distribute patrons, acting as feeder; and

40. Transportation economists typically assume that the non-administrative costs of operating buses exhibit constant returns to scale (Viton, 1980, p. 53). Consequently, if large agencies enjoyed administrative economies of scale, these should be revealed as smaller percentages of *total* operating costs absorbed by administration.

the rail, with its presumably lower operating costs, acting as line-hauler. We should note, however, that the board's policy decision to drop all parallel bus routes was based exclusively on a cost-cutting criterion—reduce the budget deficit by eliminating duplication—and not on a criterion of an optimal service mix.[41] Improving the service mix was the perspective of Metro planners.

Because many of the buses were rerouted, it was difficult for Metro staffers to estimate how much money was saved (#22). For the major alteration to date, phase two, Metro estimates range from $3.5 million (WMATA, 1976a, p. 5) to $6 million (WMATA, 1977a, p. 66) annually.[42]

This completes the record of benefits accruing from merger; we now move to the other side of the ledger.

Disadvantages of Integration and Monopoly

As with advantages, we must distinguish negative effects of integration from those resulting from eliminating redundant service. We start with the former.

When the bus companies were taken over in 1973, D.C. Transit was in a sorry state (#7, #29).[43] In addition, the route structure of the four systems had become hideously complex, even to native Washingtonians (#8). Indeed, one veteran Metro scheduler told me: "Our routes are so complicated,

41. A Fairfax County, Virginia, staff report envisaged using a service variable—travel time—as a decision criterion concerning cutbacks. This might have produced intraorganizational competition. It was not used by Metro.

42. The confidence of the jurisdictional staffs in the Metro figures varied greatly. A Virginia staffer thought Metro was producing "funny numbers on turnback savings, i.e., overestimating" (#2T). On the other hand, a Prince George's County, Maryland, staffer thought there were "tremendous savings" (#4T).

43. The suburban lines, particularly AB&W, were in better condition. The relative quality of the different systems was indicated by the fact that while D.C. residents were hoping for improvements, the Virginia commuters were fearing deterioration.

sometimes even we don't understand them" (#19). Strong management was needed to revitalize the bus system.

Such management is not impossible in an integrated organization. In General Motors, for example, divisions have historically been semiautonomous, divisional managers having considerable discretion over important decisions.[44] This type of structure was feasible for Metro in 1973. There were two variations[45] on this theme: operating the buses by contract management or creating a separate bus division, run out of different headquarters by a high Metro official (#17). Contract management is employed in several cities in the United States and was seriously considered by the board. Jackson Graham, appointed general manager in 1976, was "violently opposed" to the proposal (#15).[46] Although neither he nor his top aides had any experience in running a bus system, Graham—by all accounts[47] an extremely capable man with a successful career in the Army Corps of Engineers behind him—did not lack confidence. Characteristically, he remarked later: "I commanded more vehicles and personnel in Korea" (*Washington Post*, August 12, 1976). He scorned contract management: Metro management could handle the new task. It is fair to say, with hindsight, that Graham badly underestimated the difficulty of improving the bus system.

The second idea of Metro officials managing a quasi-autonomous bus division was also discarded. Whereas contract management was discussed publicly, the debate over which purely Metro structure should be adopted was chiefly internal. It is therefore difficult to sort out how the decision was made. In particular, it is uncertain whether Graham imposed his preferred structure of centralized management (#8, #17) or whether top Metrorail management hashed it out (#13). It does appear that this group generally supported the

44. They are, of course, financially accountable to headquarters.

45. There were several others (#17), but specifics were obtained on only these two.

46. The top bus officials, brought in primarily from D.C. Transit, opposed contract management because it would have imposed a career-mobility lid on them. It was Graham's opposition, however, that was decisive.

47. Not one newspaper report or interviewee, inside or outside of Metro, said that Graham was anything but highly competent.

idea that transit should be an "integrated show"[48] and that to manage an operationally meshed system via separate divisions would be unhealthy.[49]

In any case, the chosen structure (see Fig. 7) was far from divisionalized: bus functions were scattered across Metro's entire structure.[50] This diffuse structure contained two mechanisms for reaching decisions on bus improvements. One was Graham himself. Several interviewees asserted that this structure meant that Graham had to make most of the important decisions (#14, #17). Not surprisingly, this slowed decision-making. Even Graham, an extraordinarily hard-working executive, could not keep pace with the increased complexity of Metro: building a subway, meeting politico-financial problems, and now trying to improve a run-down bus system.[51]

The second decisional mechanism was a "bus trust" that Graham established in late 1972. This committee was composed of top Metro executives and representatives from the bus sections of operations and maintenance. How much this trust achieved is uncertain. One bus manager described a similar coordinating committee as a frustrating experience; communication between this official and other committee members was mediocre (#14). Another former Metro official thought there was "too much bureaucracy sitting around the table every Monday morning" (#17).

Neither mechanism provided the aggressive leadership and interorganizational representation of bus interests that

48. In the earthy words of one Metro official: "Give 'em the same men's room: let 'em piss together."

49. In addition, it was believed that it would have been wasteful duplication to employ separate treasurers and other general administrators (#3). This would not, however, have been necessary in a divisional organization: administrative posts that are not operationally specific could be centralized.

50. This kind of decentralization should not be confused with a decentralized competitive system. In Metro many officials had different but interdependent tasks regarding buses: their responsibilities complemented rather than substituted for each other.

51. Graham may have also made an error in judgment concerning which bus managers he did pay attention to. Apparently, he largely ignored the man—a former AB&W official—whom outside transit observers regarded as the most competent former private manager retained by Metro. This disregard may have resulted from a friction between the old D.C. Transit hierarchy and the outnumbered former Virginia bus managers (#39).

was essential. Graham was too busy; the bus trust, too un-wieldy. To make matters worse, the board of directors was dominated by Graham (#39). It therefore supplied little direc-tion and could not compensate for the unwieldy bus manage-ment structure. Bus maintenance in D.C. remained spotty, the route structure Byzantine.[52]

In early 1975 the board commissioned the consulting firm of Cresap, McCormick, and Paget to study its bus system, Metrobus, with particular emphasis on escalating deficits and service quality. With regard to management, the team recom-mended that a new position of Chief of Bus Operations and Maintenance be established for an interim period to ensure an "immediate strengthening" of that mode (Cresap et al., 1975, p. III–4). As one Cresap staffer recalled: "This organization was getting so into rail, we felt that the bus operation would suffer, and was suffering. . . . There was no one strong bus person who could get things done, short of going up to Graham" (#11). Though they accepted many nonorgan-izational recommendations, Graham and the Metro staff fought that particular suggestion with determination and skill, producing "an amazingly fast rebuttal" (#17, #11, #12). The board set the offending recommendation aside, and the management structure remained unchanged until Graham's departure.

Cresap et al.'s critique did not mean that patrons perceived complete stagnation in Metrobus. In two surveys of 1,000 randomly selected area residents in 1973 and 1975, the system received higher marks in the second study. D.C. residents registered the largest perceived improvements;[53] in the 1973 study D.C. bus service had scored lowest of the three jurisdic-

52. The delay in route improvements was not just a product of structural impediments. The top Metro planning staff had decided that to change the bus routes twice, once in 1973–75 and again in 1976 when rail opened, was a waste of time and would discomfit patrons. This is certainly defensible, but one wonders what position a strong bus division chief would have taken. This problem involves a compromise between the interests of the bus-only patrons, who would have benefited from route rationalization, and rail-bus patrons, who could accept a delay. The representation of these interests was affected by the internal organization of the modes.

53. The dimensions were routes' availability, schedule frequency, promptness of arrivals, fares, safety on buses, cleanliness of buses, skill of drivers, and drivers' courtesy.

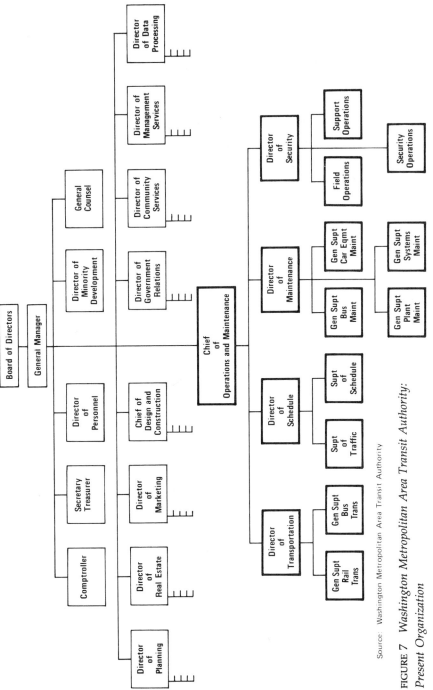

Source: Washington Metropolitan Area Transit Authority

FIGURE 7 *Washington Metropolitan Area Transit Authority: Present Organization*

tions. Maryland's improvements were considerably less. Virginia's, which had started out highest, showed an interesting pattern with increases in the second most positive category but decreases in the "excellent" ratings and small increases[54] in the "poor" ratings.[55]

Metro *had* bettered certain aspects of the bus system. Route mileage increased considerably from 1973 to 1976,[56] and over 600 new buses were purchased from American Motors in 1974. Unfortunately, the buses proved a poor purchase, compounding maintenance difficulties.[57] It is uncertain to what degree the unwise purchase decision should be attributed to the tightly integrated management structure. Certain external factors—UMTA wanted more competition in bus manufacturing and pressed Metro to accept American Motors' bid—would have affected any structure, including a decentralized one. Further, the position of bus managers at that time was not clear. Today two have said they were opposed, but if this was so, it was not widely known then (#14, #29). (This was itself a structural problem: if the bus managers did believe the purchase was a mistake, they lacked a secure organizational base from which to oppose it.) Again, a union leader recently affirmed that whereas under private ownership the union could influence bus design specifications, under Metro the union was ignored (#23). What the union's views were at the time of purchase is unknown.

The bus system needed skilled personnel—maintenance men and schedulers—as badly as it did new equipment, and

54. These responses occurred in seven out of seven and four out of seven dimensions, respectively.

55. If one assumes an interval scale and averages the scores by equating excellent = four, good = three, fair = two, and poor = one, then one finds a slight overall improvement from 1973 to 1975.

56. With it had risen the deficit, from $2.2 million in 1973 to $51.8 million in 1976.

57. Outside observers also questioned whether increasing routes and buses was the appropriate strategy at this time. The route expansions superimposed additional complexity on an already overly complicated route structure, and the new buses exacerbated the maintenance problem. But there is no direct link between these improvement strategies and organizational structure: I believe the bus officials themselves disagreed over which strategy was appropriate.

here the integrated structure worked poorly. Scheduling, an arcane craft, is essential to the economical functioning of a bus system. When Metro absorbed the bus companies, it inherited an aging cohort of schedulers.[58] New schedulers were urgently needed so they could be trained before the old cohort retired (Wilbur Smith and Associates, 1975, p. 66; #19). Yet not only was the board unresponsive to budget requests; it seemed unsympathetic, once castigating the schedulers just for raising the issue (#14, #19). Apparently the scheduling department received no help from higher-ups, which again points up the advantage of a divisional form wherein division heads are natural advocates of modal interests.

The problem of too few trained bus maintenance men was less connected to organizational structure. After merger, maintenance men, like other workers, had the right to move from one mode to the other, and many bus maintenance men moved to rail (#29). Although superficially this might appear a symptom of rail-oriented resource allocation and a direct consequence of Graham's centralized, rail-oriented style, it was not. Changing jobs was a right exercised by workers; it was not centrally directed. It could have occurred just as easily under a divisional structure or indeed if entirely distinct organizations had managed the two modes.[59] Furthermore, Metro *has* tried to hire new maintenance men, a difficult task because they are scarce and in great demand.

It is quite possible, however, that some shifts were influenced by a perception that rail was the favored mode in Metro. The union felt that the bus system was a stepchild in the integrated Metro structure. Graham was perceived as autocratic and antilabor, and Metro leadership as remote from the bus system (#32; *Washington Post*, October 31, 1975). The stepchild syndrome was probably inevitable; trains were shiny and new, buses dirty and mostly old. Indeed, Graham argued that the modes were integrated precisely in order to break down intermodal barriers (#7). In the years between merger and Graham's departure (1973–76), however, Metro

58. This is a nationwide problem.

59. For example, when BART opened, clause 13–C gave high priority to AC workers applying for BART jobs, and a number did shift.

fell short of this goal (#20, #32).[60] It would have been wiser to recognize that regardless of organizational structure, tension between workers in the two modes was inevitable.

It should be added that the problems adduced above—delays in improving the bus system and the perception that buses were second-class transit—resulted not solely from an integrated structure but also from Graham's highly centralized strategy of leadership. When Graham left in early 1976, that strategy did not long outlast him. The acting general manager, Warren Quenstedt, preferred to control transit operation in particular and internal issues in general less tightly than Graham had.

The key drama stimulating the improvement of the bus system was the July 4, 1976, fiasco when hundreds of thousands of bicentennial tourists were caught in one of the worst traffic jams in Washington's history. There were far more tourists than expected and far too few buses. Worse, buses that were available could not move for hours. The board was embarrassed by this failure in a fishbowl. Ironically, although a dramatic stimulus was needed to alert the board that the bus system needed attention, this particular breakdown was not the fault of either the bus system or its management structure. Crowd estimates were supplied by the police, and Metro could not control traffic conditions. But despite the inaccuracy of the attribution of blame, after July 4 the board strongly supported shaking up the management structure.

Quenstedt appointed Nick Roll, a hard-driving Metro lawyer, trouble-shooter for the bus system, instructing him to report on bus management. Roll's report "amazed everybody,"[61] according to one board member, because it showed "no one knows who's responsible for what" (*Washington Star*, July 24, 1976). The reorganization proceeded despite top management turnover, as Quenstedt was replaced by a former Department of Transportation undersecretary, Ted Lutz, in November 1976. Quenstedt stayed on for several months to help carry out the reorganization, as the plan adopted by the

60. One is reminded of Samuel Huntington's proposition that one cannot decrease armed services' rivalry by integration but rather by stimulating cross-cutting cleavages (1961, p. 51).

61. Why his report amazed everybody is puzzling since the board-authorized Cresap report had warned of similar problems over a year before.

board was largely his (see Fig. 8). Note that unlike Graham's structure, Metro now has a consolidated office of bus service. Bus functions are distributed less diffusely in the current organization.

In terms of some of the above problems—the delays and the remoteness of top management from operational bus problems—the new structure appears to be an improvement (#32, #2). Bus garages have been renovated, buses are cleaner, and so forth.[62]

This improvement is partly due to personnel changes. Nick Roll is considered a far more energetic problem solver than his predecessor (#2). Whereas a former bus manager lamented that it was virtually impossible to get much done through Roll's predecessor (#14), such remarks were not made about Roll during interviewing.[63] At the top, Ted Lutz is less construction-oriented and more service-oriented than Graham and is regarded by the union as treating the two modes more even-handedly (#32).

That personnel changes made a difference indicates that some of the bus system's problems in 1973–76 derived from the *timing* of merger. In 1973 Metro was deeply involved in constructing the rail system. One expression of that preoccupation was the background and expertise of its general manager, who has been described as one of the greatest public builders since Robert Moses. Hence, personnel difficulties were not random; they could have been anticipated on the basis of Metro's task involvement at the time of integration. To intertwine an ailing bus system with an organization that had devoted ten years to planning and building a rail system

62. One veteran board member, long critical of Metro management's handling of the buses, now considers the bus system to be in adequate shape (#39).

63. Critics of Metro have implied that this apparent improvement is due as much to the fact that the bus managers are not initiating many suggestions as it is to the fact that Roll is more responsive. The Washington papers have noted that the bus managers are fairly old and set in their D.C. Transit ways; though competent, they are not inclined toward the strong leadership the bus system needed. If this is accurate, it is a problem outside the analytic scope of this study because it is not primarily a structural difficulty of the organization of the two modes. Had an independent bus authority been established, it is likely that the same group of D.C. Transit managers would have predominated (#14).

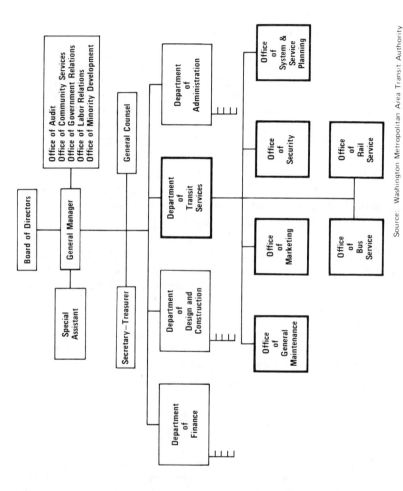

FIGURE 8 *Washington Metropolitan Area Transit Authority (1977)*

Source: Washington Metropolitan Area Transit Authority

was a mistake. It would have been less harmful by 1977 when a new general manager, one neither identified with nor personally invested in rail construction, arrived, accompanied by changes throughout the agency that made it more service-oriented.[64]

The feeling that buses are Metro's second-class mode has not, however, completely disappeared, as a recent controversy over security reveals. In May 1978 a woman bus driver was raped in southeast D.C., and drivers there went out on a wildcat strike. One of their chief complaints concerned the allocation of Metro security forces: virtually all of the 160-man force were assigned to trains and rail stations, even though there was much more crime in buses (*Washington Post*, May 19, 1978). There were reasons for this strange allocation. In Washington and the nation generally bus security falls in the local police force's jurisdiction, not the transit agency's. Furthermore, it is harder to protect many small buses than a few large stations and trains. So Metro officials argued. The drivers, however, were not appeased.

Because Metro is modally integrated, the security forces can be centrally allocated between the two modes, which would be difficult to arrange if the modes were organizationally separated. The bus drivers' aspirations concerning security are probably higher in the integrated organization than they would be in a single-mode agency, and the higher aspirations increase dissatisfaction and intraorganizational tension.

Subsequently, however, the security problem on buses improved. Metro shifted twelve transit police to buses (*Washington Post*, December 29, 1978), and "the most serious crimes have fallen sharply" (*Washington Star*, December 29, 1978). The leaders of the wildcat strike were "reasonably satisfied" with management's response (*Washington Post*, June 8, 1978; *Washington Star*, June 10, 1978).[65]

64. Metro planners would probably argue that integration was needed in that period (1973–77) in order to plan interface coordination. But that organizational integration was not a necessary condition, though it facilitated coordination planning.

65. In addition, bus-rail antagonisms were one of the three most prominently mentioned issues in a *Washington Post* interview conducted after a later wildcat strike of July 1978 (July 29, 1978).

Integration and Financial Confusion

As noted earlier, integration produces some financial advantages. What would otherwise involve drawn-out interorganizational negotiations over, for example, who should bear the fiscal burden of free transfers, is for Metro a smaller problem of intraorganizational accounting of modes' deficits. The organization's *total* deficit remains constant. There are, however, complications. Each mode operates on an annual deficit, which the political jurisdictions must cover. The formulas for allocating deficits must differ for the two modes. The bus formula is straightforward; it is based on estimated costs and revenues of operating in each jurisdiction. Because the technology is decomposable, each jurisdiction can independently decide how much bus service it wants; service additions or deletions are then reflected in the deficit the jurisdiction must pay. Although the rail deficit formula also breaks down charges to jurisdictions, rail service decisions cannot be decentralized. If the train runs in Virginia, it must do so in D.C. as well. Consequently, the Metro board must collectively decide on the annual rail service level and on the total deficit. Therefore, if jurisdictions prefer different service levels (as they do) and wish to cut service and costs individually, they can do so only by cutting the bus system.[66] Thus, the bus system, as the flexible component, becomes the financial shock absorber of Metro. As one board member remarked: "Every time we get into a financial problem, we look for bus service to cut . . . " (*Washington Star*, April 7, 1978).[67]

Nevertheless, had buses and rail been organizationally separated but the political jurisdictions maintained budgets

66. Most of the political jurisdictions have a category in their budget summaries of "mass transit subsidy costs." If a county supervisor thinks that figure is excessive, he will quickly learn that the only way to reduce it is to cut Metrobus (#3, #4T).

67. Of course, cutting bus service is merely one method of decreasing operating deficits. Probably more important is the rate of fare increases. One group, well articulated by former board member Joe Wholey, presses for increases to match inflation and for a separation of efficiency pricing (fares) and equity considerations (selling flashpasses at reduced rates to the poor). The hold-the-line group, usually the D.C. contingent, wants to keep the fare

with functional categories, a similar result might have occurred. A county supervisor, scanning the budget summary and observing that the county was spending too much on total transit, would soon learn that buses can be locally controlled whereas trains cannot. The modes' technological differences, allowing decision-makers to make certain decentralized service/budget choices but not others, probably swamp organizational differences.

Although the political jurisdictions' budget summaries contain a single mass transit entry, it is elsewhere disaggregated into the two modes' deficits. Thus, service level and subsidy decisions might also be based on how large a deficit each mode is producing by itself. Consequently, Metro's accounting rules acquire a new significance; they influence the public image of each mode's financial well-being. For example, the author was told that Metro was planning to change the accounting of transfers. Previously the free rail-to-bus transfer had been split down the middle; now the bus office would have to absorb all of it.[68] A Metro planning official said: "Therefore the bus subsidy will increase, and rail subsidy will decrease." Question: "Which could mean that more bus service will be cut back?" Answer: "It could" (#4).[69]

---

increases to one-half the Consumer Price Index increases. For other Wholey suggestions that avoid using the bus system as the financial shock absorber, see the *Fairfax Journal*, November 15, 1978.

68. This change was opposed by several staffers because they believed that a free transfer was a system benefit, unattributable to any one mode (#37). Several of the suburban board members also opposed the change, but it was one item of a compromise package, which the board passed five to one (WMATA, *Board Minutes*, April 6, 1978). The D.C. Department of Transportation is also unhappy with the new arrangement, for it is apprehensive that the cost of absorbing the free transfer—and consequently the burden on the bus system—will continue to grow (#43).

69. The author has been told that price theory yields no nonarbitrary method for allocating revenue to complementary services such as a bus-rail trip. If that is so, then the decision must either be negotiated, as it was between AC and BART, or mandated; it cannot be empirically established. Because there are two distinct deficit allocation formulas, revenue for each mode must be computed. Interdependence of complementary service makes it difficult to do this objectively.

Service Monopoly Disadvantages

Integrated organizations need not be internally unredundant, but Metro's service is nonduplicative as a matter of policy. The suburban directors in particular have stressed eliminating duplicate routes wherever possible (#4). The staff, more cautious, has in some instances pointed out to the board that apparent duplications are in fact lines serving different patrons (e.g., local and commute). Exactly how much organizational consensus prevails on this policy is difficult to discern; one staffer recalled vigorous discussion about the wisdom of at least the timing of cuts (#1). These discussions were not evident to outsiders, as Metro appeared to take a unified stand on eliminating duplication. Indeed, Metro planners had assumed since 1968 that bus and rail would be complements, not substitutes; service monopoly was a long-standing idea.

Unlike problems caused by the integrated organizational structure, where we focused on internal dynamics, disadvantages of service monopoly draw our attention outside the agency. The rail opening resulting in the most substantial bus turnback was phase two in the summer of 1977. As both suburb and city were affected, we can compare their reactions to advantage.

When the rail line to Virginia opened, most[70] Virginia lines were turned back at rail stations west of the Potomac River, and buses from southeast Washington were turned back at stations on the downtown side of the Anacostia River. At top management insistence (#15, #25), the change was not instantaneous: it took about one month to alter all the routes. This gradual staging undoubtedly eased the transition, enabling Metro to work out some of the interface's bugs and patrons to become accustomed to new travel patterns. Nonetheless, patrons complained vociferously about two problems.

70. According to the phase three plan (WMATA, 1977a), fifty-nine routes (43 percent) continued to go through, though many of these had decreased frequency. It is uncertain whether this figure is accurate: interviews and newspapers implied that a higher proportion was turned back. A Metro routing planner guessed that one-third of the Virginia lines continued to go through (#41).

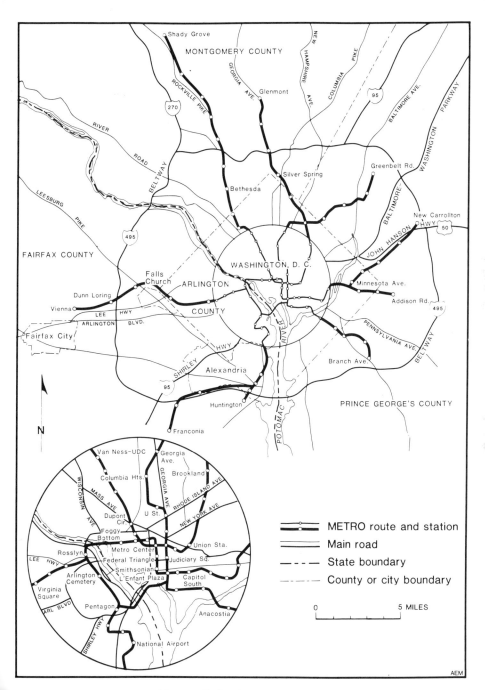

MAP 2   *Metro and the Washington, D.C., Area*

1.   Many poor people live in the Anacostia section of south-east Washington, and the bus turnbacks burdened them financially. Previously they could ride from Anacostia to downtown for $.80 round trip; after the turnback they had to transfer from bus to rail, or even bus-rail-bus in some cases, and their transit expenses as much as doubled. Compounding their grievance, the train afforded them little convenience: the train ride was short, and because the transfer station was across the Anacostia River, the buses still had to cross the Anacostia and since the worst traffic was always encountered on the bridges, patrons still had to endure the worst bottle-necks of their trips. (A Metro staffer said that some staffers thought that Metro should have waited until rail had crossed into Anacostia before starting the turnbacks [#1].)

The strength of the people of Anacostia's reaction sur-prised Metro staffers (#9);[71] they had underestimated the im-pact of the increased fare. The complaints quickly reached the D.C. board members, who were sensitive to the charge that Metro benefited affluent white suburbanites far more than poor black residents of Washington (WMATA, *Board Minutes*, August 4, 1977). The southeasterners' financial hardship was eased when Metro added buses running between transfer stations and downtown: with free bus-bus transfers, pas-sengers paid no more than the old fare. The outcries died down, suggesting that, indeed, the fare hike had mattered most.[72]

2.   In the west the more affluent Virginians seemed dis-turbed more by service changes than by increased fares (#9). The Virginia service, particularly AB&W's, had been good, and now many commuters were forced to transfer to a system that was unproven and initially unreliable.[73] Complaints

71. A Metro marketing supervisor who has handled consumer complaints observed that Anacostia riders are usually quite passive; hence the surprise when they reacted to the phase two changes (#40).

72. It puzzled me that Metro elected to install back-to-back routes rather than reinstating the old through routes. When I pursued this question, I was informed that this was done to preserve the policy of zero duplicate routes—at least in appearance.

73. The transfers were often uncomfortable because the stations, esca-lators, ticket machinery, and fare gates had been designed for train headways

peaked in the opening months of August and September (#3T). Metro responded by reestablishing a few through bus routes southwest of Washington and, more importantly, by improving the train's reliability. Metrorail's reliability improved more rapidly than had BART's, and it had another advantage over BART in its greater technical conservatism: trains were designed from the beginning to allow both automatic and manual operation. This technological redundancy enabled relatively reliable service even in the face of breakdowns. Although in July only 80 percent of train trips were completed without breakdown, by October it jumped to 95 percent, and in January it was 98 percent (*Washington Star*, September 25, 1977; WMATA, 1978a). As a result of improved reliability and customers' increased familiarity with rail, complaints tapered off after September,[74] and patronage started increasing faster[75] in November and December.[76]

When a later step of phase two opened the line to Silver Spring, Maryland, in February 1978, there were very few negative reactions (#1; *Washington Star*, February 6, 1978; *Gaithersburg* [Maryland] *Gazette*, February 9, 1978).[77] The train did

---

of two minutes; with a six-minute headway, the trains in the afternoon dumped larger pulses of people than the equipment had been designed to handle. Bottlenecks resulted. To make matters worse, some of the ticket and gate equipment were initially unreliable.

74. This claim is supported by the newspapers and local Virginia transportation staffers. Metro keeps some records on customer complaints, and I had hoped to check the newspaper accounts and human memory by constructing a trend line from Metro data. Unfortunately, the data are considered rather unreliable (#40), and two critical months (October and November 1977) are missing. However, the same official said that the complaints of rail delays have definitely diminished, suggesting that complaints about the forced shift from bus to rail have also declined.

75. Of course, one cannot say how many trips would have been made had the parallel lines been maintained.

76. While total transit ridership increased 2.64 percent from July 1976 to July 1977 (the month before turnbacks started), the increase from August to August was only 0.23 percent, September only 0.39 percent, and October 1977 0.83 percent *less* than a year earlier. But November was up 1.11 percent, and December up 2.13 percent (WMATA, 1978a).

77. However, there were complaints from the Brookland area of D.C. (*Washington Afro-American*, February 25, 1978; WMATA, *Board Minutes*, March 9, 1978).

not require a debugging period as it had during the early stage of phase two. In fact, the rail system, opening in a snowstorm, performed more dependably than either buses or autos (*Washington Star*, February 7, 1978). Because there was no Maryland-D.C. equivalent of the Shirley Highway, buses had to slog along congested roads, and the trains beat buses from Silver Spring to downtown by considerable margins.

In analyzing these reactions to the diminution of service redundancy, five points should be made.

1.   An obvious implication of redundancy theory is that the more reliable one channel is, the less are duplicates needed. Metrorail is reasonably reliable.

2.   Few commuter bus routes in Washington were or are as competitive with rail as AC is with BART. The Maryland routes in particular lack AC's freeway-plus-metered-bridge approach to downtown. We can therefore expect that when Metrorail extends out to Landover and Bethesda, Maryland, travelers will save time by switching to rail, and, as in the Silver Spring opening, few will complain.

3.   Metro's response to Anacostia's protests over service cuts indicates that users of one mode can be heard by an integrated, dual-mode organization. It is not *necessary* that modal clientele be represented by modally specialized agencies such as AC.[78] Metro's locally appointed board, combined with a rule that two members from any jurisdiction constitute a veto, ensure a measure of responsiveness to users' dissatisfactions.[79] Metro planners may resent the response to Ana-

78.   The federated political structure also permits a differentiated response to the turnbacks. For example, at the Minnesota, D.C., station opening in 1979, the D.C. government improved bus service to Bennington, D.C., while at the nearby New Carrolton station the Prince George's County, Maryland, government gave transit riders less choice (*Washington Post,* December 3, 1978).

79.   Less than one year after the Anacostia complaints erupted, the D.C. municipal government requested that Anacostia bus service be studied. The study indicated that service was inferior, particularly in midday (*Washington Post,* June 23, 1978). Metro then beefed up some of its runs. The jurisdictional governments are relatively visible alternative channels of influence; transit users that do not receive satisfaction from Metro can try their local government.

costia as an oiling the squeaking wheel that undermines economic rationality, but the response's political rationality, its stabilizing of WMATA's coalition, is evident.

4. Metrorail's expansion across the Anacostia River and across the Potomac River to the Pentagon should further placate dissatisfied ex-bus riders: the train will save them time by by-passing former bus bottlenecks. The modal transfer will make some sense to riders.

5. The flashpass, if widely used, will reduce complaints that are due to the financial hardship imposed by the first transfer procedure.

Service Monopoly, Episodic Breakdowns, and Latent Redundancies

The reader will recall that AC and BART can substitute for each other in the event of mechanical breakdown. It was conjectured, however, that most organizations possess reserve capacity in case of emergency; independent organizations are not a necessary condition for maintaining this latent redundancy.[80] Thus, when flooding rendered part of Metrorail inoperative in August 1977, buses filled the gap. This substitution has happened about twelve times since rail opened (#20) and seems to be routinized.[81] When trains are disabled and require substitutions,[82] communication between rail and bus offices appears to be swift and easy, a matter of walking a few yards from one office to another (#45).[83]

80. Whether the reserve of a single organization is sufficient for worst case emergencies is another question.

81. I do not know how formalized this arrangement is. In at least one case the bus office informally stashed extra buses in reserve (#20).

82. Thus far the communication is not reciprocal: the bus section rarely contacts the rail. For obvious technological reasons, the rail system cannot come to the aid of buses when the latter suffer from episodic breakdowns. The technological differences between bus and rail swamp the organizational differences between integrated Metro and unintegrated AC-BART: assistance tends to be asymmetrical in both cases.

83. But a Metro official observed that the organizationally and spatially more separated New York subway and bus divisions have similar assistance arrangements. A phone call suffices for these also.

As for strikes, the second kind of episodic disturbance, WMATA has suffered only one that lasted more than a day, a wildcat strike in July 1978. Because the workers belonged to the same union local,[84] the strike shut down the entire public transit system[85] of the Washington area. (Though non-sanctioned, the strike spread from mechanics to drivers.) Thus the integrated structure and monopolistic service jointly influenced the course of events: the former by increasing the probability that all operators would strike simultaneously, and the latter by ensuring that even if bus and rail crews did *not* go out together, there would be no backup for lost service.

Not surprisingly, downtown traffic was reported to be "unusually heavy" during the seven-day walkout (*Washington Post*, July 26, 1978). However, Metro management succeeded in running the trains, at a reduced level, by using supervisors and administrative personnel, so the transit system was not totally disabled. To a degree unanticipated by the author, internal substitution of personnel[86] compensated for monopolistic service's vulnerability to disruption.

The Formation of Local Bus Associations

Patrons' dissatisfaction with monopoly transit service can be signaled by complaints, switching to the auto, not traveling—or by contracting with alternative transit organizations. Transit could be supplied, à la Ostrom-Tiebout-Warren (1961), by private or public entities, and as it is a standardized service, riders could easily compare options.[87] In

84. Metro management, using court pressure, induced a merger of independent locals in the early seventies because it feared contract "whipsawing"—each local striving to outdo a contract given to a rival (*Washington Star*, July 20, 1978).

85. This excludes taxis, of course.

86. This indicates a vertical redundancy of skill. This work has emphasized horizontal rather than vertical redundancies.

87. The search for alternate suppliers of bus service is generally an instance of organizational competition rather than service redundancy; the issue is which organization shall supply the only local bus service rather than multiple suppliers providing parallel service.

the Washington area several alternative bus services have sprung up in the last half-decade. Most of these—dial-a-ride services in Anacostia, Columbia, Fairfax, and Gaithersburg—have failed rather quickly. Two have lasted longer: Montgomery County's "Ride-On" program and the community of Reston's express commuter service.

"Ride-On" was not a response to bus turnbacks and elimination of service duplication: it was created because of discontent in Montgomery County, Maryland, over the quality of local service and the high subsidy cost of Metrobus. Smaller, quieter buses for neighborhood routes and lower drivers' wages were sought. Metro could not provide the latter and was slow to provide the former.[88] The county started its program in 1976. By buying its small buses without federal aid, it avoided the sometimes costly federal labor regulations. Drivers are frequently college students working part time, and the labor situation is the main cause of the program's success. Should "Ride-On" grow much larger, Metro's union local will probably try to unionize the drivers (#32), which would wipe out the cost advantage of a county-run system. Since the county already has its preferred buses and routes, if its drivers are unionized, merger with Metro would probably not greatly change its service-cost package.[89] As a temporary program, however, "Ride-On" has proven a successful alternative to Metrobus (although success—high patronage—has worn out equipment at an unexpectedly fast rate; *Montgomery Journal*, March 7, 1979).

The presence of an alternate organization offering a different set of service characteristics did not stimulate Metro to offer a better package. Rivalry had no effect for the reason that since Metro must use unionized labor, it could not offer as attractive a program as "Ride-On" for the same price.

The suburb of Reston had formed an association, the Reston (Virginia) Commuter Bus, Inc., to arrange for special commuter express service. By 1975 the association had concluded that Metro's prices were too high and determined to contract

88. Metro will, however, negotiate with the jurisdictions over different *quantities* of service.

89. Unionization is unrelated to the issue of bus-rail merger. Had the bus firms been transformed into an autonomous bus agency, it would have been unionized.

with a private bus organization, Colonial Transit. Colonial proposed supplying the service for $45 per bus trip, plus fares, as compared with Metro's $66.91 (*Washington Post*, September 6, 1975). Metro opposed the change, and the dispute, an interstate affair involving a private carrier, went before the Transit Commission. In September 1975 the commission ruled against Metro and allowed the Reston association to contract with Colonial. By early 1979, however, there was a growing number of complaints about Colonial's service (*Washington Post*, January 12, 1979), and in March Reston ended the contract and rejoined Metro.[90]

Notwithstanding the difficulties encountered by Reston and Montgomery County, rumors circulated that the Virginia counties, wishing to reduce the bus subsidy, will eventually form their own bus agency and withdraw from Metrobus (*Washington Post*, July 31, 1978; #39). But such rumors have persisted for several years without materializing, and it remains to be seen whether they will ever do so.

Conclusions

The author had expected that the central issue in Washington would be the service (route) relations of the two modes—controversies associated with turnbacks and so forth. This was, in fact, a heated issue, as officials' reactions to questions clearly indicated. But the field research suggests that the management of service was a more central problem than the service pattern itself. I had anticipated that the two modes would be managed by two divisions; the rather chaotic structure of 1973 to 1976 was a surprise.

As argued above, the difficulties resulting from dispersed modal authority were a joint product of merger[91] and Jackson

90. Reston had difficulty in shopping around for alternative transit suppliers; no other charter company expressed an interest in supplying commute service (*Reston Times*, January 15, 1979).

91. The claim that the policy of nonduplicating service was not determined by the modes' management structure is corroborated by the fact that the reorganizations did not affect that policy in the slightest. Yet these two variables were not unrelated. Had Metro established a partially independent bus division, then the bus system would have progressed more rapidly and

Graham's management style. This conclusion is not theoretically pleasing because a leader's administrative strategy is a random variable; it is not completely determined by the simple variables of organizational structure under consideration here. Leadership, however, is partly correlated with structure: Graham personified and amplified Metro's organizational attention to the task of building a rapid rail system. One could predict, therefore, that a merged organization led by Graham would have that orientation. But this orientation would also have been consistent with establishing a separate (though not powerful) bus division. Indeed, given the preoccupation with rail and the premerger reluctance of top Metro managers to assume responsibility for buses, one might well have predicted that they would have *preferred* to set up an operationally autonomous division. Unfortunately, they did not choose that path, and the bus system was the worse for it.

The impairment of bus management due to merger had been ameliorated by the 1976 reorganization and by Ted Lutz's redirecting Metro toward operation, although certain problems, such as the excessively complicated bus route structure,[92] persist.[93] The timing of management improvement, however, has been less than ideal: the bus system's management can now better afford close intertwining with rail than it could in the years immediately following merger, yet the sequence that obtained in fact was just the reverse of this.

---

buses would have become more competitive with rapid rail. Hence, bus patrons would have been more incensed by the elimination of parallel bus routes.

92. Even the *Washington Post*, long a supporter of Metro, lamented: "Bus routes, fares, and schedules are known only to certain native Washingtonians, who learned them from the griots over the generations" (April 19, 1979). The lack of a bus route map continues to be a sore point between Metro and the D.C. Department of Transportation. The former asserts that to produce a map when the system is rapidly changing is too difficult (#41); the latter argues that riders need maps most precisely when the system is in flux (#43).

93. A veteran transit activist and rail backer remarked: "Metro still had got a lot of problems with its bus system . . . operating things that other organizations can do (with one hand) tied behind their backs . . ." (#46). He also agreed, however, that matters had improved after Lutz took charge.

Regarding the fiscal effects of integration, it will be some time yet before these have been sorted out. The problem of estimating merger's financial consequences is a reflexive difficulty: integration resulted in convoluted internal accounting rules and subsidy schemes, and these make it hard for outsiders to grasp the two modes' true financial condition.

Regarding service, it is clear that, as hypothesized in Chapter One, duplication is considered illegitimate except by its direct beneficiaries, that is, would-be users of parallel bus service. Whereas no norm inhibited the *private* bus companies from competing with or opposing NCTA, as soon as buses went public, support for creating an independent agency that would compete with Metro evaporated.

It was not the technical efficacy of redundancy that was questioned so much as its allocative efficiency:[94] the board believed that parallel service was not financially warranted.[95] Board members, in particular the Virginians, have been as concerned with representing local taxpayers as they have transit users. The enthusiasm for eliminating service redundancy is directly related to a jurisdiction's fiscal properties. Virginia, relying solely on the sensitive property tax, is most enthusiastic; D.C., recipient of more federal aid for transit, is least.

Given the financial basis of the board's antiredundancy policy, it is odd that the monetary gains from creating service monopoly are as uncertain as they seem to be (WMATA, 1977a, p. 66; WMATA, 1976a, p. 5). This combination of overt emphasis and underlying uncertainty suggests that eliminating parallel routes was as much symbolic fiscal politics as substantive, that the appearance of eliminating "excess" mattered at least as much as the actual amount of money saved. This does not imply that the board was intentionally deluding the public about the saving; board members were probably unaware that their staff's estimates were subject to a large margin of error.

94. Unlike planning redundancies, where efficacy *is* in question, it is usually obvious that operational redundancies work.

95. Certain critics of Metro, such as the *D.C. Gazette*, maintain that the board eliminated modal competition to ensure that rail's patronage figures appeared adequate.

Regarding the negative effect of service monopoly, the worst is over. First, Metrorail's period of chronic unreliability was brief, and there is no reason to believe that it will recur. Second, the most inconvenient turnbacks, where buses had to traverse the worst bottlenecks before reaching transfer stations, will be eliminated as rail extends into the suburbs. And the longer the ride, the more the train's speed advantage will pay off. Third, the pain of added fares on bus-rail transfers will be lessened by flashpasses. Routing inconveniences will persist, however, particularly in D.C., where some riders must take bus-rail-bus where once they could take one through bus.

Unanswered is the normative question of whether transit patrons should have been allowed a choice between modes. Though it is true that many patrons were and are inconvenienced by the elimination of parallelism, an *unqualified* rule of user sovereignty is not justifiable for services that are not financially self-sustaining. Conventional opposition to public redundancies resting on this fiscal principle does have a case; nonusing taxpayers must be represented as well as users. The problem in Washington is more one of equity than of undifferentiated consumer sovereignty; eliminating service redundancy hurt inner city residents disproportionately.

The Long View

Transportation planners and economists blessed with a long-time perspective may suggest that this chapter's focus on service monopoly missed a key point: the process's critical period was the sixties, before construction. It was then that the fundamental choices of mode, system size, and financing were made. If buses were ever to have provided a feasible alternative to rail, they would have had to have done so in that period, not during the operational stage (Hamer, 1976, p. 112).[96] At the very least, choice between modes should focus on extensions of the system, not on portions already built (Haefele, 1976).

96. But transportation economist Gabriel Roth (1977) has suggested considering, even after rail opened, turning the system into busways.

But even if we take the long view and examine the potential of buses versus rail in the sixties, it is doubtful that sharply different conclusions would be reached. The paucity of highways in the Washington area make buses an entirely different proposition from that in the Twin Cities or the Bay Area. Without an expansion of highways, it is unlikely that buses would have been an acceptable alternative to transit users. But given the threat that freeway construction presented to residential areas, it is equally unlikely that expanding the highways would have been acceptable. Finally, it is unlikely that removing existing lanes on highways and D.C. streets from automobile use and giving them to buses would have been tolerated. The uproar from commuters would have been deafening. Thus, a politically feasible bus solution may not have existed. Consequently, the weakness of transit planning competition, that the bus firms were more concerned with protecting their property rights than with developing detailed alternatives, was not crucial in the long run. Even if the bus companies had folded in the early sixties and had been taken over by a public bus agency, which then provided more planning competition, the final outcome probably would have been unchanged in terms of the system's basic configuration and modal mix.

6

Theory and Evidence

Authors would be saved much work if case studies could speak for themselves. Alas, to let the facts speak for themselves is a Baconian fantasy; they require interpretation. This chapter provides three analyses. First, I compare the different organizational structures conducting transit planning in the three metropolitan areas and examine how the structural variations influenced the process and outcome of planning. Second, I compare the operational redundancy of AC and BART with the operational monopoly of Metro to examine the advantages and disadvantages of those arrangements. Third, I analyze the effects of variably timed redundancy on decision-making, that is, the different effects of competitive planning and redundant operations.

Planning Comparisons

Every episode of planning prompts two major questions. First, was the outcome of planning satisfactory to the relevant constituencies? Second, how rational was the planning process itself? Was a substantial range of alternatives investigated, were they evaluated fairly, were planning estimates accurate, and were plans modified in the light of new information?

Obviously the outcome criterion is the one we are ultimately interested in, for we will not applaud a planning process, no matter how procedurally rational it seems, if it usually generates unacceptable consequences. Yet in the face of factors beyond an organization's control, a sensible planning process may produce unacceptable outcomes, and mediocre planning may occasionally produce satisfactory ones. Hence a reasonable evaluation must include procedural criteria.

The Search for Alternatives

As noted in Chapter Two, the effort devoted to designing major alternatives is at the heart of planning. If the design of alternatives is biased or given short shrift, little else accomplished in planning will matter.[1] Of course, an organization can influence a final outcome through ways other than skewing alternatives. Even if a design process had created several genuine alternatives, an evaluation could be biased to make one option appear superior. But it is harder to bias evaluation—once an array of genuine alternatives has been made available to a wide set of authorities—than to skew the design of options in the first place. The former is more visible and more risky.

In the oldest of the three cases, the search for alternatives was most circumscribed. BART planners speedily considered only rapid rail systems. AC contemplated more options, both rail and bus, but only because it was taking over the old, multimodal Key System. Thus, AC's early behavior reflected less a search for alternatives than a simple takeover orientation. In any case, AC's early multimodal position was soon whittled down to a single mode after the Public Utilities Commission allowed the Key System to abandon its trains.[2]

1. This is an exaggeration. It is possible to create a sound transit system despite an impoverished search for alternatives—AC is the obvious example. But in such cases it is the *management* of the single alternative that counts, not planning.

2. We must keep in mind that in the fifties there was no formalized planning process mandating a thorough search; that neither agency conducted one was not considered unusual at the time.

In Washington, the picture was more complex. The design of transit alternatives was initially (1959-63) more sequential than simultaneous.[3] The much-criticized Mass Transit Survey's highway-oriented plan was replaced by the rail-oriented design of NCTA, Metro's predecessor. The NCTA solution was in turn accused of paying insufficient attention to the express bus solution (Martin Wohl, cited in Hamer, 1976). Search was probably more even-handed in the first study. Though community discontent indicated that it included too many miles of freeway, it was not faulted for having completely ignored other options. NCTA's 1963 proposal, though more detailed than the Mass Transit Survey, was criticized for having treated the express bus option unimaginatively (Hamer, 1976, p. 105).

The most thoroughly examined alternative to rail was, of course, highways, but after 1963 NCTA was stripped of its authority to review highway projects. The resulting planning fragmentation produced neither an enlightening planning competition[4] nor investigations into new options. Instead, the conflict between highway planners and NCTA focused on financing. Eventually both sides grew willing to mute their

3. This sequential process strongly resembled Charles Lindblom's model (1965) of disjointed partisan mutual adjustment, a process which will be examined in Chapter Seven as an alternative to competitive planning. The Washington case is a clear example of how partisan mutual adjustment can mimic or simulate a comprehensive decision-maker with responsibility for all options in an issue area. Although at first NCTA regarded itself as the comprehensive transportation planner, capable of making decisions between mutually exclusive modal investments, this stance produced too much political controversy to be a stable position, and disjointed mutual adjustment became the dominant pattern. By late 1964 NCTA had retreated to advocating rail only; it no longer opposed highway construction. In the interim, however, neighborhood groups in D.C., opposing the building of freeways through their backyards, had organized themselves. Though the choice process had become specialized—the rail advocate, NCTA, having little to do with its former allies, the antifreeway groups—transit and highways continued to be mutually exclusive alternatives (albeit due to a thoroughly disjointed process). The *collective* result of these specialized endeavors, a rapid rail system and a greatly diminished highway network in Washington, was very close to what NCTA had tried to accomplish as a comprehensive planner.

4. The *Washington Post* editorialized: "In seven long months there have been no new engineering data, no new ideas, no new proposals. The format is now standardized" (June 11, 1962).

opposition to enable both alternatives to go through.[5] Thus, peace was achieved at the cost of highway and rail no longer being regarded as substitutes, a move the "radical" wing of the rail coalition regarded as a sellout. This logrolling among advocates is generally at the taxpayers' expense:[6] the total financial pie for transportation projects is expanded to accommodate all major alternatives.

Similarly, the intratransit conflict between rail and bus advocates was resolved by Congress protecting the bus owners' property rights rather than by evaluating the alternatives. Not only did the bus owners fail to create specific alternatives to NCTA's rail plan; even their criticism rarely rose above the superficial. For example, though they argued that rail was unnecessary, given the Washington area's low density, they presented no counterprojections of transit demand.

Thus, there is no guarantee that a policy conflict with the potential of being a full-fledged battle over options will in fact become one. Instead, it may be settled collusively, that is, by interagency negotiation smoothing over the rough edges of competition. This type of conflict resolution is not without surface appeal, for it eases "frictions" between different units of government. The *Washington Post*, during the precollusion period of intense conflict between rail and highway proponents, editorialized: "The incessant snapping and snarling among the city's transportation agencies is a reproach even to our standards of local government" (May 7, 1962). But intergovernmental calm was to be purchased at the cost of avoiding serious critical evaluations, a price that was rather steep.

In the Twin Cities, the most comprehensive search, in breadth of alternatives covered, was the first Metropolitan Transit Commission study. Even without competitive planning MTC's studies were more thorough than those in the other cases.[7] In part, this was a function of time: transit planning had become more sophisticated between the days of AC

5. However, highways were eventually defeated.

6. This logrolling would also have been at the expense of the neighborhoods that would lose territory to the intrusive projects.

7. The U.S. Office of Technology Assessment, which studied transit planning in nine metropolitan areas, concluded that the Twin Cities' was superior (U.S. Congress, 1976a).

and BART planning in the fifties and the Minnesota planning in the late sixties. Moreover, the planning teams may have been more open-minded in Minnesota than elsewhere. Competitive planning did not expand the *breadth* of search beyond the scope of MTC's efforts. Both Professor Anderson's Personal Rapid Transit group and the Metro Council covered alternatives that had been examined in the MTC's first two studies. Rather, to use the decision tree image, they increased the *depth* of search.[8] Highly innovative options such as Personal Rapid Transit had been scrutinized only cursorily and dismissed by MTC's first report. (The second report covered it in more depth.) Options such as these, having both a potential for large service improvements and much technical uncertainty, merit careful examination: their potential warrants it and their risk demands it. It turned out that even the staid bus alternative had more possibilities than MTC's early reports had indicated. In 1970, for example, bus ramp metering (giving buses higher priority at freeway entrances regulated by traffic lights) was dismissed with the remark that "the concept is untried, and a host of engineering, operational, and institutional problems are foreseen" (Voorhees, 1969). Yet ramp-metered express buses proved successful.

Although much competitive planning appeared to raise issues already covered, as MTC persistently argued, in fact only the major branches of the decision tree were retraced; the detail was often new.[9] Unfortunately, evaluating this decision process is hindered by the difficulty of appreciating the ex ante problems of estimating the value of deeper searches. After the fact, it is misleadingly easy for an observer to note missteps and missed opportunities, to criticize an organization for not investigating this or that option more intensively. Yet in all fairness one must note that the Voorhees report's conclusion on PRT systems in 1969, based on a shal-

8. The low-capital transit alternative, such as the Citizens' League idea that the concept of transit connoted vehicles that carry passengers (rather than signifying a technology), did broaden the search. MTC had not considered it in its early planning.

9. Perhaps the most important effect of this detailed search of alternatives was that the legislators were not forced into feeling that if they rejected rapid rail they would be rejecting transit altogether. There were credible alternatives they could back.

low search, turned out to be substantially correct. Though mistaken about a few particulars, it was the same conclusion reached by the much deeper investigation of the last report six years later. So to point out, ex post, that several decision branches were underexplored is to underestimate the uncertainty confronting the decision-makers, to overlook the sensible guesses they did make, and to obscure the point that they were *guessing* about the value of exploring further. Nevertheless, largely because individuals estimated the utility of different paths differently, Twin Cities transit planning had great breadth and depth.[10] Its comprehensiveness in both respects vastly exceeded that of the other cities.

Iteration in Planning

In addition to comprehensive search, transportation planning textbooks prescribe iteration. They do so on good grounds. Changes in task environments, whether changed preferences of publics or new factual premises, should be incorporated into new plans. Redesign indicates that planners have reconsidered their original concepts and have regarded them as tentative and possibly erroneous. If plans remain unchanged throughout the process, one suspects that the planning is a sham in which the final design is predetermined[11] and the technical studies mere gloss on a process determined elsewhere. Thus, the presence or absence of iteration in planning is a good indicator of whether a bureaucracy is genuinely trying to learn from experience.

In the AC-BART case, where mutual planning isolation was quickly secured, neither organization affected each other's designs, with the exception of AC's becoming an all-bus system after its loss of the Key trains in 1957. After that, AC's design changed little. BART likewise wound up with the

10. It would be interesting to examine whether the legitimacy of planning varied with the breadth and depth of search, i.e., would a more exhaustive search normally be considered more legitimate? Unfortunately, I do not have the data required to answer this question.

11. Precisely this belief was expressed to me by opponents of MTC in the Twin Cities. Those who fear rule by technocrats often believe that formal prescriptions of broad search and redesign are not genuinely followed.

technology envisioned from the beginning (Parsons et al., 1956). Though it did subsequently adapt to community preferences on system size, track location, and station siting, the system's basic configuration was set by bond election and its basic technology well before that. Subsequent modifications were marginal and achieved only by dint of considerable effort of well-organized communities.[12]

In Washington's somewhat more competitive environment, planning displayed considerable flexibility. Modal composition changed dramatically from 1959 to 1963; later, system size and routes changed considerably. The latter sequence of changes did not, however, indicate that the transit agency was learning about community preferences but rather that Congress was alternately loosening and tightening fiscal constraints. Therefore, flexibility in Metro planning resulted from a conventional hierarchical relation, which, unlike competitive planning, changed the system's size but not its technology or service strategy.

Only in the most competitive environment of Minneapolis-St. Paul did the final system depart significantly from the original designs. The expanded but noncapital-intensive bus system of 1976 *had not been sought by any of the three major planning groups in 1972.* Even the closest, the Metro Council, had first envisaged expensive busways to control the traffic environment of buses.[13] The final choice was neither predetermined nor preempted by a technical planning apparatus. Unlike the other two cases, where the basic modal selections were made quite early, in the Twin Cities planning was permeable and open to influence for almost four years. This permeability facilitated the incorporation of revised estimates of key planning parameters, such as projected regional population and financial capacity.[14] In short, in Minneapolis-St. Paul planning meant learning.

12. Probably the most important "adaptation" occurred during construction when BART, responding to community pressure for less delay in opening, decided to eliminate preoperational testing.

13. It was not then realized that for certain highways, the buses' traffic environment could be controlled by a much cheaper method, ramp metering, termed by one planner "a poor man's busway."

14. Rather than altering community preferences, these were the content of organizational learning.

Planning Differences and Outcomes

Of course the ultimate test of an organizational structure is not the procedures it follows but the effectiveness of its programs. What are the relations between the planning structure and the worth of the planning outcomes?

AC-BART is the most complicated case to evaluate. On the one hand, the systems' mutual planning isolation combined with vague promises of future complementarity to produce overlapping operations. Given BART's unexpected technical weaknesses and AC's strikes, it was fortunate that overlapping occurred. Thus, ironically, overlapping at one stage was promoted by its absence in another.

Had the two organizations competed more persistently during planning, the most likely transit outcome, given that BART's coalition was more powerful,[15] would have been BART's trains plus AC's buses without the transbay routes.[16] That outcome would have discomfited commuters, particularly during the first few years of dual service. Of course, had BART been better designed technically,[17] then operational duplication would have been less needed. In that hypothetical situation, planning isolation, by fostering the avoidance of choice between modes when that choice was cheap, might then have created wasteful duplication.[18] As it was, however,

15. Because the two had few overlaps in the East Bay and because the East Bay badly needed local transit service, even a prolonged planning fight would not have obliterated AC.

16. The only settlement that would differentiate jurisdictions without threatening the existence of *either* agency would be to give the transbay to BART.

17. During its development, BART could have benefited from a good dose of redundancy, in the sense of parallel problem solving (following Klein's model, 1962) and of more duplication built into its hardware (e.g., extra sidetracks for disabled trains and manual override in case the automatic train control system failed). These *intra*organizational redundancies at the component level are more efficient than macroredundancies at the systemic level, (Ross, 1980, pp. 320–322). The gist of the idea is that duplication of components prevents unreliability from cumulating too rapidly in a long series system.

18. However, this probably would have been correctable since had BART been a "turnkey" system (reliable from the beginning), AC would have been under great pressure to remove parallel routes.

operational redundancy was largely beneficial. Therefore, the lack of planning rivalry did have certain benign effects. This is an odd, almost paradoxical, conclusion to reach on behalf of planning monopoly.

In Washington, though transit planning competition was weak compared with Minnesota's, though noncapital-intensive options were poorly scrutinized, and though the Washington transit system would end up costing far more than the Twin Cities' system, we cannot easily conclude that the choice of rail was a mistake. For sociopolitical reasons[19] rapid rail is probably the most widely acceptable solution. Certainly it is less disruptive socially than highways or buses on new highways: few people were displaced, few homes destroyed. It is therefore doubtful that a more competitive transit planning would have produced a clearly superior out-come, that is, one preferred by all major constituencies.[20]

In Minneapolis, competitive planning proved beneficial. Perhaps that is too bold an assertion, but one grows weary of qualification, and most of those interviewed in Minnesota would agree with it as it stands. Compared with D.C., rail's financing and patronage were much riskier whereas buses were a much lower sociopolitical risk than they were in D.C. Furthermore, the actors involved almost unanimously agree that had the council avoided counterplanning,[21] the outcome would have been rail. Thus, monopolistic planning in the Twin Cities would have produced a needlessly expensive system.[22]

19. Rail is not the most cost-effective solution in terms of pure transit (movement) criteria.

20. A modally mixed system, akin to the 1965 plan wherein rail lines ended after crossing congestion bottlenecks, might have cost less than the existing system, and in terms of travel and social distribution they would have scored about the same. More extended competitive planning might have produced this outcome. However, negotiating an interjurisdictional financing formula would have been tricky.

21. That the PRT group caught the attention of the Senate subcommittee was also important.

22. Though bus operating expenses soared to unexpectedly high levels in 1976, that was partly reversible. The bus system contracted in the following years.

Negative Effects of Planning Redundancy

It must be acknowledged that planning rivalry in Minneapolis produced some negative side effects. Because the controversy involved high stakes and because the conflict, being uninstitutionalized, lacked rules of due process, the debate became personalized. This temporarily poisoned the political atmosphere. It is unlikely, for example, that current key officials, particularly legislators, could serenely contemplate any rapid rail proposals from MTC.

The personalized character of the conflict in the Twin Cities suggests that planning competition by itself cannot ensure better decision-making. How the competition is managed and resolved also matters. The less institutionalized are decision rules for resolving disagreements over factual premises, the greater the tendency to resolve issues politically, by organizational or personal influence. If planning competition is instituted without legitimating technically oriented conflict resolution, the process will tend to become politicized (see Fig. 9).

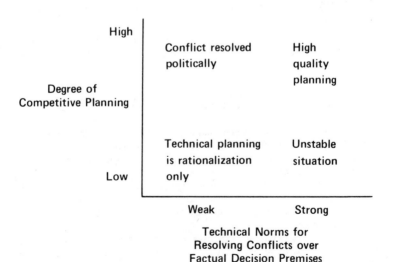

FIGURE 9   *Relation Between Competition and Technical Norms*

But if competitive planning needs to be buttressed by rules of due process, conversely those rules need the structural support of redundant planning. An excellent way to increase the probability that a bureaucracy adheres to normatively correct decision rules is to have another qualified agency check the first one by engaging in the same planning. The temptation to play funny games with a technical methodology is reduced if an agency realizes its games will be detected. In monopolistic settings, technical decision rules tend to degenerate. We need only note how often cost-benefit analysis has been distorted to serve organizational interests to substantiate this point.

Although competitive planning may politicize situations (in the absence of rules of due process), impassioned and acrimonious exchanges are also quite common in *noncompetitive* transportation planning;[23] consider, for example, the numerous, furious fights over inner-city highways. (And such heated frays have occurred in all three regions of this study.) Transit planning competition is more likely to *transform* conflict from the agency-community pattern of antifreeway conflicts into an interagency fight than it is to *create* conflict.

To summarize, the evidence presents a mixed picture on relations between planning structures and outcomes. Though planning competition was beneficial in Minneapolis, that it was limited in Washington was not devastating, and had it occurred in the Bay Area it may have proved dysfunctional.

Given the theoretical arguments for competitive planning, why do the data evince such an unclear pattern? The first reason is simple: since there are only a few *basic* options in transit planning, a single bureaucracy can design and evaluate them without missing any important possibilities. Transit system development is not equivalent in this regard to, for example, weapons systems development where significant innovations occur rapidly.

In the medium-run, fundamental alternatives[24] boil down

23. Of course the urban highway fights were intensely political, but they were noncompetitive in that the conflicts focused on a single mode rather than on a multiplicity of solutions as in the Twin Cities.

24. Personal Rapid Transit, which would be a major service gain over today's systems, will not be operational for quite some time.

to buses—with or without new highways—and rail.[25] There is thus a fifty-fifty chance that, in the grossest sense, the correct alternative would be chosen *regardless* of structure. It is therefore possible to be substantively right despite weaknesses in the planning process. And, following redundancy theory, the lower the probability of error, the fewer channels are required.

The second reason is a bit more subtle. Competitive planning is most effective when mistakes in rival proposals can be detected early in the process (Klein, 1962). Redundancy is doubly sensible in early planning because uncertainty is greatest and the cost of duplication lowest in that period. But if the uncertainty about the relative merit of rival plans is reduced slowly, then redundant planning is less economical because it is expensive to prolong the competition. Compare curves x and y in Figure 10. Curve x represents a time path of uncertainty reduction favorable to competitive planning, curve y an unfavorable path.

With this in mind we can understand why competitive planning would not have been extremely useful in Washington, D.C. Metro's major problem was cost overruns, and competitive planning might have been powerless to prevent this because the uncertainty-reducing curve for cost has the wrong shape. For planning rivalry to be effective, cost estimates must improve rapidly—before heavy construction has started. But the estimates of Metro's costs did not have that pattern; instead, they were nearly linear (see Fig. 11). Thus, even a vigorous rivalry between bus and rail planners in D.C. would have been hard put to reveal the true extent of rail's Achilles heel.

Whereas the reason why competitive planning would have had little impact in Washington is quite general, the reason why competitive planning could have backfired in the Bay Area is highly idiosyncratic. This conclusion derives from a counterfactual argument. The political resources of the potential rival planners, AC and BART, were unequal. Hence, a planning duel probably would have ended in a victory for rail.

25. Although transportation planners refer to a "virtually infinite range of alternative designs" (Morlock, 1978), that includes many variations on a few common themes.

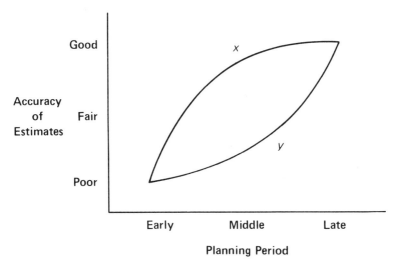

FIGURE 10 *Reduction of Uncertainty*

That outcome, *given* BART's flawed design, would have meant unredundant and unreliable transit service.

Thus, monopolistic or quasi-monopolistic planning in D.C. and the Bay Area was less harmful than the theoretical arguments of Chapters One and Two had predicted.

Competitive Planning Versus UMTA's Alternatives Analysis

To set these cases in the contemporary context of urban transit planning, we note that all predated the U.S. Department of Transportation's guidelines for transit planning. The department's Urban Mass Transit Administration (UMTA) now requires capital grant applicants to submit an alternatives analysis that specifies and evaluates plausible alternatives.

Although we have not included a study of transit planning conducted under UMTA's guidelines, it is instructive to scrutinize alternatives analysis because it institutionalizes the textbook model of planning described in Chapter Two. This

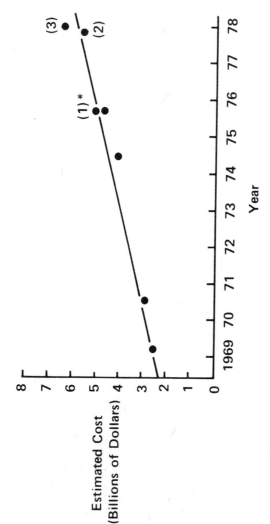

FIGURE 11 *Estimates of Metro's Cost*

*(1) includes, for the first time, an unfunded contingency of nearly $0.5 billion.

SOURCE: WMATA chronology, except for estimate (2), which is from a Baltimore *Evening Sun* interview with general manager Ted Lutz (June 22, 1978); and estimate (3), which is a *Washington Post* quote of a WMATA estimate (August 5, 1978).

model thrusts upon a single agency the responsibility for generating major alternatives, as well as for evaluating and pruning them until only one remains to be recommended to UMTA. Because only one bureaucracy generates alternatives and only one bureaucracy reviews them, specialization and monopoly, rather than duplication, characterize the process.

Alternative analysis developed over several years, having been modified in public conferences in 1975 and 1976. The manifest purpose was to compel local planners and officials to examine a greater variety of transit options than they were wont to do. UMTA promulgated five basic principles:

1. A mass transportation investment proposal must be consistent with an urban area's comprehensive, long-range transportation plan.

2. If a proposal includes a fixed guideway, then it should be developed incrementally.

3. Improved management of existing systems should be considered as a possible alternative or supplement to construction of capital facilities.

4. A proposal must determine which alternative is most economical and effective to achieve an area's social, environmental, and transportation goals.

5. There is to be "full opportunity for timely public involvement in the planning and evaluation process." (*Transportation Research Board*, 1977, p. 18)

UMTA maintained that these principles are needed because "the federal government must ensure that investment decisions premised on federal assistance are made only after full consideration of *all feasible alternatives* and with complete knowledge of the consequences" (ibid.; emphasis added). This rationalistic position, the keystone of alternatives analysis, requires that search not be limited to one predetermined option. In contrast to competitive, multiorganizational planning, alternatives analysis vests a single agency with the task of broad-spectrum search rather than relying upon a set of narrow-minded searchers.

The most obvious weakness in alternatives analysis is the naïve requirement that "all feasible alternatives" be considered. Even rationalistic planning texts warn that doing so entails investigating a hopelessly large number of options.

But UMTA's guidelines, acknowledging that constraints of time and money preclude exhaustiveness, are not wedded to this obvious mistake (ibid., p. 20). Instead, a "reasonable number" of alternatives must be considered. Replacing the definite but impossible by the feasible but fuzzy could open the door to systematic abuses, such as alternatives analyses truncated to serve applicants' interests. But vagueness was reduced by an admonition that alternatives must *sample* possible modal combinations, "so the local community can be aware of the choices available" (ibid., p. 20). In addition, the guidelines propose several nonmandatory search strategies, each informed by a different alternative-generating criterion such as investment level or service quality. Applicants using these suggestions to generate a list of options would indeed sample a wide range of possibilities. Further, though UMTA has declined to specify the alternatives that every analysis must include, the transportation planning community is now sufficiently aware[26] of a broad range of technologies so that alternatives analysis's de facto breadth is reasonably well defined.

Consequently, problems attending the development of alternatives will be due less to simple glaring omissions than to the varying degrees of intelligence, imagination, and thoroughness allocated to different options. If, for example, a transit agency had shown with flair and imagination how to exploit alternative X's best features, but treated alternative Y's potential in a lackluster manner, then the agency's analysis would be vulnerable not to the easily substantiated criticism of incompleteness but only to the subtler charge of unevenness.

If UMTA's reviewing staff has to detect subtle biases rather than mere omissions in applicants' alternatives analyses, what can we expect? How easily can its staff discern whether a specification of alternatives was even-handed or an evaluation fair? Because this is a difficult task, it is not surprising that the review of the process by the General Accounting

26. This was *not* true in the fifties and early sixties (U.S. Congress, Office of Technology Assessment, 1976c, p. 32). One could not then assume that a transit planner would be conversant with a broad spectrum of alternatives.

Office (GAO) noted several problems. Two were prominent: poor communication between Washington and local project sponsors and delayed UMTA identification of problems in submitted alternatives analyses (U.S. GAO, 1979, pp. 12, 22-23). UMTA has taken steps to correct these difficulties, including monitoring analyses while in progress (U.S. Department of Transportation, 1979). Yet UMTA's small staff is hard-pressed to avoid falling between the horns of a dilemma. Either it will not impose long delays, hence tending to rubber-stamp applications (or reject them on nontechnical grounds), or it will review and scrutinize more carefully but will consequently impose delays.

In its reply to GAO's report, UMTA admitted the difficulties of reviewing proposals at the end of a long planning sequence: "Problems . . . [such as] overoptimistic ridership and revenue forecasts, underestimated costs, . . . are difficult, if not impossible, to ferret out before the analysis is complete" (ibid., p. 4). Indeed, UMTA recognized it was not receiving the unbiased alternatives analyses beloved by planning textbooks. Instead, project sponsors adopted an "advocacy role," causing the problems cited above (ibid., p. 4). This acknowledgment tacitly recognizes that analysis guidelines cannot stop project sponsors from playing games with estimates and options.

Nevertheless, despite its recognition of advocacy in alternatives analysis, UMTA has put its faith in a single sponsor to design, evaluate, and recommend options. Organizational alternatives to monopolistic planning have been ignored. Though the alternatives analysis guidelines do not refer to redundancy in planning, UMTA's "Urban Mass Transit Act of 1964 and Related Laws" contains the Office of Management and Budget Circular No. A–95, which bans competitive planning. "The purposes of this part [IV] are: . . . to eliminate overlap, duplication, and competition in areawide planning activities assisted or required under federal programs" (U.S. Department of Transportation, 1976, p. 72). Thus, alternatives analysis is recognized and sanctioned by UMTA as *one-sided* advocacy; no competing planner provides countervailing analyses—with one exception. UMTA itself has been driven by budgetary forces to become a counteradvocate.[27] Because there are more proposals than funds, UMTA must pressure project sponsors to apply for cheaper options. Not surprisingly, local officials reacted vehemently to UMTA's early alternatives analysis proposals. They argued that UMTA's emphasis on low-capital options indicated that alternatives analysis was part of "a major thrust of UMTA . . . to allow capital development to be constrained by the budgetary process and particularly by the alternatives analysis requirement" (*Transportation Research Board*, 1977, p. 3).

Local officials, sensitive to the substantive implications of procedural change, quickly inferred that alternatives analysis was just a device to rig the process in favor of cheap solutions. Their fears were well founded. Given budgetary realities, this rigging is probably inevitable. UMTA *would* like to place the "burden of persuasion" on rail so that only regions that need aid badly would be given grants.[28] Thus, applicants' bias for rail solutions—a bias stimulated, ironically, by the greater availability of federal aid for capital than for operating expenses—will be met by UMTA's bias for low-capital solutions.

The hard facts of budgetary scarcity will constrain and shape transit system development far more than will the alternatives analysis guidelines. Since aid money will continue to be scarce, UMTA will be able to turn down new rail projects solely on the crude but effective basis of cost, regardless of the adequacy of submitted alternatives analyses. Furthermore, UMTA will be able to induce applicants to scrutinize lower-cost options more intensively.[29] In such conditions, rejecting

27. Because UMTA has neither the authority nor the resources to plan nor the ability to mobilize local support, its counteradvocacy will not blossom into full-fledged competitive planning.

28. See UMTA's "Policy Toward Rail Transit":

"There is a fairly well-defined limit to the number of rail projects that could be justified as meritorious and deserving of federal support in the foreseeable future.

Urban areas will have to demonstrate a compelling need for high-capacity, high-performance transit service in order to obtain federal assistance for rail rapid transit. (United States Department of Transportation, 1978, pp. 9428–9429; original emphasis)

29. Furthermore, UMTA staffers have greater incentive to scrutinize applications carefully if their budget is tight.

an application is based less on technical review than on the national government's unwillingness to fund many expensive grants. If, on the other hand, UMTA's budget has some slack, denying requests would be politically difficult even if they do not follow the guidelines.

Since competitive planning is unlikely to become standard practice in urban transit planning in the United States, compensation for biased advocacy must depend on a combination of limited federal money and procedural requirements such as alternatives analysis. Fortunately, alternatives analysis will not stand alone. Budgetary exigencies have driven UMTA to become a counteradvocate for cheap solutions, a development that suggests that some form of multiple advocacy of alternatives is a requisite of effective planning.

Redundant Versus Monopolistic Operations: AC-BART Versus Metro

The core function of competitive planning is to produce reliable information; the core function of redundant operations is to produce reliable service. We recall from Chapter One that there are two kinds of redundant operations: passive duplication and competition. Duplication refers to agencies peacefully paralleling each other's operations; they overlap but do not conflict. Competition connotes parallel organizations fighting over scarce resources such as patrons and taxes. It was hypothesized that passive duplication enhances systemic reliability due to the sheer multiplicity of independent alternatives whereas competition stimulates rival agencies to exhibit more adaptive, flexible behavior and provide better service. How well do the cases fit the hypotheses?

Passive transit duplication protects against developmental problems (the flaws of a new system) against mistakes in more permanent features such as the kind of service a system offers and against episodic shocks such as strikes. Taking developmental issues first, we observe that BART and Metro contrast sharply. BART, plagued by risky design and insufficient preoperational testing, has struggled to achieve reliable service whereas Metro, enjoying a more conservative technical design, attained in five months a reliability that eluded BART for years. Had Metro combined its peremptory style of turning back buses with BART's prolonged un-reliability, patrons would have reacted far more angrily. But BART needed AC as a backup system much more than Metrorail needed Metrobus.[30]

Concerning the service strategies embodied in the different modes, the AC-BART combination offers a variety the Metro riders lack. And for coping with the unknown preferences of patrons, a redundant operation is superior to a monopolistic one. But whether bus and rail offer markedly different bundles of service attributes is open to question. In a Bay Area survey, bus and rail scored quite close to each other; the differences between transit and autos dwarfed the intratransit differences. And while commuters in Washington initially resented being limited to one mode, that was partly a reaction to the easily corrected problem of increased fares. Thus, differences between modes may be either adjustable (e.g., fares) or permanent but so small that most commuters are indifferent to them.

Nevertheless, it is intriguing that the service buses offer still attracts so many commuters in the Bay Area. It is intriguing because few transit cognoscenti would have predicted, before AC and BART began operating, that buses would fare so well against a modern rail system. Although no modal choice model predicted how the two systems would split transit patronage, it is highly likely that a poll of transit planners in the fifties would have heavily favored BART. Buses were generally thought to provide unappealing service—noisy, crowded, and slow. The difference between those prior expectations and AC's success is so large as to suggest that commuters' preferences remain somewhat uncertain. Perhaps passengers value the reliability of an older technology more than we had realized (Altshuler et al., 1979, p. 115); perhaps they dislike the multiple transfers that rail often requires more than we had expected. Whatever the expla-

30. Recall that by 1974 BART was opposing Greyhound's withdrawal from transbay service and in general was concerned about having inadequate peak-hour capacity.

nation, it would be prudent to assume that riders make more distinctions between modes than surveys have been able to ferret out.

The value of duplication in mitigating episodic disturbances is hard to assess with precision because it is difficult predicting how frequent and how severe such occurrences will be. Redundancy appropriate for worst case scenarios would seem excessive when the worst does not materialize.[31] It has turned out, however, that the Bay Area has had from 1973 to 1978 more than its share of random shocks: two severe strikes by AC's union,[32] over a dozen short interruptions of BART service, and most recently a fire in BART's tube, prompting the Public Utilities Commission to order the tube closed for over ten weeks. We can say, with hindsight, that organizational duplication has served transit riders well against these disturbances.[33] It is worth noting that because no decision-maker anticipated the degree of disruption endured by the two systems, the protection afforded by redundancy was quite unplanned. The undesigned is rarely so benign.

Washington has sustained not only fewer developmental snafus but fewer episodic shocks as well: there have been no major strikes.[34] Patrons have been fortunate to enjoy this peace, for a strike would disrupt their lives more than strikes in the Bay Area have distressed Californians.[35] Unlike AC's and BART's locals, which remain independent, Metro's union has, with management's blessing, unified the locals. This merger, combined with unredundant service, bodes ill for Washingtonians. Their uninterrupted transit service rests on

31. I suspect that part of the argument over redundancy turns on decision-makers having different beliefs about worst case scenarios.

32. The first one occurred when BART, not yet in transbay service, could cover only some of AC's East Bay runs.

33. For BART's short-term breakdowns, however, a reserve fleet of buses, owned by BART and operated by AC, might have sufficed.

34. The 1978 Metro strike was unauthorized. The effects of one legitimized by the union are unknown.

35. On the other side of the ledger, transit strikes in D.C. will be less frequent than in the Bay Area because Metro has fewer unions. And if, as appears likely, transit union locals monitor one another's contracts and strive to match or outdo one another, then D.C. may endure slower wage inflation.

the shaky foundations of continued success in labor-management negotiations.

Turning now from the effects of passive duplication to those of active competition, we find some unexpected results. In general, competition had a weaker effect than the theory predicted. Though BART and Metrorail differed in many respects, particularly in their technical design, no major dissimilarity was due to the difference between competitive and monopolistic operations. Indeed, BART's operations were apparently little affected by competition, its managers having attended more to the internal problem of development than to the external problem of rivalry.

As for AC, though its service has been superior to Metrobus, most of this difference cannot be attributed to the difference between competition and monopoly. AC's service record *predated* its competitor, and its service and fare behavior seem little affected by BART.[36] Indeed, AC has a reputation as a conservative organization, responding slowly to communities' requests for altered service before *and* after BART started operations.

Metrobus's misfortunes, on the other hand, can be directly traced to organizational structure. Metrobus has been hurt, especially just after merger, by WMATA's integrated structure. Whereas AC's conservatism preserved an effective system, the Washington bus systems badly needed improvements. In that context conservatism implied stagnation.[37] Although Metro had one bus manager who wanted to move quickly, it proved difficult to obtain decisions from Metro's centralized bureaucracy. Thus, the lack of competition was less harmful than the tightly integrated organizational structure, which stifled bus managers' initiative. It is informative to compare Metrobus's torpor with AC's progress in 1958-62 when a few top managers, *unimpeded by another mode's execu-*

36. It is more difficult to discern whether BART's service or fares have been affected by AC than vice versa because AC's operation predated BART's. We have a "before" record of AC but not of BART.

37. Metro has been as slow as AC in providing new types of bus service to communities. In several cases, such as Montgomery County's "Ride-On," the communities have decided to go it alone.

tives, revitalized the ailing Key System. The central conclusion here is that AC's achievements depended more on its managerial independence than on its interorganizational rivalry.

If tightly integrated organizational structures diminish the capacity of managers to effect change, what about external channels of access as sources of change? Do modally specialized agencies provide more channels[38] for complaints by clientele than does a single integrated organization? If they do, that would join a redundancy of access to a greater managerial flexibility, a powerful recipe for adaptation.

In Washington, access to Metro has received mixed reviews. D.C.'s black press has charged that Metro is inattentive to the interests of inner-city blacks. However, Metro's federated political structure permits, and may even augment, subregional consciousness on the board, thus constituting a channel for geographically based appeals. Hence the permeability of federalism compensates for the impermeability of monopoly.

Although poor people have been better served by the Bay Area's multiorganizational system than by D.C.'s single agency, that was due to AC's historical route structure, traditionally strong in the Berkeley-Oakland urban core, not to

---

38. The classic public administration doctrine that lines of responsibility should be clear is often cited in this context as a rationale for eliminating duplication. The notion is that parallel channels, far from making it easier for citizens to register complaints, make it *more* difficult because people cannot decipher which bureau is responsible for unsatisfactory service. Duplication breeds confusion, rendering access pointless.

Actually, however, the redundant and monopolistic situations differed little on this dimension. In the AC-BART case, who was responsible for the indifferent quality of service integration was indeed a vexing question. But difficulties concerning parallel lines caused no confusion at all. AC was as clearly responsible for its strike as BART was for its technological difficulties. Redundancy does not inevitably confuse lines of responsibility, particularly if the parallel channels are independent.

Furthermore, monopoly creates dependency so that though Metro patrons *know* which agency to blame when things go wrong, inducing it to *do* something is another matter entirely. The doctrine of clear lines of responsibility must incorporate, as an implicit premise, the proposition that agency compliance is not a significant obstacle.

easier clientele access to AC's decision centers.[39] AC did not have to adapt to the demands of captive urban riders; it merely had to *resist changing* by rejecting BART's demands. The multiorganizational system was not behaviorally more responsive to clientele than was Metro; rather, it provided a richer set of options and exhibited more resistance to reducing that set.[40]

Coordination Tasks and the Advantages of Integration

Of all the problems transit integration is supposed to solve, intermodal connections are most palpable. In this context co-ordination refers not to some vague philosopher's stone of administration but to practical matters such as making patrons' intermodal transfers convenient and swift. How does the integrated structure of Metro compare with the inter-organizational structure of AC and BART in handling these tasks?[41]

39. Newspaper records indicate that interest groups rarely pressured AC. Even when they did, the congruence of interest between riders and agency makes the analysis of influence problematic. For example, when AC announced it was going to cancel, upon BART's opening, an East Bay express line, riders petitioned and the route was not canceled. But whether the petition influenced the board or whether the management and board wanted to keep the line anyway is unknown.

40. Riders are, however, only part of a public organization's constituency; there are also nonriding taxpayers. WMATA is more attentive to taxpayers than AC is. Metrobus's differentiated fares reflects the fiscal preferences and revenue-raising capacities of the polities comprising WMATA whereas AC, a special district of low salience, raised its property tax steadily for over a decade without constraint. But because this difference in fiscal accountability resulted from differences in the political rules governing the boards rather than from differences in modal organization, it is not germane to this study.

41. Since the problems involve similar technologies, we can confidently attribute the differences in outcome to the differences in organizational structure.

In the main, Metro has coordinated more effectively. Consider two differences. First, whereas Metro developed a flashpass for transfers in either direction, AC and BART took a long time to agree upon a method for transferring in only one direction, and even that required outside help.[42] Second, Metro has tried harder to smooth out logistical problems of transfer, such as buses departing just before a train arrives. These problems tend to fall into interorganizational cracks between AC and BART. In general, the interorganizational structure has been outperformed on these mundane but necessary tasks.[43]

However, some coordination tasks are more complicated to evaluate because of distributional implications. Metro's cuts of parallel routes benefit nonriding taxpayers more than commuters; AC-BART's duplicate service is just the reverse, benefiting riders more than taxpayers. Similarly, Metro's extensive rerouting of buses to improve access to rail is a boon for rail riders; it inconvenienced bus patrons. Again, the AC-BART combination reverses the distribution of advantages and disadvantages. Since BART could not persuade AC to reorient its bus routes to train stations, bus patrons are protected from inconvenience, but access to BART is poorer than to Metrorail. Because there is no clear way to evaluate outcomes with these distributional effects, one cannot conclude that monopolistic transit service in Washington has increased efficiency in any straightforward sense of that concept.

42. However, the cause of Metro's superiority, its financially integrated status, produced the offsetting disadvantage of confusing multimodal accounting. Outsiders find it harder to comprehend the financial status of the modes in Washington than in the Bay Area.

43. One argument for transit coordination is that bus and rail must mesh smoothly if a linked transit ride is to compete favorably with the auto. In D.C., in particular, buses were expected to supply a great deal of the access to rail. People, however, have their own ideas about multimodal trips. In both Washington and the Bay Area the proportion of people taking buses to rail stations is less than expected; the proportion driving cars, higher than expected. Because commuters want one leg of a trip to be demand-responsive and dependable, the trip that often competes with an all-auto ride is not pure public transit but mixed private-public, wherein coordination is decentralized.

Coordination and Antagonistic Cooperation

Popular notions of bureaucratic competition reflect a pervasive belief that conflict between agencies pursuing the public weal is undesirable. Integration, then, is a method to eliminate not only duplication but antagonisms as well. In turn, reducing antagonism should improve coordination.

But we cannot attribute Metro's superior technical coordination to less intermodal antagonism—because it is doubtful that Metro's modes enjoy better relations than those of AC and BART.[44] Bad feelings certainly exist in Metro, particularly among drivers, but hierarchical constraints limit the play of these sentiments. The AC-BART situation is, curiously enough, quite similar. There too constraints, such as fear of outside intervention, reduce the *effect* rather than the *existence* of antagonisms.

Metro's integrated structure minimizes the effects of antagonism in a second way. Some problem solving, such as figuring out transfer arrangements, is simply removed from an intermodal arena; staff working on them do not represent modal interests. Problems are settled and solutions are fixed as decision premises for modal managers. In contrast, between AC and BART antagonism may have "spillover" from competitive to complementary tasks because the two domains were poorly insulated from each other at planning and policy levels.

Redundancy in Different Contexts[45]

The most important question in using redundancy in public organizations is not whether but *when* redundancy can be efficacious. A priori, it is unlikely that

44. Indeed, one could make a good case that integration *increased* antagonisms among operators because it increased the relative deprivation of bus drivers.

45. In this section I will focus exclusively on the emergence of planning competition in Minnesota and operational duplication in the Bay Area.

redundancy is either always valuable or never valuable; the trick is specifying appropriate types of situations. The author believes that the distinction between planning and operations will prove useful.

In this section we first address an organizational question: do redundancies of planning and of operations differ in their patterns of growth and decline? The second topic is policy-oriented: which type of redundancy—competitive planning or redundant operations—gives decision-makers more information on the effectiveness of transit alternatives? This issue concerns the evaluation function performed by redundancy during different stages of decision-making.

The Emergence of Redundancy: Comparisons

Chapter One proposed that three properties characterize the growth of redundancy in the public sector: first, redundancy is triggered either by an executive deliberately seeking flexibility or as a by-product of interagency politics; second, if interagency politics is the cause, then one agency's encroachment on another's jurisdiction tends to be gradual; third, redundant agencies tend to be established at different times for apparently different purposes. Do the cases support these hypotheses?

The redundancies investigated here were not created by a central authority seeking the decisional flexibility of multiple options. Rather, both pairs of agencies were established to work on distinct problems: sewers and transit in the Twin Cities, regional and subregional transit in the Bay Area. In both cases overlap remained latent for a while—five years in Minnesota (1967-72) and, following a brief early conflict, seven years in California (1958-65).[46] During these periods it appeared that conventional, differentiated relations would take hold. Latent redundancies were activated primarily be-

---

46. Periodization is more difficult in the AC-BART case.

cause organizational integrity was threatened. In the Bay Area, operational redundancy became a serious possibility when it became clear that losing the transbay routes would hurt AC's finances and that BART would not compensate AC. In Minneapolis, the Metro Council feared its authority was being eroded by single-function agencies. In each case, creating or maintaining redundancy was a solution to a pressing problem: how to counter a threat to the organization.

In neither case was jurisdictional encroachment gradual. In Minneapolis, the council, following the arrival of new leaders, plunged rapidly into transit planning. The incorrect hypothesis of gradual encroachment assumed that rival agencies would be hierarchically equal and would therefore intrude with caution. But the council's hierarchical status enabled it to move boldly. Nor does encroachment describe the process in the Bay Area. The charters of the two organizations created an overlap potential, activated by AC's growing determination to hold its ground. BART, of course, was not incrementally encroaching on AC's turf; it was adhering to boundaries set in the early sixties. The strategy of gradualism was simply irrelevant.

The third hypothesis had two parts; one was supported, one not. Part one was the conjecture that redundancy typically results from the convergence of agencies originally established for different tasks. Indeed, this correctly described the origins of redundancy in both regions. More importantly, the reasoning underlying the conjecture was also accurate. In both cases, the agencies' early specialization enabled them to avoid the damning charge that they were wasting taxpayers' money by duplicating each other's work. Once the agencies became more secure, accusations of competing with another public organization were less threatening; hence specialization yielded to redundancy.

The second part of this hypothesis is closely related to the first. Because redundancy is generally considered illegitimate in government, anything that increases its visibility decreases its viability. If potentially redundant bureaucracies are founded simultaneously, their temporal proximity could draw unfavorable attention to their latent duplication. This is a plausible argument; its only defect is that it is wrong. Both pairs of agencies were founded close together in time. I had overlooked in Chapter One a strong counterargument.[47] If potentially redundant organizations are founded simultaneously, then none will be powerful enough to bar rivals from the field whereas if their births are widely separated, the oldest agency can mobilize opposition against new competitors. The counterargument held true here. In both cases the agencies had their hands full getting started and, aside from a brief AC-BART conflict,[48] avoided expending energy blocking each other.

When studying the growth of redundancy, understanding its timing is as important as understanding its occurrence. Why did competition emerge during planning in Minnesota when it was averted until operations in the Bay Area?

If one had examined the Bay Area in 1957 and the Twin Cities in 1967, one would not have predicted that planning rivalry would develop in the latter and not in the former. Indeed, given the closer functional similarity of BART and AC, the converse appeared more likely. How does one explain what happened? The main explanatory burden rests on the different legal conditions in the two states. Though both states' laws failed to demarcate the agencies' functions, California's statutes formally *separated* AC and BART whereas Minnesota's law formally *bound together* MTC and the Metro Council. Because the council was fiscally responsible for the region,[49] MTC was obligated to submit projects to it for review. This requirement set the stage for the council's counterplanning. Therefore, whereas it was legally feasible and politically advantageous for AC and BART to avoid each other

47. The argument of Chapter One was that if the decision-makers responsible for creating agencies had antiredundancy attitudes, then temporal separation, by increasing the chance that they would overlook a redundancy, would make duplication more likely.

48. The way this clash ended corroborates the point. The conflict was settled partly because neither organization felt it could afford to fight.

49. Neither AC nor BART had any financial responsibilities for other agencies and could, at least during system planning, virtually ignore each other.

from 1958 to the mid-sixties, avoidance was impossible for
MTC and the council. The law pitted them against each other.

From Growth to Decline: The Stability
of Redundancy

We recall from Chapter Four that Minnesota's
legislature terminated planning competition in 1975 by re-
drawing jurisdictions and banning further rail studies. The
heyday of overlap between the council and MTC lasted little
more than two years. In contrast, BART and AC's service
parallelism has lasted from 1974 to the present and shows no
signs of disappearing. Why was one redundancy more stable
than the other?

First, the Twin Cities conflict was much more visible to the
state legislature, which had the authority to liquidate competition, than was the AC-BART situation to its state legislature. Because the Minnesota legislature was the sole parent
of the Twin Cities regional agencies (unlike California's legislature, which was only partly responsible for BART and AC)
and because Minneapolis-St. Paul is the nucleus of that
state,[50] the legislature closely monitored both substance and
structure of metropolitan government. From 1967 to 1975,
significant urban governance bills were proposed in every
legislative session. Furthermore, the 1967 legislation stipulated that should the council and MTC disagree, the legislature would hear the issue. Thus, a formal procedure was
available for bringing policy conflicts—and, as it turned out,
organizational conflicts as well—to the legislature's attention.
In contrast, the California legislature had meager contact with
AC and BART in the sixties. Consequently, when the
agencies' conflict heightened in the early seventies, the state
lacked a tradition of involvement that could be easily tapped,
and the legislature remained aloof. Finally, the Minnesota
decision, involving hundreds of millions of dollars and the
regional transit system's fundamental features, was a far
more important issue than AC-BART service overlaps. In
sum, it was overdetermined that Minnesota's legislature

50. Whereas the Bay Area's population is roughly 20 percent of
California's, the Twin Cities' is about 50 percent of Minnesota's.

would pay more attention to their case of redundancy than would California's.

Although the AC-BART case did come to the attention of *local* politicians—a few mayors—these lacked authority to intervene. The only structural analogue to the Minnesota legislature for resolving interagency disputes was the Metropolitan Transportation Commission. But the commission, though fully aware of the dispute, lacked the unquestioned authority of the Minnesota chambers. In California, therefore, the conflict was invisible to those who could have ended it and visible only to those who could not.

These points explain the differential visibility of the two redundancies but not why the Minnesota legislature finally chose to eliminate overlapping.[51] There were two major reasons. Because the Minnesota redundancy was highly competitive—the agencies had much to lose—the situation was politically heated. The Bay Area case was tepid by comparison.[52] The rancor eventually disturbed important state

51. Although details of the highway-rapid rail fight were omitted from the Washington case, comparing that conflict with the Minneapolis case is interesting because it reveals varying reactions of decision-makers to undesigned competitive planning. The reaction in Washington was almost uniformly negative. Though the *Washington Post's* negative editorial reactions must be taken cautiously (a supporter of both freeway and rail construction, it was opposed to an agency conflict that delayed both), the congressmen overseeing the debate were also antipathetic. In 1962 the House Appropriations Committee scolded the partisans: "The rivalry is sowing confusion and disorder" (*Washington Post*, June 23, 1962). In 1963 Representative Basil Whitener, chairman of the hearings on NCTA's 1962 plan, said he hoped that the hearings would not degenerate into "a battle between advocates of one system over another" (*Washington Star*, July 10, 1963); Representative Joel Broyhill added: "This committee is reluctant to sit in judgment over these difficulties between experts" (ibid.).

Two themes ran through these objections. One, expressed most often by the *Washington Post*, was that the transit-highway conflict would endanger both projects. The second was a fear of becoming bogged down in an issue complex enough to make the experts disagree. This second theme was also apparent in Minneapolis, where most legislators tired of mulling over a problem on which experts could not reach consensus. However, *unlike* Washington, there was a core of legislators who did make use of agency competition.

52. The difference in the heat of the conflicts was due not to personality differences, for AC's Bingham and BART's Stokes were as feisty as the principals in Minneapolis, but to the difference in the stakes.

senators specializing on the issue, and they became eager to finish the affair. Their colleagues, involved in other issues and hence amateurs in transit policy, were perplexed by the bewildering array of options and by technical complexities and were more than happy to help end it.[53]

Indeed, it was inevitable that bureaucratic competition in the Twin Cities would be temporary, that competitive planning would not be extended into redundant operations. This extension of redundancy from one stage of decision-making to a succeeding one does happen in other policy areas. In competition over weapons systems, such as the Thor and Jupiter missiles, the armed services usually seek to plan and operate a system. Hence, if each branch has enough political support to protect its project, duplication may stretch into the operational stage. In these circumstances redundancy is quite stable, more so than cost-effectiveness criteria would justify. But in Minneapolis, the Metro Council never intended to operate a transit system.[54] Thus, the overlap, necessarily restricted to planning, had a built-in instability.

Compounding the inherent instability of competitive planning were the ambiguous authority relations of the Minnesota agencies. In California, BART could not order AC to yield the field, and to change that relationship of equal authority would have meant altering a well-defined status quo. But most Minnesotans had assumed since 1967 that the council and MTC were to work on different problems. Thus, the legislature's rearranging jurisdictional boundaries in 1975 could be seen

53. The problem of generalists arbitrating between competing specialists extends far beyond this policy area. Henry Levin, describing the difficulties of using an advocacy process in educational policymaking, quotes Justice Lewis Powell: "In view of the division of opinion among scholars and educational experts . . . the judiciary should refrain from deciding the issue" (1975, p. 239, n. 71). This quandary also cropped up in my fourth (unreported) case study of redundancies in BART's development efforts. In at least two incidents, parallel problem solving led to paralysis because an arbitrator could not choose between competing solutions. I believe, however, that if this difficulty became a persistent problem at a particular organizational level, expertise, in the guise of additional staff, would accumulate at that level. The problem is not insoluble.

54. Of course Anderson's PRT group was active only in planning.

not as departing from the status quo but as effecting old intentions.[55]

Although it was unlikely that the Bay Area overlap could have been eliminated by an external authority, redundancy can also be destabilized by bureaucracies negotiating a division-of-labor treaty or by one agency persuading another to leave the area. But neither of these strategies proved viable for AC and BART. BART became financially strapped as construction proceeded, so compensating AC for losing transbay routes was not broached. And persuasion, given AC's obvious dependence upon transbay lines, was a weak method for BART to have relied upon. As oligopolists in the private sector have found to their sorrow, collusion is not always possible.

What Do Decision-makers Learn from Duplication? Competitive Planning and Redundant Operations as Evaluation Processes

Organizations rarely can be evaluated by absolute yardsticks; the social comparison of how similar organizations are faring is often the best one can do (Thompson, 1967, p. 87). Consequently, monopolies are in a comfortable position: clients, lacking comparative yardsticks, have difficulty evaluating a monopoly's performance. But redundant organizations, whether public or private, must live with the anxiety that they can be weighed and found wanting.

This evaluative function of redundancy can be realized in either planning or operations. Competitive planning constitutes an ex ante evaluation; redundant operations, an ex post. Each has characteristic strengths and weaknesses. In parallel transit service, the evaluation of transit options is a by-product of patrons making choices. Because evaluation rests

---

55. Certainly the council's supporters viewed the arrangement as finally enabling the council to occupy its intended role. In fact, council-MTC relations were objectively hazy; it was *not* clear what the legislature had intended in 1967.

on the revealed preferences of thousands of commuters, it is far more decentralized than the evaluation produced by competitive planning. This decentralization strengthens the evaluation. Riders' modal preferences, as revealed by their modal choices, are less subject to bureaucractic distortion than are planning predictions, which are easily "gamed" to suit organizational interests.

The distortion of evaluations is a particularly vexing problem when the agencies involved have unequal political resources.[56] Alexander George has pointed out that competitive planning is in these situations quite vulnerable, the resulting evaluations reflecting more the agencies' differences in political resources than the proposals' differences in substantive merit (George, 1972).[57] Of course political resources can influence the evaluation of redundant operations as well, but they can distort evaluations less than during planning because operations produce more *evidence* about modes' merits, counteracting unequal political power. Thus, evaluation derived from service parallelism is more robust in the face of unevenly distributed resources. Since political inequality is a fact of life in much bureaucratic conflict, this robustness should be prized.

Setting aside deliberate distortions, evaluating rival transit plans is a complicated task strewn with pitfalls. Transit planners must predict the demand for the various modes, must weigh the modes' different attributes by their importance to clientele, and must perform other arcane tasks. Operational evaluations by-pass some of these difficulties. Agencies do not have to weigh transit attributes; patrons do that. Nor must agencies predict demand functions; instead, they merely observe demand behavior.

But the evaluation generated by service redundancy does have drawbacks. First, because riders do not consider the side effects of modes, such as air pollution, their evaluations are incomplete. Second, redundant operations are a more ex-

56. In George's scheme of multiple advocacy (1972), equality of resources is so important that he posits that the process requires a manager who tries to ensure equality.

57. If a politically stronger agency backs a superior mode, the cumulative inequalities of political power and evidence make the outcome obvious.

pensive form of evaluation. In comparison with the heavily subsidized operations of BART and AC, the planning studies in Minneapolis cost only about $5 million, probably saved the region many times that amount, and were a one-time rather than an annual expense.

Third, an evaluation produced by rival planners, though less reliable than that revealed by parallel service, is more usable. As projects move from planning to operations, they accrue political support, making them more difficult to kill. A decision-maker may, for example, discover that a particular transit mode falls short of predicted performance, but if that information reaches the decision-maker once the mode is in full swing, using that knowledge to terminate or cut back the service may be politically impossible. Thus, as evaluation proceeds, competitive planning and redundant operations trade off *information* for *reversibility*: letting competition extend into operations reveals more information about the modes' merits, but at the risk of permitting political momentum to foreclose choice.

To illustrate this trade-off, compare our two cases of redundancy. The information produced by Minnesota's planning rivalry was often conjectural: for example, we will never know with certainty how much patronage a *rejected* alternative, such as MTC's rapid rail, would have garnered. But on the other hand, political momentum had not predetermined choice. The Minnesota legislature had a genuine decision to make in 1975 because both bus and rail were technically *and* politically feasible. Thus the evaluations, though not flawless, were still usable.

The Bay Area's service redundancy produced the opposite mix of information and reversibility. Though operational experience had more clearly revealed the modes' comparative worth, the systems' sunk costs make them nearly invulnerable to the sting of critical assessments. The protecting shield of sunk costs particularly favors BART, its massive capital investment ensuring immunity from evaluation.

Therefore, the comparative evaluations provided by redundant operations, though generally more robust, more tractable, and more valid than ex ante assessments, suffer from one central drawback: it may be impossible to act on the basis of the acquired information.

Conclusion

These cases give us insight into the central question of this study, that is, can an organizational system perform more reliably than any of its constituent parts? Historically, organizational theorists have answered no. It was asserted in Chapter One that this negative answer was based on an unfortunate tendency to psychologize organizations. We assume, based on this tenuous analogy, that bureaucracies are marked by the same properties of routinization, of limited search capacity, of constrained ability to generate alternatives, that describe individual bureaucrats.[58]

In this study we have discarded that analogy and its implications. We have hypothesized instead that capabilities of one bureaucratic level need not correspond in a simple way to those of another. The case studies tend to support this more complex view of organizational reliability. The Minnesota case indicates that a multiorganizational system can produce an outcome, which, though unsought after by any organization, is superior to any of the alternatives designed by these organizations. In the Bay Area, the combined system of AC and BART provides more reliable service than either of its subsystems, again despite the fact that this effective multiorganizational system is an unintended consequence of bureaucratic maneuvering.

None of the above subsystems displayed unusual planning or decisional capacities; their routines for perceiving, inter-

---

58. Because the redundancies studied here are interorganizational, we have contrasted the reliability of multiorganizational systems to that of a single agency, rather than comparing the reliability of an organization to that of an individual. Strictly, therefore, there is no inconsistency between this work and that of the second generation of bounded rationality analysts (e.g., Allison, 1971), for all of us explored pathologies at the same level of analysis—the single organization.

Yet in a more important sense there are differences. The approach of Allison, e.g., did not admit of the possibility that the reliability of different organizational levels can vary sharply. And whether one is studying an individual and an organization or an organization and a multiorganizational system, assuming that a part's effectiveness is equal to the whole's is a far cry from von Neumann's vision of creating "reliable systems from unreliable parts."

preting, and acting upon their task environments were quite stable. Yet these "limits of organizations as mechanisms for computation and choice" (to paraphrase Simon, 1957, p. 200) were *not* translated into limitations of the larger, multi-organizational systems. Systems need not be as unreliable as their parts.

7

Extensions: The Desirability and Feasibility of Redundancy in Government

We close this study with an overall assessment of the role redundancy might play in American bureaucracy. The assessment is organized along three questions.

1.   Is redundancy desirable? This is the question that all readers want answered, but it is phrased inappropriately. As those noted methodologists, the Marx Brothers, have pointed out, this type of question should be comparative.[1] The relevant question is, how does redundancy compare with specific structural alternatives? Hence, we will continue to contrast redundancy with, first, monopoly and, second, with a system of pluralist (albeit nonredundant) checks and balances that Charles Lindblom has called "partisan mutual adjustment" (1965). Comparing redundancy with monopoly and with partisan adjustment gives us a broad spectrum of strategies of decision-making. Monopoly, with its emphasis on efficiency, is the most rationalistic and apolitical of the three structures

---

1.   Their famous exchange "How's your wife? Compared to what?" makes the point.

whereas mutual adjustment rests—even more than does redundancy—on the natural bureaucratic politics of a pluralist polity.

2.   When is redundancy desirable? Whereas question one is a broad-brush comparison of organizational structures, question two focuses on how political and technical differences among policy sectors affect the utility of redundancy. In this part we will return to the minicase studies of bureaucratic competition in weapons, water, and welfare presented in Chapter One.

3.   Is redundancy feasible? Here we address such issues as the natural growth and decline of competition. Is it a delicate flower that must be carefully nurtured, or is it a robust strategy in the context of American politics?

We conclude, as is customary, by pleading for further research in this domain and by giving a last look at the fundamental problem that opened this study—the fallibility of the individual decision-maker—and its relation to redundancy.

Is Redundancy Desirable?

Redundancy Versus Monopoly

In evaluating the comparative merits of redundancy and monopoly, we begin by using the five criteria described in Chapter One and repeated here (see Table 5). The evaluations are inferences based on the case studies.

Several general points about Table 5 should be made.

1.   Evaluating redundancy and monopoly is less straightforward than classical public administrationists believed. Multidimensional evaluation must replace the old unidimensional evaluation of efficiency versus waste. Moreover, the strategies entail several trade-offs (see, e.g., criterion four in Table 5).

2.   The table says nothing about the relative weights of the criteria. The criteria's significance varies over programs and over time. For example, consider the early days of the War on

TABLE 5 *Comparing Redundancy and Monopoly*

CRITERIA	PLANNING	OPERATIONS
1. Probability of error and of error detection	1. Planning in any policy arena is highly uncertain, and errors are easily made. Competitive planning is more reliable than monopolistic planning in alerting generalists and superiors to erroneous or questionable factual premises. But competitive planning is not science; the rules of the game are poorly institutionalized. Careful management is needed to exploit competitive planning's error detection potential and speed convergence to accurate premises.	1. Redundancy is more likely to increase a system's ability to *absorb* errors (reduce their costs) than reduce probability of error. (See point two below.) Using a highly routinized technology reduces error independently of organizational structure. This makes monopoly more viable than it otherwise would be.
2. Cost of error	2. Planning competition is more likely to reduce probability of error than cost of error.* (See point one above.)	2. Based on these cases, there is little doubt that redundant operations reduce the cost of errors or malfunctions.

3. Cost of redundancy versus cost of monopoly

3. *Financial* costs of monopoly planning are probably usually lower than competitive planning's, but the difference is insignificant. Much more important will be costs of *informational* overload on higher decision makers. Competitive planning burdens superiors more than does monopolistic planning.

3. Whenever redundant operations involve different technologies, mergers creating monopolies will not produce physical economies of scale, and administrative scale economies will not by themselves justify merger. When technologies are the same, the relative cost of redundancy compared with monopoly increases. Based on these cases, one cannot infer whether a redundant strategy costs more than monopoly due to an oversupply of service.

4. Interactions between type one and type two errors

4. There is no evidence that the two structures produce different strengths of interaction between error types. They may produce different frequencies. Because competitive planning is more likely to cause decisional paralysis (superiors unable to choose between rival solutions), it may increase the probability of rejecting moderately satisfactory

4. In operations, type one error means providing service to people who should not receive it; type two means not providing it to people who are eligible. Monopoly increases the probability of type two errors, redundancy, the probability of type one. Refining administrative procedures to make services more discriminatingly targeted is more likely to reduce *total* errors

TABLE 5 (continued)

CRITERIA	PLANNING	OPERATIONS
	plans. Monopolistic planning, due to momentum built up when a single agency dominates the choice set, creates a higher probability of accepting a weak plan.	than are changes in organizational structure.
5. Search behavior and the possibility of significant innovation	5. Monopoly bureaus' search for alternatives may be broad but will tend to be superficial. High-risk, high-potential options tend to be ignored. Monopoly bureaus have little reason to offer innovative programs since doing so disrupts standard operating procedures and personnel. Redundancy increases depth of search into high-risk, high-potential options. Individual	5. There is less scope for significant improvements during operations than during planning under *either* organizational forms.

competing agencies are no more inclined to disrupt their own personnel and standard operating procedures than are monopolies, but the risks of *not* innovating in a competitive environment are greater than those in a monopolistic one. Further, bureaus new to a policy field may be able to offer programs that are novel to sector but not to the agency itself, thereby reducing the costs of innovation.

---

*In the case study on competitive planning, the selected alternative (buses) would have been a less costly error than rail would have been had the latter been chosen and turned out poorly. Therefore, in this case planning competition could have reduced the cost of error. But I do not know whether or not this is a general consequence of competitive planning, for this would depend on the details of the alternatives in a given case; and whether or not competitive planning will result in, e.g., more reversible options than will monopolistic planning is uncertain.

Poverty. With a prosperous economy supporting new government programs, a strong president leading a coalition to reduce poverty, and a widespread belief that the old welfare programs were ineffective, the most important criterion may have been number five, the possibility of discovering significant innovation. But when times are lean and a welfare backlash is threatening, decision-makers may have to worry most about the trade-off politics of criterion four—providing benefits to ineligibles versus omitting eligibles. We can expect other variations across different policy areas.

3.   The table does not describe the characteristic *temporal* distribution of the two strategies' benefits and costs. Redundancy constitutes an investment whose return is deferred and sometimes uncertain. Monopoly, on the other hand, frequently pays in the short run (removing parallel service does save money) but hurts in the long run when unexpected problems disrupt a taut system.

4.   Critics may suggest that the table's inductive generalizations have a slender empirical base and that the case for redundancy is inconclusive. To this I reply, they do and it is. But it must be kept in mind that the empirical warrant for monopoly in government *is yet more slender*. Indeed, it is virtually nonexistent. (Organizational ideologies have a way of persisting despite the absence of evidence.) If we imposed equally rigorous standards of evidence upon both strategies, we would become far more agnostic about organizational structure—and possibly more experimental.

5.   Finally, the criteria of Chapter One said nothing about the power implications of redundancy. But in Chapter Two it was hypothesized that redundancy, particularly in planning, shifts power away from bureaucracies and toward elected officials. This conjecture, supported by the Minneapolis case study, taps a theme of long-standing interest in organization theory and political science—the issue of bureaucratic power. Dating back to Max Weber, social scientists have been troubled by the political power of bureaucracy. Weber himself was ambivalent, praising bureaucracy's technical efficiency and criticizing its political influence. In his view, politicians, mere dilettantes compared with career bureaucrats, were helpless

against the officials' monopoly of expertise. Curiously, though Weber worried about this problem, the founder of sociological organization theory never proposed a structural remedy for the excessive political power of bureaucracy. Yet his own diagnosis suggests a prescription. To the extent that the "overtowering position" (Weber, 1972, p. 61) of bureaucrats derives from their monopoly of expertise, one should be able to reduce their power in any policy domain by introducing competition. Oddly, though this measure follows directly from his analysis, Weber apparently never considered it.

After Weber, organization theorists and political scientists have displayed a similar ambivalence toward bureaucracy, admiring its technical virtues and fearing the "Prussian boot" of authoritarianism. In the last few decades, however, the attitudinal mix has changed. A fear that the large-scale formal organization is generally incompetent has supplanted Weber's hymn of praise (see, e.g., Landau, 1973b). But the other component of Weber's ambivalence, the distrust of bureaucratic power, is with us still. The strategy of redundancy holds out some promise of addressing both concerns, of increasing reliability as well as diminishing untoward bureaucratic influence.

Of course redundancy is not the only strategy for reducing bureaucratic power. An always popular approach is to bind bureaucrats ever more tightly with legislation and rules (Lowi, 1969). In Lowi's "juridical democracy," bureaus, though monopolies, would have little influence over public policy because they would have little discretion. In a legally minded society, this reform is appealing. It has serious flaws, however. First, it is questionable whether legislatures in general and Congress in particular are competent to pass laws specific enough to constrain bureaus in the desired manner. Congress has good political and technical reasons for making laws both ambiguous and general. Ambiguous laws shift the politically controversial task of resolving value trade-offs to the bureaucracy; general laws economize on congressional resources, for Congress has neither the expertise nor the time to draft highly detailed statutes that take into account particulars of place, time, and condition.

Second, the legal approach to controlling bureaucratic influence intensifies a problem Merton (1940) alerted us to over forty years ago, the organizational tendency to displace ends with means. This danger of goal displacement evokes the other theme of our ambivalence, the belief that bureaucracy is sluggish and ineffective. In a juridical democracy, bureaus might not be politically overtowering, but they would not be fountains of energy either. What is needed is a strategy that restrains bureaus' excessive political influence without stripping them of their initiative. The rules approach would not fulfill both objectives; a competitive strategy might.

Not all of the advantages of redundancy over monopoly were anticipated prior to my field research, which merely corroborates the proposition that when doing empirical work, one should expect the unexpected. There were two such unanticipated benefits, and they concern the relation between managerial attention and redundancy and a larger political function of redundancy.

Managerial attention is a scarce and valuable resource in any organization, and its allocation is influenced by organizational structure. Functional organization sweeps programs related to the same goal into one agency, with no institutional mechanism for ensuring a reasonable distribution of managerial attention across programs. And attention often is maldistributed due to the presence of an *organizational mission*.[2] An organizational mission includes more than an agency's function or goals; it usually identifies a specific *solution* or means as central to accomplishing a function. And in a functionally organized agency, the solution identified as part of the organizational mission will receive the lion's share of managerial attention.[3]

2. Morton Halperin's definition is slightly different: "The organization's *essence* is the view held by the dominant group in the organization of what the missions and capabilities should be" (1974, p. 18). Halperin observes that in some agencies, leaders may disagree about the organizational essence.

3. Managerial attention could be misallocated even if programs do *not* functionally overlap because attention, a scarce resource, could be devoted to any programs, redundant or complementary. But skewing is particularly likely when programs overlap because their substitutability strengthens the conviction that a commitment must be made to one or the other.

Organizational missions develop for several reasons. (1) An important leader may identify himself with, and lend prestige to, a particular program. (2) An organization may have integrated backward into education, as do the armed services, and during the intensive college years recruits learn specific skills which they identify as belonging to the central mission. (3) Some alternatives are more glamorous than others. The sex appeal of a public policy is rarely examined in academic journals, but it exists and it matters.[4] Glamour influences the content of organizational missions by making certain options more prestigious. (4) Identifying *a* solution as organizationally central reduces uncertainty and simplifies training and procurement in the bargain.

Whatever the causes of organizational missions, their effect in monopolistic, functionally integrated agencies is to focus managerial attention on the program defined as the mission. Though occasionally this allocation reflects clientele preferences, more often it results from intraorganizational conditions (such as the above) *unrelated* to clients' welfare. The Washington Metro case illustrated this point dramatically.

The second unanticipated point concerns a larger political function of redundancy. In Chapter One it was hypothesized, following Ostrom et al. (1961), that rivalry (competitive redundancy) should make bureaus more responsive to the wishes of citizens in the bureaus' jurisdictions. It follows from Ostrom's conjecture that because responsiveness becomes more difficult the more heterogeneous a jurisdiction's citizens are (diverse clients may require different skills, equipment, or even specialized programs), a monopoly is likely to perform particularly poorly in a heterogeneous environment. A monopoly bureau will often tailor programs for a specific interest group while overlooking other groups' interests. The pressure of competition is needed to stimulate agencies to attend to variations among citizens.

This is, however, too narrow a formulation. It is not merely the subset of *competitive* redundancies that promotes better

4. I define the glamour or sex appeal of a policy as its instrumentally irrelevant attractiveness. The glamour of a policy is hard to articulate but easy to recognize. In this study many interviewees spontaneously remarked that rapid rail is much sexier than buses.

service for a diverse clientele; it is duplication *in general,* including passive redundancy, that serves this function. We recall that the combination of AC and BART satisfied a wider set of patrons (local riders as well as commuters) then did Metro, which discomfited many inner city riders by bending bus routes to serve rail. But we must stress that this difference was not due to the rivalry between AC and BART making them more responsive to clients. Redundancy, in the broader sense of functionally equivalent programs rather than in the narrower sense of active competition, produced the greater diversity of options.

Whatever the cause of selective orientation, the political costs of monopoly bureaus in heterogeneous task environments can be substantial. To those not in the chosen, narrow clientele group, bureaucratic behavior will appear arbitrary and capricious.[5] Service designed for a group will appear unfair to others. Blacks in southeast Washington, for example, considered the arrangement of their transit system unreasonable—and so it was, from their perspective and for their interests. Yet it made good sense for long-distance commuters. Multiple bureaus, using personnel with different expertise, with different equipment, and with diverse programs, usually satisfy a broader range of persons.

A corollary of this argument is that redundancy in heterogeneous task environments is more desirable when representative political institutions are weak. When agencies of representation are strong, diverse interests can use them to influence even monopolistic bureaus. But if they are weak, redundant bureaus, by offering programmatic choices, can produce a protodemocracy and crudely substitute for electoral representation. We recall that whereas in the AC-BART case, elected officials were uninvolved, in Washington, D.C., Metro is closely watched by electoral institutions, compensating for Metro's monopolistic tendencies.

---

5. If a monopolistic bureau is in a *homogeneous* task environment, it is much less likely to behave willfully. Monopolies can afford to be more arrogant than competitive bureaus, but even they cannot ignore a homogeneous clientele.

Redundancy Versus Partisan Mutual Adjustment

In the context of American public bureaucracy, it is insufficient to compare redundancy only with monopoly. Although monopolistic bureaus do exist, they do not operate in vacuums but in environments studded with other agencies working on related issues. Even if there is only one bureau in a policy area, its programs will often be scrutinized by agencies affected by the monopolist's actions. These other bureaus will often criticize a monopolist's plan or program and argue over the merits of alternatives.

This criticism by differentiated but interdependent agencies Lindblom has called "partisan discussion" (1965, p. 28). A member of the larger set of strategies denoted by partisan mutual adjustment,[6] which includes bargaining, negotiation, and the like, partisan discussion is the American political system's undesigned remedy for the informational deficiencies of monopolistic planning. It has been argued (see below) that partisan discussion squeezes information out of reluctant bureaus much as does competitive planning. Moreover, partisan discussion is well adapted to enduring features of American politics. Consider Lindblom's definition of partisan discussion: it is composed of decision-makers "who [do] not assume that there exist some knowable criteria acceptable to [all] decision-makers that is sufficient, if applied, to govern adjustments among them" (ibid., pp. 28–29). This definition of partisan discussion is an apt description of the nature of problems faced by senior bureaucrats, indicating that it is eminently suited to the political contexts of American bureaucracy. And, indeed, partisan discussion is well established in the United States. Few major issues arise about which interdependent decision-makers do not argue. Partisan discussion

6. To compare redundancy with the entire scope of partisan mutual adjustment processes would be pointless, as the latter embraces so many substrategies. Indeed, a key weakness of Lindblom's analysis (1965) is that it is unclear what is *not* partisan mutual adjustments, apart from highly centralized decision-making. Consequently, it is too easy to make performance claims on its behalf.

and partisan mutual adjustment generally rest on the dispersed authority, interdependent policy sectors, and goal conflict that characterize American politics. And because it is such a practical alternative to redundancy, it proves a much tougher comparison than does monopoly.

Though they are alternatives, the two strategies are not totally dissimilar: they derive from similarly skeptical traditions, sharing the same doubt about any claims to administrative certainty, sharing the same concern over unintended consequences, and sharing the same appreciation of the benefits of multiple decision-makers. In a series of works culminating with *The Intelligence of Democracy* (1965), Lindblom has delineated how multiple decision-makers can ameliorate problems caused by limited cognitive abilities and by political conflict.[7] This line of analysis is highly congenial to redundancy theory.

But Lindblom emphasizes that in partisan mutual adjustment, decision-makers are differentiated rather than redundant (ibid., pp. 151, 156). His scheme does not assume that agencies functionally overlap; *specialization* is the hallmark of partisan mutual adjustment and partisan discussion. For example, the Environmental Protection Agency (EPA) specializes in environmental policy, the Council of Economic Advisers (CEA) in macroeconomic policy. If the CEA believes a policy alternative of EPA might aggravate inflation, for example, it will criticize the proposal on those grounds, thus initiating a cycle of partisan discussion between agencies whose primary responsibilities do not duplicate each other.

Several readers of drafts of this work acknowledged these *process* dissimilarities between partisan discussion and redundancy but wondered whether those differences affected policy *outcomes*. More than one reader conjectured that an iterative cycle of partisan discussion, in which an agency makes a proposal that is criticized, modified, put forward again, and so on, would be functionally equivalent to competitive planning.[8] Lindblom himself suggests that partisan discussion

7. This was his task in part. The major purpose of his study was to show how coordination could occur without a coordinator.

8. For similar claims about the information-producing effects of a for-

provides the same cross-checking of information that competition provides. He quotes a legislator speaking of interest groups. "Both sides come to you, so you can balance off all one-sided presentations (and they're all one-sided)" (1968, p. 66).[9]

But the author doubts that the two processes are functionally identical; their structural differences make that unlikely. Instead, each probably has distinctive strengths and weaknesses. We start the evaluation with the advantages of partisan discussion.

1.   Partisan discussion is a politically robust strategy because it does not presuppose that decision-makers agree on goals. Though several formulations of redundancy are compatible with goal conflict (Landau, 1969; George, 1972), the more formal models of problem-solving redundancies (Nelson, 1961) presume more consensus than does partisan discussion.[10] In these narrow formulations of redundancy, parallel problem-solving efforts are directed toward well-defined objectives.[11] Rarely do issues in the public sector admit of such

---

malized partisan discussion procedure, see Serge Taylor's probing study of the Environmental Impact Statement process in the federal bureaucracy (1984).

9. See also *The Intelligence of Democracy*: "No one decision-maker is motivated to undertake the comprehensive investigations envisaged by the advocates of an overview, but, taken together, a group of partisan adjusters may generate a great deal more information and analysis than will a central coordinator. Again, they will not necessarily do so but they may" (Lindblom, 1965, p. 174).

10. However, solutions to reasonably complex problems are invariably multidimensional, and without a set of weights that collapse the dimensions into a single metric, quasi-political fights over competing solutions arise as the dimensions become proximate goals. This tendency is enhanced if the dimensions are differentially important to different bureaus, as in, e.g., the fight between the Navy and the Air Force over the design of the F–111 fighter plane (Art, 1968).

11. These works assume simpler goal sets than do the discursive expositions of Klein and Landau in order to facilitate formal modeling and computation of optimal amounts of redundancy in development projects. Introducing goal conflict makes it difficult to calculate how much duplication is optimal.

pristine strategies.[12] Partisan discussion is more realistic in this respect.

2.   Partisan discussion is more robust because it is predicated on specialization, which is far more legitimate in the American political system than is duplication.

3.   Partisan discussion does not require a simultaneous evaluation of alternatives. Partisan critics of one policy

> are not required, as they would be by the synoptic ideal, to bring their anticipation of failures to bear as an objection on the very policy that stimulates the anticipation. Instead they more simply employ the anticipation by designing a next step to deal with the anticipated failure or adverse consequence of the last step.   (Lindblom, 1965, p. 156)

This is less demanding than the competitive planning model, which, though not synoptic, requires a functionally simultaneous[13] review of rivals' programs.

4.   Partisan discussion does not depend on a carefully orchestrated multiple advocacy requiring resource parity and centralized management (George, 1972). Thus partisan discussion is both easier to start and easier to maintain. (Of course, precisely because Lindblom does not stipulate demanding prerequisites for partisan analysis, he does not make powerful normative claims for it.)[14]

12.   See also Lindblom's point that "by definition cooperative problem solving through discussion in the light of adequate and agreed criteria is ruled out as not belonging to the present category of partisan adjustment" (1965, p. 69).

13.   Competitive planning is functionally simultaneous if all alternative solutions are reviewed before one is chosen. The review need not be literally simultaneous.

14.   Actually, both multiple advocacy and partisan mutual adjustment are subject to the trade-off between practicality and effectiveness. If George's scheme (1972) did not require resource parity, it would be more robust and widespread, but inequality would increase the risk of technical distortions. Similarly, partisan mutual adjustment is liable to distortion if the actors are of unequal strength, but if parity were a defining attribute, the process would be far less common.

The central weakness of George's design is implementation. As Destler (1972) noted, it is unlikely that such a complex design will be established by the White House or other political executives. Lindblom (1965), on the other hand, emphasizes the feasibility of partisan mutual adjustment and skirts the

5. Finally, partisan analysis does not require creating detailed alternatives, but only critiques and modifications of others' options. Therefore, it is more easily accomplished by nongovernmental groups with limited resources.[15]

In exchange for these advantages, partisan analysis has several weaknesses. It is less likely than competitive planning to produce detailed policy alternatives because an initiating agency has a vested interest in its option and because all too often the criticism phase of partisan discussion comes too late in the policymaking sequence to have much effect.[16] Partisan discussion's sequentiality requires that mistakes be correctable,[17] that systems have the ability to avoid being locked in to old solutions.[18] In the policy studied here, that assump-

---

issue of its desirability. George pays more attention to such dysfunctions as partisans dividing up a policy sector, buying off weaker competition, and so forth (1972, p. 761). Indeed, even generally undesirable behavior such as collusions between bureaus would in Lindblom's scheme be an instance of partisan mutual adjustment! I think it is fair to say that Lindblom's analysis does not specify the conditions in which partisan mutual adjustment is benign and for whom. But given the context in which by definition the strategy functions—goal conflict—devising criteria to evaluate it would be a difficult exercise in normative political theory.

The case of competitive planning studied in this work, involving undesigned and unmanaged redundancies, represents a more practical type of redundancy than George's multiple advocacy. However, precisely because "due process" is not a defining attribute of competitive planning, it is more likely to produce technically distorted outcomes than is multiple advocacy.

15. The Minneapolis case, however, indicates that redundant generation of policy alternatives is not restricted to governmental organizations: the Personal Rapid Transit group was nongovernmental.

16. This conclusion partly depends on the political clout of the generating and commenting bureaus and the salience of the values they are guarding. In the example chosen (environment versus inflation), the importance of the latter to the nation—and, more to the point, to the White House—ensures that criticisms will be heard.

17. Purely sequential forms of redundancy may not work well either. In an experiment on different kinds of duplication, Felsenthal and Fuchs found the sequential type to be ineffective, particularly if a redundant problem solver was answering a question that preceding problem solvers had solved incorrectly (1976, pp. 474–475).

18. In Chapter One, however, it was assumed that the sequential decision-making would be carried out by one group whereas Lindblom posits that the sequence of new moves would be undertaken by *critics* of the first move.

tion was not satisfied. In general, there is a greater chance of becoming locked in to a particular alternative under a differentiated structure of partisan discussion than under a redundant one. In policy fights, it is hard to beat something with nothing, and partisan criticism frequently seems like nothing.

One might argue that policies in partisan discussion systems *do* change; they just do so incrementally. One could further argue that *most* bureaus, whether redundant or monopolistic, change their programs only incrementally. They do so deliberately to conserve the knowledge and equipment invested in status quo solutions; they do so unintentionally because of bounded rationality factors such as limited search (Simon, 1947; Braybrooke and Lindblom, 1963). But this point would not vitiate the contention that *systems* composed of monopolistic bureaus are more prone to programmatic sluggishness than those composed of redundant agencies. The limited adaptability of a single organization translates into *systemic* incrementalism only if organizational incrementalism is compounded by monopoly. Consider the following.

Suppose we accept that bureaus change incrementally.[19] Nevertheless, an incremental shift for a *new* actor in a policy arena may be quite novel for established actors. For example, when congestion confronts highway engineers, the standard operating procedure of this profession is to increase highway capacity. Transportation economists, facing the same stimulus, would probably recommend peak-load pricing of the scarce resource. Measured by the history of highway planning, that would certainly be a nonincremental response. Yet applying scarcity pricing to transport facilities is not very novel to economists; for them it is just an incremental extension of a well-established principle.

Thus, innovation at the systemic level and incrementalism at the subsystemic level are compatible, but only in systems with redundant policy designers.[20] In systems of partisan dis-

19. Incrementalism here connotes small departures from the status quo. Lindblom originally emphasized the property of sequential error correction. These two properties are probably connected less tightly than Lindblom thought. See Wildavsky (1974, p. xiii) on this distinction.

20. Of course, even in such systems proposals that depart drastically from the status quo may be modified by opposing groups (e.g., car drivers, in the

cussion, in every sector one bureau monopolizes policy design. Hence, if the bureau changes only incrementally, as by assumption all bureaucracies do, then the system changes incrementally.[21] The sluggishness of an entrenched bureau is challenged only by critics who themselves offer no alternatives. Criticizing a program that departs incrementally from the status quo is unlikely to make the program innovative. The criticism of partisan discussion is more likely to spot holes in weak options than to produce strong (high-potential, high-risk) alternatives.

I have ended this section by comparing redundancy with partisan discussion because it is the toughest comparison I, or my readers, could think of (far tougher than comparing redundancy with monopoly), and not because I advocate replacing one by the other. Partisan discussion is indispensable: it is flexible, easily deployed, and easily produced by a variety of interorganizational arrangements. Indeed, unless a president muzzles his subordinates, partisan discussion is a routine feature of bureaucratic politics in the United States. Yet its practicality should not obscure the possibility that for important issues it may have to be supplemented by redun-

---

above example). But the incrementalism that results is due not to the bounded rationality of individuals but to conflict between groups.

21. Serge Taylor, suggesting to me that economists outside the transportation agency (perhaps in a central budget office) might well advocate scarcity pricing as an alternative to construction, has argued that partisan discussion systems can be as innovative as competitive planning. If, however, a commenting agency such as the Office of Management and Budget has the expertise to produce detailed alternatives to a lead agency's plan, then I would argue that the distinction between partisan discussion and competitive planning vanishes. In such circumstances, the two agencies' functions overlap, though they are not identical, and overlapping is a type of redundancy. (Analogously, if two diversified firms have only one product in common, they nevertheless compete in that market.) It may be that initially specialized bureaus, locked in ongoing partisan discussion, develop redundant expertise—witness the spread of economists in federal bureaus—and redundant expertise in turn creates the potential for competitive planning. Thus, partisan mutual adjustment may be *transformed* into redundancy. Further, I conjecture that a partisan adjustment system becomes adept at generating policy innovations only when a growing redundancy of expertise is quietly transforming the system into one of competitive planning.

dancy, which promises a more probing exploration of a wider range of options.

Whatever their differences, both strategies find a common theoretical justification in the framework of bounded rationality. And pragmatically, both seek systemic compensation for subsystemic unreliability. Their pragmatic similarity is rooted in their shared theoretical justification: if one thinks about organizational design in the light of bounded rationality, one is led to think about systems with large disparities between the reliability of part and whole. This is exactly the opposite of the equivalence implied by Allison (1971) between individual and collective limits on rationality. Although his case descriptions of organizational unreliability are reasonably accurate, one cannot explain these instances *solely* by referring to the bounded rationality of individuals inside the organizations, for though individual bureaucrats are always of limited rationality, bureaucracies are not always unreliable. And when doing prescriptive work, one should view the relation between the reliability of part and whole with more subtlety.[22] The popular literature on bureaucracies is replete with examples of smart people in mediocre organizations; the converse—ordinary people in smart organizations—remains a design problem.

When Is Redundancy Desirable?

The Utility of Redundancy in Different Policy Sectors

All designs or strategies, including those of proven utility, have domains of application, problem areas for which they are suited. As a method for improving bureaucratic reliability, redundancy is not restricted to urban transit. Nevertheless, it is not immediately obvious what its domain

22. Of the works following in the Carnegie tradition, the most widely read in political science is probably Graham Allison's *Essence of Decision* (1971). In that study, insofar as cognitive capacities are concerned, governments are persons writ large, limited by the same constraints. There are two reasons why Allison overlooked the possibility of systemic compensation for

of application is. Could it be that redundancy has more utility in certain sectors than in others?

The three short case studies of Chapter One—redundancy in weapons systems projects, in water projects, and in anti-poverty programs—were introduced to give a basis for comparing the effects of redundancy in different domains. The cases were chosen to represent three general types of policy sectors that have markedly different political properties. As we shall see, these political properties interact in sometimes troubling ways with the more technical problem of uncertainty reduction and containment that is the fundamental justification for duplication.

The three types of policy sectors are drawn from an analysis of federal programs by Douglas Arnold in his *Congress and the Bureaucracy* (1979). Arnold suggests that from the perspective of congressmen, or legislators in general, programs and projects usually fall into one of three sets. First, some projects confer benefits mostly upon local constituencies. Water projects such as dams are the prototype. When congressmen evaluate such projects in terms of their general (nationwide) value, most of them are indifferent. The distribution of con-

---

subsystemic deficiencies. First, Allison's second model (Organizational Process) implicitly assumes that organizations would be no more diverse—concerning mind sets and action routines—than the individuals composing them. At the next level up, the analogous assumption would be that governments, as multiorganizational complexes, would be no more diverse than a single organization.

Second, the omission may have resulted from Allison's distinction between Model Two and Model Three (Bureaucratic Politics) and from the lack of interplay between them. The Organizational Process model ignores the role that conflict might play in organizational decision-making; conflict is relegated to Model Three. Allison's Model Two bureaucracy lives in a placid environment where there is no danger of jurisdictional displacement. Consequently, whether or not there might be tension between the internal routines of a single agency and external threats to the monopoly status of those routines was not explored. His Model Three actors, on the other hand, live in a world filled with interagency conflict, but the model ignores how this politicized environment can change bureaucratic routines over time.

It is a pity that these aspects of Models Two and Three were not combined. A Model Four, of a population of rigid, competing, and programmatically diverse bureaus, could have produced insights about the relation between subsystemic inflexibility and the capacities of a larger system.

gressional preference on general benefit grounds is represented by Figure 12a. Some programs, such as defense, confer significant general benefits upon the entire population. The corresponding distribution of congressional preference is indicated by the positively skewed curve of Figure 12b. Finally, some programs, either because they are redistributive (welfare programs) or because they involve profound moral questions (abortion), confront polarized preference distributions in Congress (see Fig. 12c).

The evaluation of redundancy varies significantly across these three types of policy sectors, as does the extent of disagreement on this question. Let us consider the hardest category first. Antipoverty programs plausibly fall into category three, polarized preferences; whereas liberals usually feel that income or in-kind aid programs should be augmented *and* made less demeaning, conservatives are prone to cut them. Consider then how variably redundancy will be evaluated. First, the question of the sheer amount of welfare: if liberals and conservatives agree on the factual premise that independent, parallel welfare programs produce higher total budgets, then *ceteris paribus* liberals will prefer to maintain redundancy whereas conservatives will advocate consolidation.[23] Second, consider the weighting of different types of operational errors. Liberals worry more about poor people who remain unaided because they fall through the cracks of the welfare system; conservatives worry more about the opposite error, that is, giving aid to ineligibles.

Third, consider the differing reactions to technical uncertainty. It was argued in Chapter One that the "Let One Hundred Flowers Bloom" period of the War on Poverty produced a diversity of approach that was beneficial given how little we knew about poverty. The theoretical and, ultimately, programmatic variations were crudely similar to Burton Klein's design scheme of parallel problem-solving teams. But the po-

23. Because conservatives do want a particular kind of reliability—a welfare system that rarely helps ineligibles—they should support a corresponding kind of redundancy. This type would not be parallel programs but duplicate control procedures designed to prevent waste, fraud, and abuse. This is equivalent to the serial redundancy (preventing an invalid message from being communicated) discussed in Chapter One.

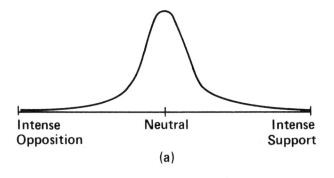

Intense
Opposition

Neutral

Intense
Support

(a)

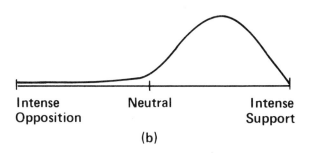

Intense
Opposition

Neutral

Intense
Support

(b)

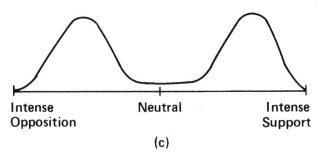

Intense
Opposition

Neutral

Intense
Support

(c)

FIGURE 12 *Patterns of Political Support and Opposition*

litical environment of the War on Poverty was so turbulent that Klein's vision of duplicate R&D as simply a knowledge-producing strategy is only partly relevant. In the polarized politics of type three sectors, technical uncertainty and pro-grammatic failure become political Rorschach tests. For liberals, failure of one approach means that society has learned something; failure of several means that we must try new strategies. For conservatives, failure of one program provides an opening for an attack upon the entire venture; failure of several is "proof" that the problem cannot be solved.[24] As Donald Campbell has regretfully acknowledged, when the "experimenting society" is also a politically driven society, experimental findings become political weapons (see Tavris, 1975, p. 52). Polarized political environments strain the parallel problem-solving strategy enormously.[25]

What, then, can be said about organizational design in this type three sector? It is very difficult to reach agreement on a design in specific problem contexts if (1) solving the problem entails much redistribution, (2) everyone knows their interests, and (3) there is a clear connection between organizational designs and outcomes. If these three conditions are satisfied, then

> each [decision-maker] will rank the [designs] according to their desirability to him, and these rankings are strictly opposed; this substitutes another game over the [organizational designs] for the original bargaining conflict over payoffs of a game. Not much is accomplished.
> (Luce and Raiffa, 1957, p. 122)

Therefore, to reach agreements on the design of organizational structure in type three contexts requires that "a veil of ignorance" be laid over decision-makers: they must choose structures without knowing their particular interests.

24. That this was an overgeneralized response to a variegated set of programs (some failed, other succeeded) has been pointed out by many analysts, but to little avail.

25. Henry Aaron has argued that the normal processes of programmatic learning, criticism, and modification tend to tear apart the coalitions that created the programs in the first place (1978, p. 159). If he is right, there is a deep contradiction between the functional requisites of programmatic learning and of coalition maintenance.

To make this idea more concrete, imagine that a set of citizens are voting on two alternative organizational structures, redundant versus nonredundant, for managing welfare policy. Though we assume the citizens vote with self-interest in mind, the veil of ignorance prevents them from knowing their future incomes. Thus no one knows whether in the society to come he will be affluent (hence a taxpayer) or poor (hence a recipient of welfare). He does know, however, certain facts about the structures. (1) There is a reliability trade-off: a redundant welfare system is less likely to overlook eligible people; a monopoly is less likely to give aid to ineligibles. (2) A redundant system provides higher per capita aid to eligible people. (3) The total welfare budget is higher under a redundant system. With these facts in hand, the citizens vote.

Within this framework a variety of results is possible. If we follow Rawls (1971, p. 152) in assuming that citizens do not know even the probability distribution of their future incomes and that they therefore use a cautious maximin decision rule (maximize your minimum gain, i.e., choose the alternative whose worse outcome is better than the worst outcome of the other alternatives), then clearly they will choose the redundant system, for if the worst befalls a citizen in the future society, that is, he will be at the bottom of the income ladder, he will be better off with redundant welfare agencies than a monopolistic one.[26]

Of course Rawls's assumptions are not the only plausible ones. If we assume that citizens know the overall income distribution but not their individual fate, they could use the decision rule of maximizing expected utility instead of the more conservative maximin. To derive how a majority of citizens would vote would then require a more detailed specification of the two organizational systems (how much is the per capita aid difference? how likely is a monopoly to over-

26. The significance of the maximin rule for those worried about extreme poverty has been noted by students of peasant societies. A Chinese image makes the point vivid: "There are districts in which the position of the rural population is that of a man standing permanently up to the neck in water, so that even a ripple is sufficient to drown him" (Scott, 1976, p. 1). Rawls's analysis (1971) is not devoid of pragmatic content.

look eligibles?). In addition, one must specify whether the citizens are risk-neutral, risk-averse, or risk-seeking.[27] Suppose all are risk-neutral. They then simply compare their expected after-tax incomes under the two alternatives and choose the higher one. But if they are risk-averse, the dispersion in the income distribution is itself distasteful[28] (see Fig. 13). Assuming System 1's mean equals System 2's mean, a rational, risk-averse citizen would choose System 2 since it is more predictable. Tough choices occur only if the mean and riskiness traded off so that one could reduce risk only by accepting a lower expected value[29] (see Fig. 14). To deduce how risk-averse citizens would vote under these conditions requires specifying exactly how the two systems' means and riskiness compare and what the citizens' indifference curves (varying combinations of expected value and dispersion to which the citizens are indifferent) look like.

We shall not proceed with these elaborations, hoping that this brief exercise shows how the device of the veil of ignorance can aid normative appraisal of organizational designs. Though this method may seem a bit bizarre, it serves an important function. In the ordinary course of politics, self-interest is a strong force; ideals such as fairness are weak forces. Hence, real world evaluations of, say, the organizational structure of our welfare system, though couched in

27. A person is risk-averse if, given two alternatives with equal expected values, he prefers the one with lower risk. The other two concepts are defined with the obvious substitutions.

28. Even if we step out of the veil of ignorance setting, a redundant welfare system might have smaller variance in the following sense: if one receives help from several programs whose budgetary fluctuations are not perfectly correlated, one will have an aid package with lower variance than if all the programs were consolidated. Thus, if poor people in the United States are risk-averse, they would be quite rational in opposing welfare reformers who want to merge transfer programs. Of course, just as a diversified portfolio cannot protect investors from the *systematic* risk of a recession, so a diversified welfare bundle cannot protect the poor from the systematic risk of a presidential attack on the welfare state.

29. We define the set of *efficient* organizational designs as all undominated feasible alternatives. A design is efficient if no feasible alternative has a higher expected value and the same dispersion (risk), or a lower dispersion and the same expected value. An optimizing risk-averse citizen would choose only from the efficient set.

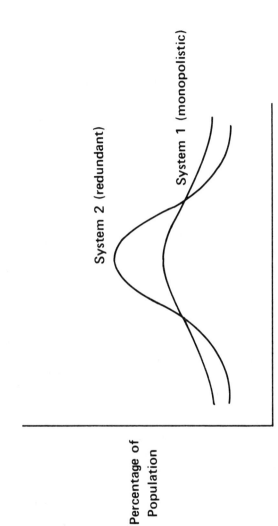

FIGURE 13 *Alternatives with Equal Means and Differing Riskiness*

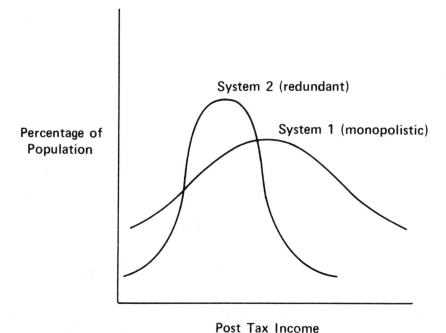

FIGURE 14 *Alternatives with Different Means and Differing Riskiness*

general, nonegoistic terms, are subject to the substitution game pointed out by Luce and Raiffa (1957): arguments purportedly over the general virtues of organizational designs are actually arguments over payoffs to particular groups or individuals. Though this is empirically understandable, it is normatively unacceptable. Most political theorists, from Kant on, agree that rules and procedures "should be general. That is, it must be possible to formulate them without the use of what would be intuitively recognized as proper names, or rigged definite descriptions" (Rawls, 1971, p. 131).[30] But though Americans seem to accept this as an ideal, achieving it in

30. One reader objected that the veil of ignorance has been used to analyze constitutions, not organizational designs. But choosing an organizational structure is in many ways similar to choosing a constitution. A constitution and an organizational design are both procedures for solving specific classes of problems. Both should be more stable than the problems they work on. Thus, both choices are *meta* choices, posing similar kinds of difficulties of evaluation.

practice is difficult. The spirit is willing but the flesh is weak. The veil of ignorance helps us out by creating a thought experiment in which an alternative's general virtues must be considered since its particularistic effects are unknown. This is, of course, only a theoretical proposal. Real decision-makers are as likely to accept vows of chastity as they are veils of ignorance. But it does suggest a method for scholars thinking about the problem of choosing an organizational structure in the face of severe political conflict. We now leave the polarized world of class three policies with a sigh of relief. Organizational design in such circumstances is a tricky process; its products, fragile. Evaluating redundancy is easier, though still nontrivial, in the other two types.

In the benign world of class two policies, congressmen believe programs confer general benefits (recall Fig. 12b). Consequently, if redundancy increases reliability in either planning or operations, then it produces these benefits for the entire population. Naturally, therefore, redundancy will create much less political controversy than it does in class three sectors.

Yet despite the consensual character of these issues, certain problems persist. First, because the demand for even a pure public good varies within a population, the demand for reliable performance must also vary. Therefore, even if everyone agreed on the factual issue of the effectiveness of different organizational structures, there would continue to be disagreement about the preferred amount of redundancy. But the conflict created by this kind of disagreement is far less intense than the conflict created by polarization over a program's basic objectives. Second, in the context of redundant planning or R&D, decision-makers would still be faced, as Defense Secretary Charles Wilson was, with pruning problems: when should parallel problem-solving paths be trimmed back? When do the costs of redundancy outweigh its benefits?

As the Thor-Jupiter case study illustrated, producer interests may distort the answer to this question. Armacost put it well:

> Since deferred choice between competing projects permits not only the accumulation of knowledge but the development of vested interests in the maintenance of programs, political ob-

stacles to clear-cut decisions emerge as the intellectual obstacles are being removed.

(1969, p. 17)

Thus, there may be a systematic tendency for redundancy, once begun in development projects, to be oversupplied.[31] Nevertheless, to say that a program is overly redundant is not to say, as does the conventional wisdom, that operational duplication is totally without merit. Rather, it is to make the less dramatic point that one can have too much of a good thing. Finally, even if producer interests in a class two policy sector cause duplication in a program to continue too long, at least the benefits of redundancy (though not worth the cost) are distributed to the population at large. Hence, excessive amounts of redundancy in this sector will never provoke the controversy that would develop in a class three sector.

Class one policy sectors present an intermediate degree of evaluation difficulties. On the one hand, excessive duplication—for example, so many dams built in the same watershed that marginal costs exceed marginal benefits—is socially more wasteful than in class two, the redistributive effects less acceptable. A small group, such as the water users in the Kings River case, is enjoying normatively excessive benefits at the expense of the rest of the nation. And unlike antipoverty programs, the particularistic projects common to class one are not explicitly redistributive; they are legitimized on other grounds. Therefore if a project is overly reliable, due to a superabundance of redundancy, that benefit cannot be rationalized on the basis that needy people are being helped. There is little reason to believe that the poor are the primary recipients of pork barrels.

The above pertains to operational redundancy. If duplication occurs during planning, it is somewhat less problematical, for it may be managed so that better information about a project's effects is squeezed out of the bureaucratic rivals. But even in planning there is risk, namely, that the agencies seeking the support of local interests will engage in

31. In practical terms, decision-makers may face a difficult choice: the risk of having parallel projects continue past the optimal pruning point versus the risk of starting off with insufficient redundancy. Thus, the practical choice may not be between efficient versus excessive redundancy, but too much versus too little.

a bidding war by "gold plating" the project, thus exacerbating the transfers from the general population to the local groups. Though this kind of bidding war did not occur in the Kings River case, we cannot dismiss it out of hand.

On the other hand, redundancy causes less controversy here than in class three sectors. The reason is obvious: if there are net transfers from the nation to a local group, they are small compared with those of class three, and political conflict is thereby less intense.

So much for differences; some common themes cover all three sectors. First, it is possible to have too much redundancy. Nothing in this work should be taken as a denial of this obvious point. "Wasteful redundancy" is not a contradiction in terms. One can have too many weapon systems, too many antipoverty programs, too many dams on the same river. Second, and more subtly, it is even possible to have too many competing *plans* for such programs. Top decision-makers are limited in their ability to assess the worth of alternative designs. What the limits are remains to be discovered, but we are confident they exist. And given a "reasonable" amount of diversity in the solutions explored by the first n rivals, search by $n + 1$ may be excessive.[32]

Third, the intrapolicy sector analysis of Chapter Two, breaking decision-making into planning and operations and assessing the relative value of redundancy in those phases, pertains to all three types of sectors. In all three, uncertainty is the greatest and cost lowest during planning; the former decreases and the latter increases as programs move from blueprint to being. Letting "n flowers bloom" is therefore applicable to each sector; what varies is the value of n and the date of pruning.

Implementing Redundancy: Problems of Performance Monitoring

Thus far the analysis of sectoral differences has centered on a rather salient variable, the distribution of decision-makers'

32. To make this idea precise, one should represent it as a search-for-information problem. To reach conclusions about when search is excessive, one may have to make rather strong assumptions about the probability distributions of solutions in the search space.

preferences. But policy sectors differ on a second dimension, which, though less eye-catching to the political scientist, nonetheless affects the utility of redundancy. The *measurability* of a bureau's performance raises several knotty questions about redundancy's domain of application. Let us compare competition in four policy areas, moving from the easily measured to the poorly measured.

1.   When cities contract out their garbage collection, they can specify the kind of service they desire. Curbside or non-curbside pickup? Once or twice a week? These and a handful of other easily observed variables constitute, with the price, the service contract. Competitors know what they must do to outperform rivals; contracting cities know what to look for when comparing competing suppliers. The agreements do not suffer from problems of observing performance.

2.   As mentioned in Chapter One, many small cities in the greater Los Angeles area participate in the Lakewood Plan, buying public services from Los Angeles County, each other, and private vendors. One service delivered on a contractual basis is police services. Unfortunately, specifying a sensible contract for police protection is more difficult than for garbage collection. What should be stipulated? Arrests? That could mean that if crime increases, the police's performance record improves. Convictions? That could give police perverse incentives to avoid expending effort on difficult cases. Numerous performance measures are subject to similar distortions. In fact, many of the Lakewood arrangements suffer from contractual incompleteness: they do not include performance criteria at all. Instead, they refer to *effort*, inputs such as patrol cars and man-hours. As several researchers have discovered: "It is not entirely unexpected that the contract services plan, especially as it operates in Los Angeles County, does not appear to have improved police performance noticeably" (Mehay, 1978, p. 320). The contract provides an incentive for diligence, as effort is specified and partially observable, but not for effectiveness or efficiency.

3.   Problems may develop if performance is partially measurable but the service supplier's behavior is hard to observe. Consider the idea of vouchers as a way of increasing com-

petition in education. Parents, armed with vouchers, contract with a school to educate their children. How would education be described in the contract? Parents would not wish to repeat the mistake of the Lakewood Plan by including only effort in the agreement; quality of education must somehow be captured. Suppose state government were to establish standardized tests to evaluate children's progress. What goes unobserved is teachers' classroom behavior. The danger is that they would skew their efforts toward preparing students for the standardized tests. The measures are obtrusive, the measurement process corruptible.

4.   Lastly, consider a domain where performance is almost unmeasurable: foreign policymaking. Unlike police contracts, for which performance indicators are conceivable even if incomplete and corruptible, anything but the most subjective standards in foreign affairs is hard to imagine. But the process of foreign policy formation is partly observable by a superior. It is therefore quite appropriate that Alexander George (1972) proposed procedural controls in his scheme of multiple advocacy in foreign policymaking. The rule is, when one cannot evaluate performance, regulate the process. It is a second-best solution, but a solution nonetheless.

We have analyzed four different policy situations exemplifying different degrees of contractual completeness (see Fig. 15). Garbage collection criteria are easily covered in a formal contract; behavioral control is therefore unnecessary. This is an ideal situation for competition among public organizations. Technologically certain domains such as garbage collection do not exhaust this set; perhaps the most impressive results of governmental competition arise where means are uncertain but results spectacularly observable, as in competition within the Manhattan Project over key components. For the police and schools there is significant contractual incompleteness in the form of poor and partial performance measures. The poor indicators combine with serious difficulties in observing suppliers' behavior to create the risk that indicators will be gamed.

In the third class of domains, performance measures fall entirely by the wayside, and one must rely on managing the

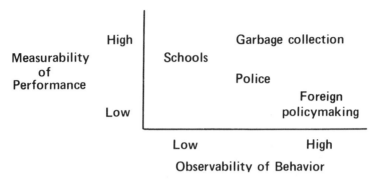

FIGURE 15 *Types of Policy Sectors*

process. Clearly, the difficulties of managing public sector competition increase as we move from situation one to situations two or three. It is not just that problem solving and service delivery become objectively more difficult in two and three than in one; the relevant question is whether the competitive strategy *intensifies* problems.[33] In the case of schools and vouchers, competition may increase the gaming of standardized tests. Of course one should expect a certain amount of distortion of such critical numbers under monopoly as well, but in a competitive environment a school faces greater risks and hence greater temptation to manipulate the numbers.

Similarly, Samuel Huntington pointed out twenty years ago that rivalry intensifies the armed services' public relations activity and cultivation of congressmen as well as their rivalry over military strategy and program. The task-oriented and

33. In one respect, however, difficulties in measuring performance affect all organizational designs. In Chapter Six it was noted that the amount of information about a project trades off with the usefulness of the information: the longer a decision-maker waits, the more information is generated about rival solutions, but using those data to terminate inferior options becomes increasingly difficult. Measurement problems inherent in certain policy sectors exacerbate this trade-off. If one wished to have as much information about, e.g., a weapon system as one can obtain about a transit system, one would have to accept a less reversible decision. (Full-scale testing of weapons fortunately occurs only sporadically, i.e., during wars, whereas transit systems can be tested continuously.) But this is not a function of organizational design; the trade-off curve between information and reversibility is intrinsically worse in defense than in transit.

nontask-oriented behaviors are a *joint* product of competition; one cannot have one without the other. From the point of view of a competitor, outperforming a rival is only one way to win. One can also lobby congressmen or engage in "unfair practices." The task facing superiors who are managing competition is to induce rival bureaus to pick improved performance as their action option. Achieving this is of course easier if rewards are linked to performance measures, but as the experience with program evaluation showed, it is far from simple to develop such measures in government. More often than not, superiors will have to fall back on regulating competitive due process rather than rewarding the fruits of competition. Using the strategy is bound to cause disappointment if, as in the Lakewood Plan, there is contractual incompleteness, yet officials fail to regulate the process. In such situations competition will often generate instrumentally irrelevant behavior.

Is Redundancy Feasible?

Desirability is one issue; practicality, another. Theory and some evidence may suggest that instituting redundancy in certain policy sectors could improve the performance of public organizations. But is the strategy organizationally and politically feasible? A desirable but infeasible strategy is utopian, and it would be ironic if redundancy fell into that trap, for redundancy theorists like von Neumann saw the theory as an alternative to the utopian dream of making systems reliable by perfecting their parts. In view of that design philosophy, it is germane to investigate conditions that increase redundancy's feasibility.

1.   The probability of a premature quashing of redundancy is diminished if overlapping agencies use different technologies. As in the AC-BART case, different technologies promote a (possibly false) expectation of functional specialization, that is, the different technologies will be deployed for different ends, whereas identical technologies make redundancy highly visible and vulnerable. Indeed, until a problem

is sufficiently salient to be categorized as a policy area on the national agenda, alternative technologies may not even be *considered* functional substitutes. It has been suggested, for example, that until the energy crisis broke in 1973, congressmen were not troubled that no department monopolized jurisdiction over energy programs.[34] Though coal was under the aegis of the Interior Department and nuclear issues under the Atomic Energy Commission, there was no hue and cry to eliminate fragmentation and organize functionally. Because congressmen categorized programs by technology rather than by use, they did not see them as alternatives.

2.   If bureaus overlap rather than exactly duplicate each other's functions, redundancy is more tolerable politically. Organizational existence is less threatened by overlap, for it enables agencies to retreat to domains that are theirs alone. Consequently, they will try less vigorously, and less viciously, to oust interlopers in the overlapped domains. This argument also points up the wisdom of encouraging bureaus to diversify functionally. A functionally diversified bureau is less likely to be precisely duplicated by another agency, and its diversity reduces the threat posed by a rival in one programmatic area. Portfolio theory applies to bureaucracies as well as to investors.

3.   The above point is complemented by this one. A well-established agency can mobilize its political resources to bar newcomers to its policy field. It is not accidental that both redundant cases in this study involved agencies that started almost simultaneously. None of the organizations was sufficiently entrenched to repel others from their turf. This complements point two above because in each pair, each agency deluded itself into believing that *eventually* the relationship would become completely differentiated. In the Twin Cities the organizations, during their fragile early years, devoted themselves to different missions. In the Bay Area, the different technologies required different lead times, producing in their early years nonoverlapping activities (AC operating, BART planning). And the technological differences mandated partly disjoint service areas. Hence both tempo-

34. Stuart Ross brought this example to my attention.

rally and spatially these two overlapped rather than fully duplicated (see Fig. 16).

4. Redundancy is more stable, and therefore more practical, if overlapping bureaus do not have a powerful superior close at hand.[35] In Minneapolis, where the state legislature is active in metropolitan politics, the redundancy was ended quickly whereas in the Bay Area, where state government has historically been remote from regional government, the overlap persists. Though a few executives encourage duplication, superiors more often reorganize duplication out of existence than promote it.

For this reason redundancy is probably more feasible among special districts than among regular line departments because districts are less commonly embedded in hierarchies. It also follows that among line departments, redundancy is more feasible in decentralized organizations. In these, bureaucratic entrepreneurs can intrude on each other's domains without a nice regard for jurisdictional proprieties and without fearing that their actions will be killed by hierarchical fiat.

If the ideology of administration in the public sector changes and redundancy is legitimized, then point four may become invalid. For as we shall see below, hierarchical supe-

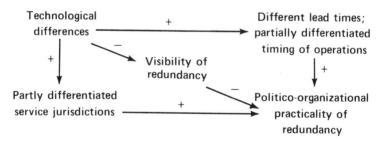

FIGURE 16 *Effect of Technological Differences on Feasibility of Redundancy*

35. The proposition does not necessarily hold if there is more than one powerful superior. For example, Serge Taylor has suggested to me that the fragmented nature of the congressional committee structure has helped prevent the merger of overlapping programs in the executive branch.

riors are apt to eliminate redundancy more because they hold to incorrect beliefs than because their political interests are threatened.

5. Chapter One explored the practicality of lateral redundancies, wherein agencies are hierarchically equal. A second kind of duplication, vertical redundancy, involves superiors and subordinates. We recall that it was easy for the Twin Cities' Metro Council to assert itself and move in on transit planning. First, it had the authority to do so. Second, the means-end relations between it and the MTC were intrinsically fuzzy. And this ambiguity is inherent in hierarchy, for the superior's ability to specify goals can go far toward selecting means.

But the feasibility of vertical redundancies is constrained by the limited resources of superiors. They can only intervene selectively in subordinates' jurisdictions. Further, vertical redundancies are inherently unstable. What hierarchy giveth, hierarchy taketh away. If a superior wants a jurisdiction, the subordinate will usually be removed from the field. The result is a substitution of one actor for another, rather than redundant actors.

6. Finally, the reader will recall that redundant agencies must retain some diversity in order to produce the full fruits of duplication. The probability of parallel agencies remaining independent is the knottiest problem in the pragmatics of redundancy theory. It is particularly problematic during planning. Heterogeneous planning require a diversity that comprehends mind-sets, planning assumptions, and predispositions about solutions.

This obstacle to implementing redundancy has not gone unnoticed. Steven Chan claims that homogeneous patterns of recruitment and socialization in the intelligence community militate against genuine diversity in intellectual perspectives and methods (1979, pp. 177–178). Lawrence Pierce, describing fiscal policymaking, refers to an "incestuous process" linking similarly trained economists whose "interbreeding ideas" seem to come out the same (1971, pp. 56–57).[36]

36. I suspect that Pierce exaggerates the similarities. For example, Chicago- and Yale-trained economists regard governmental intervention in the economy very differently.

In addition to recruitment and socialization difficulties, competing bureaus may reduce programmatic differences by converging toward a middle position in a policy space (Downs, 1957, p. 117).[37] Then competing bureaus, like competing political parties, would be offering a Tweedledum-Tweedledee choice: the shadow but not the substance of diversity.

What can we infer from our data?

1.   The cases show that diversity can be sustained for a while at least. It does not *inevitably* decay.[38]

2.   Diversity does not necessarily require that agencies employ different specialists. As in Minneapolis, generalists can develop visions of the future. Passionate commitments to visions, though they also produce negative side effects, sustain diverse approaches over long periods.[39]

3.   A conscious effort by agency leaders to preserve a sense of organizational culture helps maintain independence.[40] Every organization develops its own folkways and traditions.[41] These can internally inhibit convergence toward median policy positions. Although bureaucracies are not representative institutions, leaders are influenced by the led, and a widespread sense of organizational identity can inhibit opportunistic blurring of differences by leaders.

37.   This point was raised by several listeners during a talk on redundancy given at the Stanford Business School.

38.   Though there is no guarantee that the cases are typical, it is reassuring that diversity persisted in both pairs of agencies: MTC and the Metro Council and BART and AC.

39.   This is, to borrow Thomas Kuhn's phrase, one positive function of dogma.

40.   I thank Martin Landau for suggesting this point.

41.   It may appear that this point contradicts the argument on organizational missions. Earlier I noted negative effects of missions; here I point to positive effects of unique organizational traditions. Yet central to an agency's tradition is its mission. The difference is that the discussion on missions presumed an integrated agency monopolizing its policy sector whereas the discussion on organizational culture presumed several competing organizations in the same sector. If an organizational mission develops in a monopoly, it will usually cover only one of the functionally equivalent programs in the agency, starving the others. But if there are redundant bureaus, then unique cultures, rather than imposing homogeneity, preserve diversity.

4. Investment in durable equipment sustains diversity. AC is unlikely to discard buses for trains; the Navy is unlikely to discard the Polaris missile for ICBMs. (Obviously this point pertains more to operations than to planning.)

5. Finally, whether duplicating bureaus remain independent will often depend on diversity in the surrounding social system, on the educational system and the structure of professions and skill groups in society. If functional specialities are broken down into subspecialties, with their own technologies and traditions, then organizations will be staffed more diversely. For example, in transportation schools, students might be directed into subspecialties of highway planning and mass transit planning, or they might all be trained as broad-gauged transportation planners. Although the narrower education may promote "the deformation of the specialist," collectively it inhibits the creation of a bland sameness within a functional area. If all experts in a policy area have been exposed to the same options (and biases), then bureaus will have less diversity to draw upon. Of course, because bureaus rarely influence the degree of differentiation in the larger social system, it is a parameter to which they must adapt.[42]

Above and beyond the obstacles of organizational politics, there may be psychological obstacles to institutionalizing competition in government. The aversion to redundancy may have deep roots in our conceptualizations of collective, organized action. The cognitive feature that may interfere with implementing redundancy lessens the strategy's *accessibility* to decision-makers. In experiments on concept formation, Jerome Bruner and his colleagues found that disjunctive concepts—something is an x if it has property p *or* q—were much less familiar to subjects than conjunctive ones—something is an x if it has properties p *and* q. Their subjects, after viewing a set of objects, were asked to infer the category that described the set. Bruner et al., finding that subjects were

42. There are exceptions. The United States' armed forces' tradition of educating their own officers breaks down the functional group of "experts in violence" into subspecialties. Higher French public administration also has its own schools, but these may increase homogeneity.

much less likely to discover disjunctive than conjunctive concepts, concluded:

> In spite of the fact that the disjunctive concepts had been carefully explained, subjects showed regularly what can only be called "conjunctive tendencies". . . . strong antidisjunctive tendencies exist in intelligent adults that probably require prolonged buffeting before they are abandoned.
>
> (1956, pp. 168, 173)

If we recognize that the logical representation of redundant systems is disjunctive, we will grasp the significance of this finding. In logic diagrams in reliability engineering, a system's redundant components are connected by "or" links: to brake an automobile, component p or q will suffice. Nonredundant systems are represented by "and" links: to reach a goal one must do p and q. Conjunctive categories, which are so much more familiar to most people, are the conceptualization of nonredundant series systems. Thus, Bruner et al.'s study, suggesting that the idea of parallel systems is cognitively inaccessible, predicts that decision-makers would have a powerful bias in favor of nonredundant systems— even in the face of *no evidence* about the effectiveness of the two designs!

However, Bruner et al. observe that the "antidisjunctive tendencies" may succumb to "prolonged buffeting." One type of prolonged buffeting is repeated failure. Rightly or wrongly, government is often considered ineffective. Numerous programs are thought to be failures. These experiences may be the prolonged buffeting that is needed to make decision-makers think disjunctively, to think of reaching programmatic goals either by pathway p or pathway q, rather than thinking serially. But we cannot be overly optimistic. There are two reasons why decision-makers may not learn to introduce more redundancy: the ambiguity of experience and budgetary constraints.

More often than not, the lessons of the past are ambiguous (March and Olsen, 1975). The buffeting of failures may lead decision-makers to reassert the primacy of the nonredundant serial design rather than exploring the strategy of redundancy. We need only note the efforts of recent presidents to assert control over the permanent bureaucracy. Control rarely assumes the form of Roosevelt's competitive strategy; instead, it involves tightening a hierarchical, serial chain of command from the president through his political appointees down to the bureaucracy, tightening the links in the chain rather than duplicating them. Perhaps asserting presidential control via a hierarchical chain is too temptingly direct not to be tried. Perhaps cognitive psychologists are correct: decision-makers overestimate the probability of getting what they want via serial systems (see below for evidence on this point). Certainly it is true that one "lesson" recent presidents have learned from their predecessors' failure to control the bureaucracy is that control was poorly executed. Thus, saved by a residual category of diagnosis, "implementation failure," the failure of nonredundant hierarchical control merely intensifies attempts to control (Landau and Stout, 1979, p. 151). The lesson learned paraphrases George Bernard Shaw: "Control systems haven't failed; they haven't been tried."

There is a second reason governmental ineffectiveness may not induce decision-makers to think of using redundancy: money. This period of fiscal retrenchment is an inhospitable budgetary climate for bureaucratic duplication. As noted in that, contrary to conventional political science, which emphasizes the clash of interests above all else,[48] and contrary to conventional economics, which acknowledges imperfect com-ineffective; rather, the conventional wisdom, enduring in an evidential vacuum, is bolstered by short-sighted efforts to economize.

The relation between budgetary constraints and the political viability of redundancy can be summarized in a simple proposition: the amount of programmatic redundancy in government varies directly with the total budget's real growth rate. If the budget is decreasing in real terms, then programmatic duplication declines. However, the *proportion* of redundancy that is competitive, where bureaus fight over scarce funds, changes inversely with the total budget's real growth rate. The reason is simple: if the growth rate becomes negative, slack is squeezed out of the system (Cyert and March, 1963). Slack permitted duplication without contestation for funds, hence, noncompetitive redundancies. As slack vanishes, some noncompetitive duplication is eliminated outright and some become competitive redundancies as once-peaceful parallel bureaus start fighting over a shrinking pie.

We conclude that in periods of fiscal retrenchment it would be tactically sensible to emphasize competitive rather than noncompetitive redundancy. The former extends the promise of holding down costs; the latter does not.

Some of these limitations on redundancy's feasibility may be only temporary. Budgets expand as well as contract; certain psychological obstacles, such as a bias for conjunctive (nonredundant) systems, once recognized, may be overcome. One factor, however, is quite durable: the feasibility of duplication in government is certain to fluctuate indefinitely with the strategic interests of bureaucrats and politicians. This is particularly true for the subset of competitive redundancies, for in terms of political power, competition is an elaboration of the centuries-old political axiom of divide and conquer. As such, it may well be included in savvy politicians' working theories of power. But savvy bureau chiefs probably share the politicians' theory, and any strategy that reduces an actor's power will elicit a counterstrategy. Thus, bureaucratic leaders, perceiving that it is in their interest to resist becoming redundant, may collude to reduce competition. This points up that a competitive bureaucracy may be neither self-regulating nor self-stabilizing. The framework of competition must, as Alexander George has suggested, be sustained from without. But just as organizational interests often dictate collusion, so can there be an organizational interest in "cheating," in stealing a march on a bureaucratic rival by moving into an important policy area. Political management of bureaucratic competition means promoting these latter tendencies, arranging incentives so bureaus compete rather than collude. But because bureaucratic leaders will be simultaneously devising strategies to secure monopolistic positions, it will be a game of move and countermove.[43] Like most seqences of offense and defense where new tactics can be created, this game has no end.

43. Depicting only two strategic actors oversimplifies the situation. Redundancy is a game that can be played at all organizational levels, and a smart bureau chief may wish to eliminate external competition while simultaneously maintaining internal redundant channels below him, just as a firm

Future Lines of Research

Most research monographs include a plea for further research. This work follows that sensible tradition of urging others to help solve problems left unsolved by the author.

Incentives and Redundancy

We do not understand with any depth when and why bureaus compete instead of collude. That they choose sometimes one and sometimes the other is indisputable; *why* is more perplexing. Undoubtedly the configuration of budgetary incentives is part of the story, but only part. Bureaucracies will sometimes avoid a task, even one accompanied by extra funds, if it conflicts with a sense of organizational mission or if accepting the task would plunge the agency into a polarized issue environment (Hammond, 1979). To create a theory of the origins of public sector competition, we must develop a finer-grained understanding of bureaus' incentive structures. One approach would be to model jurisdictional politics as a sequential prisoners' dilemma, in which there are short-run organizational interests to cheat (compete) but long-run interests to cooperate (collude).

The Political Environment of Bureaus

This study can be faulted for overemphasizing the supply side of redundancy. The demand for redundant or competitive programs has been scanted. We need to know more about coalitions in different policy sectors that may influence the creation or elimination of redundancy. How does, for example, the distribution of a program's costs and benefits

---

prefers to sell its goods monopolistically while buying goods from competing sellers. To figure out the aggregate implications of this multilevel game requires mathematical modeling.

affect the demand for bureaucratic competition? James Wilson (1980) has suggested a simple typology of policy sectors (see Fig. 17). The effective demand for redundancy should vary as the distributional patterns of programs vary. For example, the effective demand for redundant projects under cell two conditions in Figure 17 will be less than the demand under cell three conditions. Thus a study of bureaus' political environments may help us estimate the empirical distribution of redundancy by policy sectors.

Complementing this would be an analysis of the role of representative institutions in articulating demand for redundancy. Under what circumstances do legislators have an incentive to oppose conventional wisdom and press for bureaucratic competition? Niskanen (1975) and Miller and Moe (1983) have made promising starts here.

Greater Realism in Formal Theories of Bureaucracy

The formal modeling of bureaucratic competition and monopoly will receive major inspiration from the public choice school. Trained in economics, public choice theorists are predisposed to view bureaucracy in these terms. Since the bulk of formal modeling will be produced by this school, it is essential to our understanding of bureaucratic competition that the models be empirically plausible.

Public choice models of bureaucracy have generally been characterized by three assumptions: (1) decision-makers are egoistic; (2) technical certainty prevails, that is, bureaucrats know their own production functions; and (3) time is inessential, that is, the models are single-period constructs. The

		Diffuse	Compact
Distribution of Benefits	Diffuse	1	2
	Compact	3	4

FIGURE 17 *Distribution of Costs and Benefits*

first assumption is the distinctive characteristic of public choice models and may be worth retaining. But the second and third assumptions must be relaxed. Because some bureaus have highly certain technologies whereas others are highly indeterminate, public choice models must allow for technical uncertainty. As for time, the difference between redundancy and monopoly will be fully understood only through multiperiod models. With single-period models one comprehends only static efficiency or how well different organizational designs perform *within* fixed choice sets. With multiperiod models one can assess dynamic efficiency or how well different organizational designs *expand* choice sets. And how well bureaus learn over time is more important than their short-run efficiency (Stinchcombe, 1975).

Innovation and Redundancy

Innovations in government policies have been studied from the perspectives of diffusion (Gray, 1973) and leadership (Downs, 1976), among others, but the effect of bureaucratic competition is underexplored. Not so in economics. Since Joseph Schumpeter, economists have debated whether competitive or oligopolistic firms are more innovative. (Significantly, none has bet on monopolies.) We need to address this question in public administration.

The conventional wisdom advocating monopolistic bureaus comports with our notion that agencies' structures should be simple, neat, and easy to grasp. We believe control and, especially, pinpointing responsibility to be facilitated by such simplicity. But it is reasonable to hypothesize that agencies without rivals lead "the quiet life" of monopolists, that is, they rarely innovate. And noninnovative monopolistic bureaus will not develop the "requisite variety" in their response repertoires that is needed to cope with complex task environments (Ashby, 1963). As Ashby's theorem on requisite variety implies, failure to innovate—stagnation—will, in a changing task environment, generate anomalous and unpleasant consequences. Thus, we may have to decide whether we want surprising competitive bureaus that produce unsurprising (intended) policy consequences or unsurprising monopolistic bureaus that produce surprising (unintended) consequences.

Conclusion: Man's Frailties Revisited

The most basic argument for redundancy rests on the practicality of increasing a system's reliability without increasing the reliability of its constituent elements. Duplication is a substitute for perfect parts. In bureaucracies, the most important parts are decision-makers; hence it is the fallibility of decision-makers that justifies organizational redundancy. And as we argued in the introduction, error, due to the limited capacities of the human mind, is an ever-present threat.

Could this be an overly pessimistic view of the cognitive abilities of human beings? After all, the works that were cited in Chapter One to support this view (Merton, 1940; Simon, 1947; Cyert and March, 1963) are several decades old. Perhaps in the intervening time we have discovered that Simon's theory of bounded rationality is incorrect, that in fact decision-makers do not labor under the cognitive constraints he imputed to them.

On the contrary. Far from being disconfirmed, Simon's insights have been sustained, broadened, and deepened. In the last fifteen years there has been a tremendous outpouring of experimentation in cognitive psychology showing that people, in order to cope with the discrepancy between the "booming, buzzing confusion" of reality and their cognitive abilities, use simplifying strategies, known as heuristics, to make problems manageable.[44] (Indeed, the heuristic best known to organization theorists, satisficing, is now considered only one member of a large set, and perhaps not the most fundamental one at that.) These mental strategies, though they enable us to cope with a complex world, are not costless:

44. For an excellent overview of this work, see Nisbett and Ross (1980), and also Einhorn and Hogarth (1981). For a review from the perspective of political science, see Kinder and Weiss (1978); for one from the perspective of organization theory, see March and Shapira (1982).

they lead us into making systematic errors. In the context of bureaucratic decision-making, two kinds of problems are particularly worth noting: difficulties of predicting the future and of learning from the past.

As Landau has argued (1972), public policies should be regarded as hypotheses, as conditional conjectures of the form, "if a bureau carries out actions X and Y, then Z will result." Accordingly, pragmatic success rests, in large measure, on the ability of decision-makers to predict the future. Unfortunately, individuals tend to overestimate their capacity to do so and to underestimate the uncertainty confronting them.[45] Two political psychologists note that these tendencies imply that "decision-makers [are] more confident that they understand the problem and more satisfied that their policies will achieve the predicted ends than the evidence really justifies" (Kinder and Weiss, 1978, p. 723). This overconfidence, if uncorrected by other bureaucratic tendencies, would make an agency's leader underestimate the value of redundancy: like BART's planners, he would expect everything to go according to plan. In the context of such expectations, duplication is considered wasteful.

Worse news is yet to come. There is evidence that our predictive errors cumulate. The cumulative bias occurs when people try to predict the probability of compound events, for example, the probability of A and B and C occurring. One study concludes that the overestimations grow *exponentially* with the number of subevents (Cohen et al., 1972).

The significance of this finding for organizational decision-making is clear. Two leading researchers in this field, Daniel Kahneman and Amos Tversky, note:

> Biases in the evaluation of compound events are particularly significant in the context of planning. The successful completion of an undertaking, such as the development of a new product typically has a conjunctive character: for the undertaking to succeed, each of a series of events must occur. Even when each of these events is very likely, the overall probability

45. There are two specific manifestations of this problem in experimental settings. First, subjects set overly narrow confidence intervals around their estimates of an event's probability. Second, their subjective guesses of events' probabilities often correspond poorly with objective relative frequencies.

of success can be quite low if the number of events is large. The general tendency to overestimate the probability of conjunctive events leads to unwarranted optimism in the evaluation of the likelihood that a plan will succeed or that a project will be completed on time.

(1974, p. 1129)

In the light of this research, it is sobering to realize that the conventional wisdom in public administration, in extolling the virtues of streamlined organizations, has advocated precisely the structure most conducive to overconfident predictions, for a streamlined agency is nothing more than a series system wherein long chains of compound events (A tells B who instructs C who . . .) must be executed flawlessly. And though we realize that any break in a chain disables it, we underestimate how likely *some* break is. Thus, the proverb "a chain is only as strong as its weakest link" is overly optimistic; a chain, or series system, is *weaker* than its weakest link. If, for example, the probability of completing acts A, B, and C is 0.9, 0.8, and 0.9, respectively, then the probability of completing the whole chain is, assuming statistical independence, $0.9 \times 0.8 \times 0.9 = 0.648$. This is less than the weakest link probability of 0.8. More generally, a series system will be weaker than its weakest link unless the probability of completing *all* the other links is one. Folk wisdom partakes of the same overconfidence that cognitive psychologists think plagues decision-makers.[46]

Yet prediction is, after all, a hard task. Perhaps we excel at

46. If the heuristics responsible for these biases are not culturally bound, then we should find problems such as decision-makers overestimating the reliability of nonredundant systems in other nations. Joseph Berliner has inferred the existence of this particular bias in the Soviet Union. Commenting upon the paucity of competition in Soviet research and development, he conjectures:

It is not surprising that the concept of parallel R&D effort should not have developed in the Soviet context. The Soviet philosophical outlook has a strong rationalist element. The system of control planning draws support from the belief that if one plans rationally what each unit should do, and if each unit would indeed do it, one's problems would be solved. (1976, p. 123)

It is thus a tenable hypothesis that cognitive biases against redundancy are not confined to the American context.

learning from our mistakes; perhaps decision-makers muddle through by adapting rather than by anticipating. If so, then in the long run a system of redundant planning would do no better than a system of monopolistic planning, for both would converge to the same (correct) solution. The latter would merely take longer.

Alas, it is a central finding of recent work in cognitive psychology that people do not learn as easily, rapidly, or correctly from experience as an optimistic Bayesian statistician might think (Nisbett and Ross, 1980, pp. 167–192). We reinterpret ambiguous evidence to suit our beliefs; we have a regrettable tendency to hold fast to our beliefs in the face of disconfirming evidence;[47] we rarely search for disconfirming evidence; when we encounter negative evidence, we criticize the methods that produced the data, but when we encounter confirming evidence produced by *exactly* the same methods, we turn off our methodological criticism. The list of our adaptive shortcomings is a long one.

It is therefore unlikely that adaptation solves all the problems created by our predictive weaknesses, and it is equally unlikely that the sole advantage of competitive planning is its greater speed in reaching good solutions. Given the strong tendency to cling to one's beliefs, a decision-maker or planner who starts off with a poor solution in mind has a good chance of never reaching a satisfactory one. Individual decision-makers find it difficult to follow Walter Lippmann's advice that one should hold hypotheses lightly and modify them gladly.

These inferential difficulties uncovered by psychologists appear, at least in part, to be aspects of "cold" cognition, by-products of the heuristics we use to make a complex world comprehensible. One does not need to postulate "hot" cognition—reasoning distorted to serve motivational drives such as self-esteem or ego defense—to explain these phenomena; the information-processing characteristics of human be-

47. Some philosophers of science have argued, quite reasonably, that one should not overthrow a well-corroborated theory (belief) on the basis of one piece of negative evidence. Quite so, but the belief perseverance of experimental subjects goes beyond normatively justifiable conservatism. See Nisbett and Ross, 1980, pp. 169–172, 175–179, for some telling experiments.

ings suffice to account for them (Nisbett and Ross, 1980, pp. 228–248). Thus, even if public officials were to surprise James Madison by developing the hearts of angels, motivated not by self-interest but only by the public weal, even if politicians never distorted economic predictions to further their political ambitions, even if bureaucrats were never reluctant to admit administrative blunders in order to protect their careers, nevertheless, they would still commit errors of "cold" cognition. The persistence of such mistakes, caused not by self-interest but by fundamental heuristics of human thought, indicates that, contrary to conventional political science, which emphasizes the clash of interests above all else,[48] and contrary to conventional economics, which acknowledges imperfect competition but not imperfect computation, the strategy of redundancy would still be relevant in a government led by (fallible) angels.[49]

But whether we cannot trust decision-makers because they are egoistic or because they reason imperfectly is ultimately irrelevant. Both tendencies are here to stay. The durability of that fact implies that we would do well to set aside the utopian dream of perfecting the individual decision-maker and concentrate instead, following von Neumann's advice, on "building reliable systems from unreliable parts."

48. Robert Jervis has similarly argued that the concepts of belief and perception have been underemphasized and that of interest overemphasized in explanations of foreign policymaking: "Knowing what a person's interests are does not tell us how he will see his environment or go about selecting the best route to reach his goals. . . . It was not in Chamberlain's interest to see Hitler as appeasable, [or] in Acheson's interest to believe that China was not likely to enter the Korean War . . ." (1976, pp. 8–9).

49. In such a world, only the subset of competitive redundancies would become unnecessary. In economic theory, competition is typically justified because of the play of self-interest; decision-makers' reasoning may be perfect but their motives are impure. This points up that the idea of redundancy, focusing on the *existence* of unreliable components rather than on any particular cause of unreliability, is a more general concept than competition.

Bibliography

Aaron, Henry J. 1978. *Politics and the Professors: The Great Society in Perspective.* Washington, D.C.: Brookings Institution.

Adler, Seymour. 1978. "The Early History of Relations Between the Alameda-Contra Costa Transit District and the San Francisco Bay Area Rapid Transit District." University of California, Berkeley. Unpublished paper.

———. 1980. *The Political Economy of Transit in the San Francisco Bay Area, 1945–1963.* Washington, D.C.: Urban Mass Transit Administration.

Alameda-Contra Costa Transit District. 1958. *Facts About the ACCTD Plan.* Oakland, Calif.

———. 1955–77. *Board Minutes.* Oakland, Calif.

Allison, Graham. 1971. *Essence of Decision: Explaining the Cuban Missile Crisis.* Boston: Little, Brown.

Altshuler, Alan. 1977. "The Politics of Urban Transportation Innovation." *Technology Review* 79(6) (May):50–58.

Altshuler, Alan, James Womack, and John Pucher. 1979. *The Urban Transportation System: Politics and Policy Innovation.* Cambridge, Mass.: MIT Press.

Armacost, Michael. 1969. *The Politics of Weapons Innovation: The Thor-Jupiter Controversy.* New York: Columbia University Press.

Arnold, Peri. 1976. "Executive Reorganization and Administrative Theory: The Theory of the Managerial Presidency." Paper presented at the annual American Political Science Association Convention. Chicago.

Arnold, R. Douglas. 1979. *Congress and the Bureaucracy.* New Haven: Yale University Press.

Art, Robert J. 1968. *The TFX Decision.* Boston: Little, Brown.

Ascher, William. 1978. *Forecasting: An Appraisal for Policymakers and Planners.* Baltimore: Johns Hopkins University Press.

Ashby, W. Ross. 1963. *An Introduction to Cybernetics.* New York: John Wiley.

Barlow, Richard, and Frank Proschan. 1965. *The Mathematical Theory of Reliability.* New York: John Wiley.

Barton-Aschman Associates, Inc. 1972. *Feasibility of a Low-Risk, Incremental Investment Strategy for the Twin Cities Regional Transit System.* Minneapolis, Minn.

Berg, Thomas, and Peter Petrafesso. 1975. *Metropolitan Transit.* St. Paul, Minn.

Berliner, Joseph. 1976. *The Innovation Decision in Soviet Industry.* Cambridge, Mass.: MIT Press.

Braybrooke, David, and Charles Lindblom. 1963. *A Strategy of Decision: Policy Evaluation as a Social Process.* New York: Free Press.

Bruner, Jerome, Jacqueline Goodnow, and George Austin. 1956. *A Study of Thinking.* New York: John Wiley.

Califano, Joseph, Jr. 1981. *Governing America.* New York: Simon & Schuster.

California Department of Transportation. District 04 Toll Bridges. 1979. *Summary Toll Collection Record: San Francisco-Oakland Bay Bridge.* August 1968–August 1979.

Chan, Steven. 1979. "The Intelligence of Stupidity: Understanding Failures in Strategic Warning." *American Political Science Review* 73(1) (March):171–180.

Chandler, Alfred. 1977. *The Visible Hand: The Managerial Revolution in American Business.* Cambridge, Mass.: Belknap Press.

Citizens' League. 1973. *Building Incentives for Drivers to Ride.* Minneapolis, Minn.

————. 1974. *Transit: Redirect Priorities Toward a Small-Vehicle System and Shorter Trips.* Minneapolis, Minn.

Cohen, David K., and Eleanor Farrar. 1977. "Power to the Parents?—The Story of Education Vouchers." *Public Interest* 48 (Summer):72–97.

Cohen, J., E. Chesnick, and D. Haran. 1972. "A Confirmation of the Inertial-psi Effect in Sequential Choice and Decision." *British Journal of Psychology* 63(1) (February):41–46.

Cohen, Michael. 1981. "The Power of Parallel Thinking." *Journal of Economic Behavior and Organization* 2(4) (December):285–306.

————. 1984. "Conflict and Complexity: Goal Diversity and Organizational Search Effectiveness." *American Political Science Review* 78(2) (June):435–451.

Coker, Francis. 1922. "Dogmas of Administrative Reform." *American Political Science Review* 16(3) (August):399–411.

Creighton, Roger. 1970. *Urban Transportation Planning.* Urbana: University of Illinois Press.

Cresap, McCormick, and Paget, Inc. 1975. *A Study of Bus Management and Operations.* Washington, D.C.

Cyert, Richard, and James March. 1963. *A Behavioral Theory of the Firm.* Englewood Cliffs, N.J.: Prentice-Hall.

Daniel, Mann, Johnson, and Mendenhall, and Midwest Planning and Research, Inc. 1971. *Transit Options for the Twin Cities Metropolitan Region.* Reports 1 and 7. Minneapolis, Minn.

Deen, Thomas. 1974. "Critical Decisions in the Rapid Transit Planning Process." In *Out of Cars/into Transit: A Critical Look at Urban Planning Strategies.* Edited by Andrew Hamer, pp. 41–63. Atlanta: Georgia State University.

DeLeuw, Cather, and Company. 1957. *Report on an Initial Transit Plan.* Berkeley: Alameda-Contra Costa Transit District.

———. 1962. *Report on the Effect of Rapid Transit on the Alameda-Contra Costa Transit District Operations.* San Francisco.

DeRoos, Robert. 1948. *The Thirsty Land.* Stanford: Stanford University Press.

Destler, I. M. 1972. "Comment: Multiple Advocacy: Some 'Limits and Costs.'" *American Political Science Review* 66(3) (September):786–790.

Dickey, John W. 1975. *Metropolitan Transportation Planning.* New York: McGraw-Hill.

Dimock, Marshall. 1936. "The Criteria and Objectives of Public Administration." In *The Frontiers of Public Administration.* Edited by John Gauss, Leonard White, and Marshall Dimock, pp. 116–133. New York: Russell & Russell.

Doty, David. 1972. "Legal Opinion Concerning Power of Metropolitan Transit Commission to Plan and Engineer Transit System." Letter to MTC chairman Douglas Kelm. November 28. St. Paul, Minn.

Douglas, Walter. 1955. "Remarks." Commonwealth Club. January 28. San Francisco.

Downs, Anthony. 1957. *An Economic Theory of Democracy.* New York: Harper & Row.

Downs, George. 1976. *Bureaucracy, Innovation, and Public Policy.* Lexington, Mass.: D. C. Heath.

Einhorn, Hillel, and Robin Hogarth. 1981. "Behavioral Decision Theory: Processes of Judgment and Choice." *Annual Review of Psychology* 32:53–88.

Felsenthal, Dan, and Eliezer Fuchs. 1976. "Experimental Evaluation of Five Designs of Redundant Organizational Systems." *Administrative Science Quarterly* 21(3) (September):474–488.

Galambos, Louis. 1975. *The Public Image of Big Business in America, 1880–1940*. Baltimore: Johns Hopkins University Press.

George, Alexander. 1972. "The Case for Multiple Advocacy in Making Foreign Policy." *American Political Science Review* 66(3) (September):751–785.

Gomez-Ibanez, Jose, and John Meyer. 1977. *Improving Urban Mass Transportation Administration*. Washington, D.C.: Urban Mass Transportation Administration.

Gordon, Robert. 1957. "Optimum Component Redundancy for Maximum System Reliability." *Operations Research* 5(2) (April):229–243.

Gray, Virginia. 1973. "Innovation in the States: A Diffusion Study." *American Political Science Review* 67(4) (December):1174–1185.

Grossman, Jonathan. 1973. *The Department of Labor*. New York: Praeger.

Gulick, Luther. "Notes on the Theory of Organization." In *Papers on the Science of Administration*. Edited by L. Gulick, L. Urwick, and J. D. Mooney. New York: Institute of Public Administration, Columbia University.

Haefele, Edwin. 1976. *Making Metro Work: Press Summary*. Washington, D.C.: Washington Center.

Hagstrom, Warren. 1974. "Competition in Science." *American Sociological Review* 39(1) (February):1–18.

Halperin, Morton, with the assistance of Pricilla Clapp and Arnold Kanter. 1974. *Bureaucratic Politics and Foreign Policy*. Washington, D.C.: Brookings Institution.

Hamer, Andrew. 1976. *The Selling of Rail Rapid Transit: A Critical Look at Urban Transportation Planning*. Lexington, Mass.: Lexington Books.

Hammond, Thomas. 1979. "Jurisdictional Preferences and the Choice of Tasks." Ph.D. dissertation, University of California, Berkeley.

Hart, Henry C. 1957. *The Dark Missouri*. Madison: University of Wisconsin Press.

Haveman, Robert. 1977. "Introduction: Poverty and Social Policy in the 1960s and 1970s." In *A Decade of Federal Antipoverty Programs*. Edited by Robert Haveman, pp. 1–19. New York: Academic Press.

Hay, Thomas. 1973. "MTC Proposed Development Program." Letter to Metropolitan Council chairman Albert Hofstede. January 25. St. Paul, Minn.

Hays, Samuel. 1959. *Conservation and the Gospel of Efficiency*. Cambridge, Mass.: Harvard University Press.

———. 1964. "The Politics of Reform in Municipal Government in the Progressive Era." *Pacific Northwest Quarterly* 55(4) (October):157–169.

Herring, Pendleton. 1936. *Public Administration and the Public Interest.* New York: McGraw-Hill.

Hirsch, Werner Z. 1970. *The Economics of State and Local Government.* New York: McGraw-Hill.

Huntington, Samuel P. 1961. *The Common Defense.* New York: Columbia University Press.

Hutchinson, B. G. 1974. *Principles of Urban Transport Systems Planning.* New York: McGraw-Hill.

Hyneman, Charles. 1950. *Bureaucracy in a Democracy.* New York: Harper.

Janis, Irving. 1972. *Victims of Groupthink.* Boston: Houghton Mifflin.

Janis, Irving, and Leo Mann. 1977. *Decision-Making: A Psychological Analysis of Conflict, Choice, and Commitment.* New York: Free Press.

Jervis, Robert. 1976. *Perception and Misperception in International Politics.* Princeton: Princeton University Press.

Johnson, Michael. 1975. *Going to Work by Car, Bus, or BART: Attitudes, Perceptions, and Decisions.* Berkeley: University of California, Institute of Transportation and Traffic Engineering.

Joint Program. 1967. Notes: March. St. Paul, Minn.

———. 1968. *Twin Cities Area Metropolitan Development Guide.* Report 5. St. Paul, Minn.

Jones, David, et al. 1974. *The Metropolitan Transportation Commission: An Innovative Experiment in Incremental Planning; a Cautious Experiment in Regionalism.* Stanford: Center for Interdisciplinary Research.

Kahneman, Daniel, and Amos Tversky. 1974. "Judgment Under Uncertainty: Heuristics and Biases." *Science* 185 (September): 1124–1131.

Kaufman, Herbert. 1977. "Reflections on Administrative Reorganization." In *Setting National Priorities: The 1978 Budget.* Edited by Joseph Pechman, pp. 391–418. Washington, D.C.: Brookings Institution.

Kelm, Douglas. 1973. *Roles and Relationships of the Metropolitan Council and the Metropolitan Transit Commission.* St. Paul, Minn.

Kennedy, Norman. 1971. *The Alameda-Contra Costa Transit District. A Review of Ten Years of Public Ownership and Operation.* Berkeley: University of California, Institute of Transportation and Traffic Engineering.

Kinder, Donald, and Janet Weiss. 1978. "In Lieu of Rationality: Psychological Perspectives on Foreign Policy Decision-Making." *Jour-*

nal of Conflict Resolution 22(4) (December):707–735.

Klein, Burton. 1962. "The Decision-Making Problem in Development." In *The Rate and Direction of Inventive Activity*, pp. 477–497, 503–506. Report of the National Bureau of Economic Research. Princeton: Princeton University Press.

Klein, Burton, and William Meckling. 1958. "Application of Operations Research to Development Decisions." *Operations Research* 6(3) (May-June):352–363.

Landau, Martin. 1969. "Redundancy, Rationality, and the Problem of Duplication and Overlap." *Public Administration Review* 29(4) (July–August):346–358.

———. 1972. *Political Science and Political Theory*. New York: Macmillan.

———. 1973a. "Federalism, Redundancy, and System Reliability." *Publius* 3(2) (Fall):173–196.

———. 1973b. "On the Concept of the Self-Correcting Organization." *Public Administration Review* 33(6) (November): 533–542.

Landau, Martin, and Russell Stout. 1979. "To Manage Is Not to Control: On the Folly of Type II Errors." *Public Administration Review* 39(2) (March):148–156.

Levin, Henry. 1975. "Education, Life Chances, and the Courts: The Role of Social Science Evidence." *Law and Contemporary Problems* 39(2) (Spring):217–240.

Lindblom, Charles. 1959. "The Science of 'Muddling Through.'" *Public Administration Review* 10(1) (Spring):79–88.

———. 1965. *The Intelligence of Democracy: Decision-Making Through Mutual Adjustment*. New York: Free Press.

———. 1968. *The Policymaking Process*. Englewood Cliffs, N.J.: Prentice-Hall.

Lippman, Steven, and John J. McCall. 1981. "The Economics of Uncertainty: Selected Topics and Probabilistic Methods." In *Handbook of Mathematical Economics*. Edited by Kenneth Arrow and Michael Intrilligator, pp. 211–284. New York: North-Holland.

Long, Norton. 1954. "Public Policy and Administration: The Goals of Rationality and Responsibility." *Public Administration Review* 14(1) (Winter):22–31.

Lowi, Theodore. 1969. *The End of Liberalism*. New York: W. W. Norton.

Luce, R. Duncan, and Howard Raiffa. 1957. *Games and Decisions*. New York: John Wiley.

Lynn, Laurence. 1977. "A Decade of Policy Developments in the Income-Maintenance System." In *A Decade of Federal Antipoverty*

Programs. Edited by Robert Haveman, pp. 55–117. New York: Academic Press.

Maass, Arthur. 1951. *Muddy Waters.* Cambridge, Mass.: Harvard University Press.

McConnell, Grant. 1966. *Private Power and American Democracy.* New York: Vintage Books.

McCulloch, Warren. 1960. "The Reliability of Biological Systems." In *Self-Organizing Systems.* Edited by M. G. Yovitz and S. Cameron, pp. 264–281. New York: Pergamon Press.

Macmahon, Arthur. 1937. "Departmental Management." In *The President's Committee on Administrative Management,* pp. 249–274. Washington, D.C.: U.S. Government Printing Office.

McNulty, Paul. 1967. "A Note on the History of Perfect Competition." *Journal of Political Economy* 75(4) (August):395–399.

March, James, and Johan Olsen. 1975. "The Uncertainty of the Past: Organizational Learning Under Uncertainty." *European Journal of Political Research* 3(2) (June):147–171.

March, James, and Zur Shapira. 1982. "Behavioral Decision Theory and Organizational Decision Theory." In *New Directions in Decision Making.* Edited by Gerardo Ungson and Daniel Braunstein, pp. 92–115. Boston: Kent Publishing.

Markowitz, Harry. 1959. *Portfolio Selection: Efficient Diversification of Investments.* New York: John Wiley.

Mehay, Stephen. 1978. "Governmental Structure and Performance: The Effects of the Lakewood Plan on Property Values." *Public Finance Quarterly* 6(3) (July):311–325.

Meier, Kenneth. 1980. "Executive Reorganization of Government: Impact on Employment and Expenditures." *American Journal of Political Science* 24(3) (August):396–412.

Merton, Robert. 1940. "Bureaucratic Structure and Personality." *Social Forces* 18(4) (May):560–568.

———. 1973. *The Sociology of Science: Theoretical and Empirical Investigations.* Edited and with an introduction by Norman Storer. Chicago: University of Chicago Press.

Metropolitan Council. 1970. *Status of Transit Planning in the Twin Cities Metropolitan Area: A Joint MTC-Metro Council Staff Conclusion.* St. Paul, Minn.

———. 1971. *Metropolitan Development Guide.* St. Paul, Minn.

———. 1972a. Memorandum from staff to the Development Guide Committee re *Decision Sequence for Transportation Planning.* January 5. St. Paul, Minn.

———. 1972b. *Transportation Planning Materials,* Books 1 and 3. St. Paul, Minn.

Metropolitan Transit Commission. 1971. *Transit in Transportation: A Commission Statement.* St. Paul, Minn.

Metropolitan Transportation Commission. 1974. *Transit Development Program for the SFBA, 1975–84.* Berkeley, Calif.

Meyer, John, John Kain, and Martin Wohl. 1965. *The Urban Transportation Problem.* Cambridge, Mass.: Harvard University Press.

Miller, Gary. 1981. *Cities by Contract: The Politics of Municipal Incorporation.* Cambridge, Mass.: MIT Press.

Miller, Gary, and Terry Moe. 1983. "Bureaucrats, Legislators, and the Size of Government." *American Political Science Review* 77(2) (June):297–322.

Millett, John. 1959. "Concepts of Organization." In *Elements of Public Administration.* Edited by Fritz Morstein-Marx. Englewood Cliffs, N.J.: Prentice-Hall.

Morlock, Edward. 1978. *Introduction to Transportation Engineering and Planning.* New York: McGraw-Hill.

Murin, William. 1971. *Mass Transit Policy Planning: An Incremental Approach.* Lexington, Mass.: Heath-Lexington.

Nelson, Richard. 1961. "Uncertainty, Learning, and the Economics of Parallel Research and Development Efforts." *Review of Economics and Statistics* 43(4) (November):351–364.

Nisbett, Richard, and Lee Ross. 1980. *Human Inference: Strategies and Shortcomings of Social Judgment.* Englewood Cliffs, N.J.: Prentice-Hall.

Niskanen, William, 1971. *Representative Bureaucracy.* New York: Aldine-Atherton.

———. 1975. "Bureaucrats and Politicians." *Journal of Law and Economics* 18(3) (December):617–644.

Ostrom, Vincent. 1973. *The Intellectual Crisis in American Public Administration.* University, Ala.: University of Alabama Press.

Ostrom, Vincent, Charles Tiebout, and Robert Warren. 1961. "The Organization of Government in Metropolitan Areas." *American Political Science Review* 55(4) (December):831–842.

Parsons, Brinckerhoff, Hall, and MacDonald. 1956. *Regional Rapid Transit, 1953–1955: A Report to the San Francisco Bay Area Rapid Transit Commission.* New York.

Pierce, Lawrence C. 1971. *The Politics of Fiscal Policy Formation.* Pacific Palisades, Calif.: Goodyear Publishing Co.

Pierce, William. 1965. *Failure-Tolerant Computer Design.* New York: Academic Press.

Popper, Karl. 1963. *Conjectures and Refutations: The Growth of Scientific Knowledge.* London: Routledge & Kegan Paul.

Rawls, John. 1971. *A Theory of Justice.* Cambridge, Mass.: Harvard University Press.

Robacker, John. 1957. "Note on 'Optimum Component Redundancy for Maximum System Reliability.'" *Operations Research* 5(6) (December):847–848.

Roberts, Norman. 1964. *Mathematical Methods in Reliability Engineering.* New York: McGraw-Hill.

Robinson, Edward A. 1958. *The Structure of Competitive Industry.* Chicago: University of Chicago Press.

Ross, Sheldon. 1980. *Introduction to Probability Models.* New York: Academic Press.

Roth, Gabriel. 1977. "Should Metro Be Derailed?" *Washington Post,* July 31.

Rothschild, Michael, and Joseph Stiglitz. 1971. "Increasing Risk II: Its Economic Consequences." *Journal of Economic Theory* 3:66–84.

Salamon, Lester. 1978. *Welfare: The Elusive Consensus.* New York: Praeger.

San Francisco Bay Area Rapid Transit District. 1964. Memorandum to file re impact of BART on AC Transit.

———. 1969. Memorandum from Transportation and Traffic Analyst to Central Operations re AC's reroute plans. November 19.

———. 1970a. Letter from B. R. Stokes to Alan Bingham re AC-BART coordination. August 7.

———. 1970b. Memorandum from Malcolm Barrett to B. R. Stokes re AC-BART competition. November 13.

———. 1970c. Memorandum from E. R. Preston to Lawrence Dahms re AC-BART coordination. November 16.

———. 1971a. Memorandum from Henry Bain to the assistant general manager for Planning and Public Service re AC-BART coordination. January 5.

———. 1971b. Memorandum from Henry Bain to Lawrence Dahms re AC-BART coordination. January 22.

———. 1971c. Letter from B. R. Stokes to the board re AC-BART coordination. January 27.

———. 1971d. Letter from B. R. Stokes to Robert Rinehart re AC-BART coordination. June 18.

———. 1972. Memorandum from P. H. Mattson to Lawrence Dahms re public relations coordination between AC and BART. March 20.

———. 1975. *Patronage Report: June.*

———. 1977. *Patronage Report: December.*

Sapolsky, Harvey. 1972. *The Polaris System Development.* Cambridge, Mass.: Harvard University Press.

Scheff, Thomas. 1963. "Decision Rules, Types of Error and Their Consequences in Medical Diagnosis." *Behavioral Science* 8(2) (April):97–107.

Scherer, Frederic. 1962. "Comment." In *The Rate and Direction of*

Inventive Activity, pp. 497–503, 506–508. Report of the National Bureau of Economic Research. Princeton: Princeton University Press.

Schlesinger, Arthur. 1958. *The Coming of the New Deal*. Boston: Houghton Mifflin.

Scott, James C. 1976. *The Moral Economy of the Peasant*. New Haven: Yale University Press.

Seidman, Harold. 1970. *Politics, Position, and Power: The Dynamics of Federal Organization*. London: Oxford University Press.

Simms, Denton H. 1970. *The Soil Conservation Service*. New York: Praeger.

Simon, Herbert. 1947. *Administrative Behavior: A Study of Decision-Making Processes in Administrative Organization*. New York: Macmillan.

———. 1957. *Models of Man*. New York: John Wiley.

———. 1964. "On the Concept of Organizational Goal." *Administrative Science Quarterly*. 9(1) (June):1–22.

———. 1966. "Political Research: The Decision-Making Framework." In *Varieties of Political Theory*. Edited by David Easton, pp. 15–24. Englewood Cliffs, N.J.: Prentice-Hall.

Simon, Herbert, and Allen Newell. 1972. *Human Problem-Solving*. Englewood Cliffs, N.J.: Prentice-Hall.

Simpson-Curtin. 1967. *Coordinated Transit for the San Francisco Bay Area—Now to 1975*. Springfield, Va. U.S. Clearinghouse.

Smith, Wilbur, and Associates. 1975. *Integrated Metrobus Services for the Washington Transit Zone: Final Report*. Washington, D.C.

State of Minnesota. 1967. *Session Laws*. Enacted by the Sixty-fifth Legislature. St. Paul: Department of Administration.

———. 1969. *Session Laws*. Enacted by the Sixty-sixth Legislature. St. Paul: Department of Administration.

———. 1971. *Session Laws*. Enacted by the Sixty-seventh Legislature. St. Paul: Department of Administration.

———. 1974. *Session Laws*. Enacted by the Sixty-ninth Legislature. St. Paul: Department of Administration.

Steiner, Gilbert. 1971. *The State of Welfare*. Washington, D.C.: Brookings Institution.

Stinchcombe, Arthur. 1975. "Social Structure and Politics." In *Handbook of Political Science*. Vol. 3. Edited by Fred Greenstein and Nelson Polsby, pp. 142–192. Menlo Park: Addison-Wesley.

Stockfisch, Jacob. 1973. *Plowshares into Swords: Managing the American Defense Establishment*. New York: Mason & Lipscomb.

Tavris, Carol. 1975. "The Experimenting Society: A Conversation with Donald T. Campbell." *Psychology Today* 9(4) (September): 46–56.

Taylor, J. Serge. 1984. *Making Bureaucracies Think: The Environmental Strategy of Administrative Reform.* Stanford: Stanford University Press.

Thompson, James D. 1967. *Organizations in Action.* New York: McGraw-Hill.

Todd, Thomas. 1977. *A Presentation to the House Committee on Local and Urban Affairs, with an Addendum.* State of Minnesota, House of Representatives: Research Department. St. Paul, Minn.

Transportation Planning Program. 1974. *A Summary Report of Travel in the Twin Cities Metropolitan Area.* St. Paul, Minn.

Transportation Research Board. 1977. *Urban Transportation Alternatives: Evolution of Federal Policy.* Special Report 177. Washington, D.C.: National Academy of Science.

U.S. Congress. House of Representatives. 1963. *Transit Program for the National Capital Region.* Hearings before Subcommittee 6 of the District of Columbia Committee. Eighty-ninth Congress, First Session. Washington, D.C.

———. Office of Technology Assessment. 1976a. *An Assessment of Community Planning for Mass Transit: Minneapolis–St. Paul Case Study.* Washington, D.C.: U.S. Government Printing Office.

———. Office of Technology Assessment. 1976b. *An Assessment of Community Planning for Mass Transit: San Francisco Case Study.* Washington, D.C.: U.S. Government Printing Office.

———. Office of Technology Assessment. 1976c. *An Assessment of Community Planning for Mass Transit: Summary.* Washington, D.C.: U.S. Government Printing Office.

———. Senate. 1965. *Rapid Rail Transit for the National Capital Region.* Hearings before the Senate Committee on the District of Columbia. Eighty-ninth Congress, First Session. Washington, D.C.

———. Senate. 1972. *Bus Systems Acquisition by WMATA.* Joint hearings before the Committee on the District of Columbia of the Senate and the Subcommittee on Business, Commerce, and Fiscal Affairs of the House District of Columbia Committee. Ninety-second Congress, Second Session. Washington, D.C.

U.S. Department of Transportation. 1976. *The Urban Mass Transit Act of 1964 and Related Laws.* Washington, D.C.

———. 1978. "Policy Toward Rail Transit." *Federal Register* 43(45):9428–9430. Washington, D.C.

———. 1979. *Reply to GAO Report of February 22, 1979, on Need for UMTA to Improve Management of Its Planning Requirements for Major Transit Projects.* Washington, D.C.

———. 1982. *National Urban Mass Transportation Statistics.* Washington, D.C.: U.S. Government Printing Office.

U.S. General Accounting Office. 1979. *Communication and Manage-*

ment Problems Hinder the Planning Process for Major Mass Transit Projects. Washington, D.C.

Viton, Philip A. 1980. *The Profits of Competition in Public Transit.* Washington, D.C.: Urban Mass Transit Administration.

Voorhees, Alan, and Associates. 1969. *Development of a Long-Range Transit Improvement Program for the Twin Cities Area: Technical Report 3 to the Twin Cities Area Metropolitan Transit Commission.* McLean, Va.

————. 1970. *Screening and Evaluation of Public Transit Vehicle Systems: Technical Report 1 to The Twin Cities Area Metropolitan Transit Commission.* McLean, Va.

————. 1974. *AC Transit/BART Service Coordination.* McLean, Va.

Wallace, Schulyer. 1941. *Federal Departmentalization: A Critique of Theories of Organization.* New York: Columbia University Press.

Warren, Robert. 1966. *Government in Metropolitan Affairs.* Davis, Calif.: Institute of Governmental Affairs.

Washington Metropolitan Area Transit Authority. 1968. *Traffic, Revenue, and Operating Costs: Adopted Regional System.* Washington, D.C.

————. 1975. *Resident and Metrobus Rider Attitudes Toward Metrobus.* Washington, D.C.

————. 1976a. *Phase II Interface: Proposed Plan.* Washington, D.C.

————. 1976b. *Legislation Relating to the Development of Rapid Transit in the Washington Metropolitan Area.* Washington, D.C.

————. 1977a. *Phase III Transit System Planning Study.* Washington, D.C.

————. 1977b. *Quarterly Report: Metrobus and Metrorail Ridership.* Washington, D.C.

————. 1978a. *Quarterly Report: Metrobus and Metrorail Ridership.* Washington, D.C.

————. 1978b. Memorandum to file re train trips completed. Office of Rail Services. Washington, D.C.

————. 1977–78. *Board Minutes.* Washington, D.C.

Webber, Melvin, 1976. "The BART Experience—What Have We Learned?" *Public Interest* 45(Fall):79–108.

Weber, Max. 1972. "Essay on Bureaucracy." In *Bureaucratic Power in National Politics.* Edited by Francis Rourke, pp. 53–63. Boston: Little, Brown.

White, Leonard. 1939. *Introduction to the Study of Public Administration.* New York: Macmillan.

Wildavsky, Aaron. 1974. *The Politics of the Budgetary Process.* 2nd ed. Boston: Little, Brown.

Williamson, Oliver. 1975. *Markets and Hierarchies: Analysis and Antitrust Implications.* New York: Free Press.

Willoughby, W. F. 1927. *Principles of Public Administration*. Washington, D.C.: Brookings Institution.

Wilson, James Q. 1980. "The Politics of Regulation." In *The Politics of Regulation*. Edited by James Q. Wilson, pp. 357–394. New York: Basic Books.

Wilson, Woodrow. 1887. "The Study of Administration." *Political Science Quarterly* 2(1) (June):197–222.

Wolin, Sheldon. 1960. *Politics and Vision: Continuity and Innovation in Western Political Thought*. Boston: Little, Brown.

Zwerling, Stephen. 1974. *Mass Transit and the Politics of Technology*. New York: Praeger.

Index

Aaron, Henry J.: on antipoverty theories and strategies, 16–17; on programmatic learning and modification, 268n25

AC-BART transit planning: and iteration, 214–15; monopoly in, 22, 82, 95–102; outcome of, 216–17, 220–21; search for alternatives in, 210

AC-BART transit redundancy, 21–22, 79–80, 85–118; and antagonistic cooperation, 106–9, 234; benefits of, 109–17, 244; compared with monopolistic transit, 227–32, 233–34, 256; developmental problems in, 109–11, 227–28; division-of-labor agreements in, 92, 93, 95, 101; emergence and growth of, 87–95, 236, 237; episodic shocks in, 111–12, 229; and feasibility of redundancy, 279; financing and costs in, 104–5, 107; future uncertainties in, 117; information and reversibility in, 113–16, 243; intermodal coordination in, 107, 232–33; legal restrictions in, 95–96, 237; vs. merger proposals, 102–4, 113; modal choice in, 90–92; origins during the planning stage, 87–95; passenger service requirements in, 113–16; po-

litical support in, 89–90; popularity of bus transport in, 228–29; reliability of, 113–14, 118, 244; rivalry effects in, 116–17, 234; special districts in, 89; stability of, 102–4, 238–41; vs. strategies for monopoly, 95–102

Adler, Seymour, 95; on AC-BART planning, 87n1, 88, 89, 91, 92n

Administrative economies of scale, 29; in bus-rail mergers, 102n27, 181–82; in monopolistic transit operations, 75

Administrative integration of bus-rail transport: advantages of, 179–82, 232–33; compared with interorganizational coordination, 232–33; disadvantages of, 183–93; financial effects of, 181–83, 194–95, 206

Agencies: independence and diversity of, 282–84; overlapping domains of, 280–81; partisan discussion between, 258; role in the stability of redundancy, 43

Aid to Families with Dependent Children (AFDC), 18, 20

Alameda–Contra Costa Transit District (AC), 21–22, 79–80, 95–102. *See also* AC-BART transit planning; AC-BART transit redundancy

311

Designer:	Barbara Llewellyn
Compositor:	Interactive Composition, Inc.
Printer:	McNaughton & Gunn, Inc.
Binder:	John H. Dekker & Sons
Text:	10/12 Palatino
Display:	Palatino